"NO-WIN WARS"

"Under this new conception, we are required in the midst of deadly war to soften our blows and send men into battle with neither promise nor hope of Victory."

GENERAL DOUGLAS MACARTHUR

WHO denied us Victory in Korea? WHY is Victory denied in Viet Nam? WHERE will our sons next face death in a no-win war?

Major Roberts not only answers these provocative questions but also presents the necessary legal action which must be taken to restore to America's valiant sons the promise of Victory.

This book is dedicated to Victory over international tyranny; that America's soldier sons, sacrificed in foreign military adventures, shall not have died in vain.

VICTORY DENIED

by
Arch E. Roberts
Major, A.U.S. (Ret.)

CHAS. HALLBERG & COMPANY
Publishers
CHICAGO, ILLINOIS 60610

E
839.8
.R6

Library of Congress Catalog Card Number: 66-20665

About the Author

Arch E. Roberts, Major, AUS (ret.), soldier, writer, lecturer, and author of the famous Pro-Blue Troop Information program which taught "Citizenship in Service" to members of the 24th Infantry Division in Germany, played an important role in the "Military-Muzzling" controversy which resulted in a lengthy Senate investigation. On August 30, 1961, the entire text of the Pro-Blue program was inserted into the *Congressional Record* by Senators J. Strom Thurmond and John G. Tower.

Major Roberts was critically attacked by the national press for defying Pentagon "muzzling" in an address before the Seventy-First Continental Congress, Daughters of the American Revolution in Washington, D.C. In this talk, which is included in the proceedings of the Congress for April 19, 1962, he noted that all citizens, ". . .in and out of uniform are very concerned about civilian control (over the army) when one channel of that control terminates in the office of a Communist."

Anti-anti-Communists in the Pentagon at once effected the confinement of Roberts to the limits of his post at Fort Lee, Virginia and relieved him of military duties pending "an investigation." On May 7, denied a hearing or review, Major Roberts was ordered to inactive duty by the Secretary of the Army and directed to return to his home in Colorado.

Vigorously protesting this unprecedented action, the D.A.R. petitioned the Congress of the United States to investigate this ". . . arbitrary exercise of power."

Roberts, a veteran of eighteen years, nine months active duty at the time of his ouster (one-third of that time spent overseas) subsequently brought suit against the Army Secretary, charging violation of public law and abridgement of Constitutional rights.

On June 18, 1964, the U.S. District Court of Appeals directed that Roberts be reinstated and that further proceedings be conducted to determine ". . . the extent of the relief required."

Restored to active duty by Department of the Army (order dated August 5, 1965) and paid back pay in the amount of $34,000.00, Major Roberts applied for Voluntary Retirement effective September 30, 1965, terminating twenty-six years service.

This retired officer whose family traces its military lineage to the Revolutionary War, is now working to mobilize resistance to a United Nations take-over of the U.S. military establishment and seeks to halt the "internationalizing" of the American fighting man.

Major Roberts is an ex-paratrooper and served with the 11th Airborne Division, the 187th Airborne Regimental Combat Team, the 101st Airborne Division, the 3rd Infantry Division, Office of the Surgeon General, Army Information Digest, and Office of the Chief of Information as an army information officer. A graduate of the Command and General Staff College, the Armed Forces Information School, the Medical Field Service School, and Officer Candidate School, he enlisted in the Regular Army at Denver, Colorado on June 2, 1939.

He is a member of the Reserve Officers Association, the Airborne Association, International Platform Association, and Sons of the American Revolution.

Chicago Tribune

FOUNDED JUNE 10, 1847

J. HOWARD WOOD, Publisher
W. D. MAXWELL, Editor

Saturday, September 4, 1965

ONE MAN'S BATTLE

Three years ago Maj. Arch E. Roberts was removed from active duty status for making a speech before the Daughters of the American Revolution which offended army censorship and government officials. Roberts, after 18 years' service, stood to lose his service pension as well as his place in the army.

He went to court and finally won a verdict that he should be restored to duty with "all the rights, privileges, and emoluments" he had previously enjoyed. The ruling will protect all army reservists with 18 or more years of service from summary separation in future without a hearing.

Roberts is now back in uniform and has received $24,000 in accumulated back pay, after deduction of $12,000 for income tax and other claims. But his fight for reinstatement left him broke. He had to borrow $20,000 to keep his family going, and legal fees took another $20,000.

The secretary of the army dismissed him in violation of a specific statute preserving the rights of veteran reservists. Altho the secretary was the offender, the burden of proof was placed on Maj. Roberts, and also the expense of justifying himself.

The major was a casualty of the campaign to censor utterances of military men instituted during the administration of President Kennedy. The campaign to gag the military grew out of the celebrated "Fulbright memorandum," sent to Mr. Kennedy in 1961 by Sen. J. William Fulbright, chairman of the foreign relations committee.

Sen. Fulbright felt that military officers were talking

too much about the menace of communism, and that their disposition to speak out showed them to be infected with the virus of right-wing radicalism." He thought "the danger is great" if the military engaged in educating the public.

Among Fulbright's contentions was that the "right wing" equated social legislation with socialism, and the latter with communism, and that accordingly such utterances constituted an attack on the Democratic administration's social welfare programs and foreign policy.

As an exercise in anti-anti-communism, this is just about what could be expected of Sen. Fulbright. But it was sufficient to embark the administration on a campaign to suppress any statements by military men which might be offensive to the Kremlin, which, in the view of the administration, was "mellowing" and moving toward "convergence" with the United States and the west. As a consequence, the blue pencil was overworked in Washington and all seminars and troop indoctrination programs relating to the real nature of communism were discouraged.

Maj. Roberts was swept up in the administration's war against the hard-line anti-communists because, as as an information officer with the American 24th division in West Germany, he had been concerned with drawing up a program of indoctrinating the troops and giving them information about communist objectives and methods.

He was relieved from that duty after the division commander, Maj. Gen. Edwin A. Walker, was "admonished" by superior authority for intimating that some political personages entertained flabby views on communism and for expressing a preference for the election of conservatives. Walker soon resigned from the army.

The Roberts case is unlikely even to provide a footnote in the history books, but it nevertheless provides an interesting reflection of the fantasies cherished in Washington these last few years. Chief of these is that the way to deal with communism is to give it assurance that the United States entertains only the kindest thoughts about it and in no circumstances will speak ill of it.

TABLE OF CONTENTS

PREFACE

The Korean betrayal motivated this work and the war in Viet Nam constitutes the urgent reason for its publication.

The book is partly based upon public speeches presented by the author during the period 1962-1965 and on intelligence gathered by private investigators employed by the author during the process of exposing *Overseas Weekly*, a civilian newspaper distributed to American troops overseas through Army channels. It incorporates some material previously disseminated at personal expense in broadside form.

Reliance on public records and reports is acknowledged, including those of the United States Senate Subcommittee to Investigate the Administration of the Internal Security Act and Other Internal Security Laws; The United States House of Representatives, Committee on Un-American Activities; Military Cold War Education and Speech Review Policies, Hearings Before the Special Preparedness Subcommittee of the Committee on Armed Services, United States Senate, and other official references as indicated in the text.

The assistance and inspiration generously given to the author by many dedicated and erudite patriots has materially contributed to the accuracy and authority of the manuscript.

Apologies are offered where brief passages have been quoted, and through the author's oversight, may appear in this work without prior permission. These will be corrected in succeeding printings of *Victory Denied. . . Why Your Son Faces Death in "No-Win" Wars.*

Arch E. Roberts, Major, AUS (ret.)
P.O. Box 986, Fort Collins, Colorado

CHAPTER I

THE STRANGE CASE
OF GENERAL VASILIEV

"The U.S. (upon admission of Red China to the
United Nations) will push for approval of a joint
U.S.-Philippine plan to weld the military forces of all
sixty member nations into a workable international
army."—*New York Sunday News*, September 12,
1954

Millions of Americans today are deeply troubled by
political pressures which, under the guise of "International
Peace and Security," undermine the Constitution
of these United States.

Those who have studied the United Nations and its
Charter believe that the greatest threat to our national
survival is embodied in the thrust to centralize world
military power in the Security Council of the United
Nations Organization.

Public and private spokesmen for the U.N., with increasing
regularity, loft trial balloons extolling an imaginary
world security to be achieved by establishing an
international "Peace Force" — a Peace Force which
Americans are to man and finance.[1] These dubious pro-

[1] "Six House GOP's Seek Backing on U.S. Force for U.N." *Denver
Post*, June 20, 1965.

motions have convinced many citizens that the build up of an international army under U.N. control will lead inevitably to a totalitarian one-world government.[2]

Present war-making capability of the United Nations Security Council is substantial and alarming. The authority which this supra-government war department exerts over Americans in uniform is succinctly spelled out in the articles of the U.N. Charter.

"In order to ensure prompt and effective action by the United Nations," states Article 24, "its Members confer on the Security Council primary responsibility for the maintenance of international peace and security."

The scope of this "responsibility" is unlimited. It provides, under Article 42, for U.N. military action "by air, sea, or land forces as may be necessary, to maintain or restore international peace and security," e.g.: Korea, Katanga, Dominican Republic, Viet Nam, and in the near future, South Africa.[3]

Weaponry and manpower for such military adventures as may be embarked upon by the Security Council are provided by member nations which make "available to the Security Council, on its call and in accordance with a special agreement or agreements (i.e.: NATO, SEATO, CENTO, OAS, etc.)[4], armed forces, assistance and facilities, including rights of passage, necessary for the

[2] "52 Prominent Americans Urge World Government Formation," *Denver Post*, October 6, 1965.

[3] "Apartheid and United Nations Collective Measures," Carnegie Endowment for International Peace, U.N. Plaza, N.Y.

[4] North Atlantic Treaty Organization, Southeast Asia Treaty Organization, Central Treaty Organization, Organization of American States.

purpose of maintaining international peace and security." [5]

These contributions of men, hardware, and national sovereignty to the cause of, "international peace and security," as defined by the United Nations Charter and by those who implement its policy, are not subject to debate or veto — at least not by America. The Charter irrevocably binds the signatory nations and their citizens to the decisions of the Security Council. "The Members of the United Nations," directs Article 25, "agree to accept and carry out the decisions of the Security Council in accordance with the present Charter."

The pre-eminence of the United Nations Treaty agreements in American domestic and international affairs, irrespective of the misleading insertion of paragraph 7, Article 2 barring U.N. intervention in matters, "which are essentially within the domestic jurisdiction of any state," has been deliberately blurred by a public relations image of the U.N. as a benevolent world body responsive to the consensus of its members.

This popular and erroneous concept is fraught with peril.

Whether U.N. purposes and objectives are benign or malignant is, of course, the subject of this study. However, a quick corollary may be drawn by comparing pro-U.N. publicity with the strange case of General Vasiliev.

Lieutenant General Alexandre Ph. Vasiliev was the Soviet representative on the United Nations Military

[5] United Nations Charter, Article 43.

Staff Committee from 1947 until the USSR withdrew from the committee on January 19, 1950. This former chairman of the U.N. Military Staff Committee was thereupon ordered to North <u>Korea</u> where he was placed in command of all Chinese Communist movements across the thirty-eighth parallel.

The Vasiliev case history of international deceit begins with *U.S. State Department Bulletin Number 442A*, dated August 3, 1947, titled, "Arming the United Nations." On page 239 of this official document our State Department says:

"On April 30, 1947, Lieutenant General A. Ph. Vasiliev, of the Red Army, chairman of the Military Staff Committee of the United Nations, forwarded to Trygve Lie, Secretary-General, for transmission to the Security Council, a report of the Military Staff Committee containing recommendations on the general principles governing the organization of the armed forces made available to the Security Council by member Nations of the United Nations.

"Article 43 of the Charter," this report continues, "appears in Chapter VII, 'Action with Respect to Threats to the Peace, Breaches of the Peace, and Acts of Aggression.' This article contains the undertaking assumed by members to make military forces available to the Security Council."

Following a quotation of the text of Article 43, this State Department report continues:

"Authorization for the Security Council to employ such forces is contained in article 42." [6]

[6] "Arming the United Nations," *U.S. State Department Bulletin* 422A, August 3, 1947, page 239.

Most Americans, of course, assume that U.S. Army organization tables and battle plans are prepared in the Pentagon at the direction of the Congress.

The U.S. State Department, however, reveals that war plans for the employment of American soldiers are now prepared by foreign generals under the direction of Soviet Communists at the United Nations military headquarters.

The spectacle of a Red Army general drawing up plans for the assignment of our soldiers in an "Armed United Nations" is a shocking expose of the casual manner in which our government has become party to gross violations of the United States Constitution.

By following the spoor of General Vasiliev it can be revealed how he applied his plans for "Arming the United Nations." The trail next leads to the Pentagon.

On May 15, 1954 the Office of Public Information, Department of Defense, released a paper titled, *The Truth about Soviet Involvement in the Korean War.* On page five of this official intelligence digest is the following information:

"One prisoner of war, a Major of North Korean engineers, said that as the flow of Russian equipment to Korea increased during the period immediately preceding the initial attack, the flow of Russian advisors increased with it. All orders, he said, came from these advisors, and he, who spoke Russian, was given the job of translating them into Korean.

"Many Russian 'advisors' were attached to the North Korean Army advance headquarters established in June, 1950. They wore civilian clothing, the Major added, and it was forbidden to address them by rank. They were introduced as 'newspaper reporters' but they had supreme authority. They took the lead in making operational and mobilization plans, and in commanding and manipulating troops. They treated the Korean officers who were nominally their chiefs, the Major said, 'like their servants, or children.'

"The North Korean Major identified two of these Russian 'Advisors' as Lieutenant General Vasiliev and Colonel Dolgin. Vasiliev, he said, apparently was in charge of all movements across the thirty-eighth parallel.

"Another prisoner interrogation report identified Colonel Yun, a Russian who spoke Korean haltingly, as advisor to the Tank Command of the North Korean Army in June, 1950. It named as head of communications along the frontier before and during the initial attack a Russian colonel named Gregor. This prisoner also said he actually heard General Vasiliev give the order to attack on June 25." [7]

This General Vasiliev is, of course, the same Alexandre Ph. Vasiliev of the Red Army who, as Chairman, U.N. Military Staff Committee, directed the preparation of plans for an "Armed United Nations." He later directed the Chinese hordes who were let loose to murder United Nations soldiers in Korea — including many thousands of Americans who were killed or captured to be tortured in Chinese Communist Prisoner of War cages in North Korea.

Korea is a savage example of United Nations "nonwars" in which scenario and stage-management are under the exclusive direction of professional internation-

---

[7] *The Truth about Soviet Involvement in the Korean War.* DOD, Office of Public Information, May 15, 1954, page 5.

alists operating behind a "front" of national militarists.

The stomach-churning case of General Vasiliev constitutes grounds for American victims of the Korean bloodbath to bring charges of mass murder against members of the Security Council of the United Nations.

This evidence strongly supports the conviction of many U.S. citizens that the Korean War was engineered by the United Nations and the State Department so that the supreme military authority of the U.N. might be established by force of arms and endorsed before the world. There can be no more shocking evidence of United Nations cynicism than the concealed duplicity of General Vasiliev; nor a more terrible indictment of our own military and political leadership.

It is ironic that Vasiliev was not in violation of the high-sounding U.N. Charter which, in paragraph 1, Chapter XV, announces:

"In the performance of their duties the Secretary-General and the staff shall not seek or receive instructions from any other authority external to the Organization. They shall refrain from any action which might reflect on their position as international officials responsible only to the Organization." [8]

There is little question that, as United Nations "advisor" to the Chinese Communists, General Alexandre Ph. Vasiliev of the Red Army was ". . . responsible only to the Organization."

There exists the rationale that Korea "happened a long time ago" and the conditions which applied then do not threaten Americans today. In rebuttal to this

[8] U.N. Charter, Article 100.

specious argument it is pertinent now to submit for examination two points of evidence. The first is Senate Concurrent Resolution Number Thirty-two, introduced by Senator Joseph S. Clark of Pennsylvania on April 8, 1965, requesting that the President formulate as speedily as possible "specific and detailed proposals for the implementation of the foreign policy objectives of the United States regarding the establishment of an international authority to keep the peace under conditions of general and complete disarmament;" secondly, the United Nations War in Viet Nam.

Resolution Number 32 reveals that our Congress is seriously considering enactment of the final tyranny by inserting into federal statute the supra-government provisions of the United Nations Charter, i.e.:

(a) an International Disarmament Organization,

(b) a permanent World Peace Force,

(c) World Tribunals for the peaceful settlement of all international disputes,

(d) other International Institutions necessary for the enforcement of world peace, and

(e) appropriate and reliable Financial Arrangements for the support of such peacekeeping machinery.[9]

It requires small knowledge of the semantics of professional internationalists to understand that Resolution 32 is to be the legal machinery for establishing United Nations control over U.S. national defensive armaments and atomic weapons, and to make absolute the U.N. power to wage war and make peace; to transfer Amer-

---

[9] Senate Concurrent Resolution 32, 89th Congress, April 8, 1965.

ican military personnel under direct United Nations Command; to create a world-wide bureaucracy enabling the United Nations to control all of the world's people and resources, and lastly, to establish a United Nations revenue bureau with the authority to directly tax all Americans so as to "reliably finance" a one-world United Nations government.

All of these proposed legislative-executive acts are in contradiction to the limited and delegated powers enumerated in the United States Constitution. The Constitution is very explicit about the powers of making war, keeping peace, the jurisdiction of the courts and the methods of amending those powers. Nowhere in the Constitution is to be found the power of relegating those functions to any other body, or to an international organization of any kind.

It is apparent, therefore, that Resolution 32 springs, not from the United States Constitution, but from the United Nations Treaty agreement. It is intended to strip away the public pretense that the United Nations Charter is merely a "treaty." The United Nations Charter is to be proclaimed the "supreme law of the land" by congressional statute, say its supporters.

Senate hearings on this pending world socialist legislation have been completed and recorded in a public document titled, "Planning for Peace."[10] The testimony contained therein represents largely the views held by one-worlders, collectivists, and socialists who are government financed and/or supported by tax-exempt founda-

[10] "Planning for Peace", Hearings before the Committee on Foreign Relations, USS, 89th Congress, on Sen. Con. Res. 32, May 11-12, 1965.

tions. There is a thin sprinkle of opposition by citizen-backed organizations. This "Minority opposition" is intended to create the fiction that the hearings constitute a national consensus of opinion and agreement. Random extracts of testimony, deliberately organized in the order of the five principles presented in Resolution Thirty-two, illustrate the technique:

1. International Disarmament Organization:
   Adrian Fisher, Deputy Director, Arms Control and Disarmament Agency (pages 135 and 136)
   "We are, however, giving continuing study to the kinds of organization which might monitor a comprehensive test ban treaty, a freeze on the numbers and characteristics of strategic bombers and missiles, major arms reduction measures and comprehensive disarmament. . . These steps would clearly require considerable change in the existing practice and attitudes of nations."
2. Permanent World Peace Force:
   Professor Emile Benoit, Americans for Democratic Action (page 104)
   "The basic unsolved issues underlying disarmament are essentially those involved in the substitution of a supra-national inspection and defense establishment, for national defense establishments, and the transfer to this supra-national inspection and defense establishment of the essential obligations to enforce not only the continued disarmament of the nation-states but also their continued politico-military security — in short, a substitution of supra-national security guarantees for security based on the nation's own defense forces." *Shelby Southard,* assistant director, Cooperative League of the USA (page 152)
   "A peacekeeping force is needed that will be responsive to the collective moral conscience of freedom-loving people everywhere — one that will act for all of them."

Douglas MacArthur II, Assistant Secretary for Congressional Relations, for the Secretary of State (page 5)

"The earmarking of standby forces for emergency U.N. service by the Scandinavian countries, Canada, and others is an example of the kind of steps which are contributing significantly to the U.N.'s capacity to keep the peace within the limits of what nations are now willing to undertake."

Honorable Joseph D. Tydings, United States Senator from the state of Maryland (page 17)

"Until called into service by the United Nations, these units would be financed and controlled by their own governments."

3. World Tribunals:

Harlan Cleveland, Assistant Secretary of State for International Organization Affairs (page 126)

"The goal is clear ... It is to work everlastingly at the tough, practical jobs of strengthening U.N. machinery for keeping the peace and for peaceful settlement . . . of extending the reach of the international Court. . ."

C. Maxwell Stanley, United World Federalists (page 58)

"Peace demands a world-wide system of justice, law, and order."

4. Other International Institutions:

Honorable Jacob K. Javits, United States Senator from the state of New York (page 107)

"First, most people agree that sometime, somehow, somewhere, there will be an international peace-keeping organization, supra-national in character, which will probably be built upon the new concept of regionalism in the affairs of mankind, which is very quickly developing right under our very eyes — and we are undoubtedly going through a stage of transition from nationalism, perhaps the first really historic transition since medieval times which saw the birth of nations, the beginning of the birth of nations, and now into regionalism."

5. Reliable Financial Arrangements:
   Clark M. Eichelberger, chairman, Commission to
   Study the Organization of Peace (page 56)
   "My theory has been that the United Nations must
   have sovereignty of its own and it must have its own
   taxing power. It must have the power of the purse."

The shocking contempt for the Constitution and for
the American people revealed in this sampling of official
and private political philosophy is a shrill warning signal
of impending United Nations world tyranny. Unless the
respective state legislatures act quickly to assert their
sovereignty, the people will be committed to support
and obey the one-world government plans of the internationalists in Washington. Senator John P. Sparkman
(D-Ala.), for example, is wholly favorable to dismantling the United States military establishment. Sparkman's
anti-American conviction was identified as early as July
21, 1958, when, practically single-handed, he succeeded
in passing a Senate resolution calling for a permanent
United Nations police force.

Senator William Jenner denounced the manner in
which the resolution was slipped through the Senate by
Sparkman and warned that "the plan is to build up
U.N. military power step by step and cut down U.S.
military power step by step.

"How long," he asked, "before troops from Poland
and Czechoslovakia or Indonesia will be posted at key
points on American soil?"

The "Planning for Peace" testimony before the U.S.
Senate Foreign Relations Committee has a direct bear-
ing on the conduct of the United Nations war in Viet
Nam as the provisions of the SEATO agreement reveal.

The Southeast Asia Treaty Organization (SEATO),
signed at Manila September 8, 1954, binds the signatory

nations, including the United States, to the United Nations Organization and to the provisions of the United Nations Charter. "Reiterating their faith in the purposes and in agreement with the principles set forth in the Charter of the United Nations," states Article one of SEATO, the participants "undertake to refrain in their international relations from the threat or use of force in any manner inconsistant with the purposes of the United Nations." [11]

Under Article IV, paragraph one, the SEATO agreement further directs that, "measures taken under this paragraph shall be immediately reported to the Security Council of the United Nations."

It should be noted parenthetically that NATO and CENTO treaties contain identical wording.[A]

SEATO is, therefore, a "front" organization or regional arrangement for the United Nations military command in New York City and Articles 53 and 54 of the U.N. Charter apply as they did in Korea; i.e.: "The Security Council shall at all times be kept fully informed." [12]

Operational control of the U.N. Security Council, the U.N. military headquarters, is exercised by its executive officer, who also holds the title of "Undersecretary for Political and Security Council Affairs." This executive officer is the custodian of all United States plans for self-defense and he controls all military forces placed at the disposal of the United Nations in consonance with

[11] Southeast Asia Treaty Organization, Article 1.
[A] Exhibit — NATO "The North Atlantic Treaty"
[12] U.N. Charter, Chapter VIII, "Regional Arrangements," Article 54.

U.N. Charter Articles 44, 45, and 46. The Undersecretary of Political and Security Council Affairs is easily the most powerful man in the United Nations.

The individual now holding this U.N. military post, as will be noted subsequently, is Vladimir P. Suslov, a Soviet Communist. Suslov is also the third member of the U.N. Marxist "troika," consisting of U Thant, Ralph Bunche and Suslov.

The authority exercised by the U.N. Security Council in the Viet Nam "war of liberation" has been confirmed by the administration in Washington. On Tuesday, July 13, 1965, President Johnson told the American people that American troops are dying in Viet Nam because of our commitment to the SEATO agreement. ". . . we expect to keep that commitment," said the President. "Our national honor is at stake." [13]

The accuracy of the President's statement is beyond question, for Article 25, United Nations Charter, states:

"The Members of the United Nations agree to accept and carry out the decisions of the Security Council in accordance with the present Charter."

America's soldier sons in Viet Nam are, therefore, again committed to a United Nations "no win" war under the same kind of internationally-programmed scenario as existed in the Korean conflict.

The men and the system which has transferred the U.S. military establishment to United Nations control will be critically examined in succeeding chapters.

[13] "Increased Cong Action may force Step-up by U.S.", *Denver Post*, Wednesday, July 14, 1965.

CHAPTER II

UNITED NATIONS
ONE-WORLD GOVERNMENT

Americans must halt the build-up of a United
Nations Army, or we will soon find ourselves supervised by sociological drovers on a one-world animal
farm.

My interest in United Nations cabalistic nuance began in Korea where I observed the American flag and
the United Nations banner flying side by side at the
Pusan headquarters, Supreme United Nations Command, Korea. It was also in Korea that, for the first time,
I observed American dead being buried under a foreign
device in a United Nations cemetery.

This curiosity increased during the course of my
struggle to comply with military orders which directed
the establishment of pro-American troop educational
programs in Germany. These military directives, I found,
were sabotaged by concealed forces in the Pentagon
and in the Department of State. I was to discover later
that these policy moves originated in the United Nations
under authority of the United Nations Charter.

Additional evidence of a strange ambivalence regarding official statements concerning troop information objectives and the field application of those principles

was revealed during the course of the Senate "military muzzling" investigations which sprang from this struggle. It then became apparent that hidden policy planners at an international level were in fact directing a propaganda campaign which opposed the principles set forth in the United States Constitution; the Constitution which I have sworn to "defend and preserve."

Confronted with the divided allegiance demanded by the new military morality I determined to trace the origins of this mischief and to make it my mission to seek the means for correcting the misdirection of armed forces policy and which would end the exploitation of America's soldier sons in international adventures.

The information gleaned during the course of my personal investigations, and the situations which produced such evidence, are presented in this book. This compendium of international deceit is drawn from actions in which I was personally involved or which are the result of related research and examination of public and private documents.

The following factors will be disclosed as having a material bearing on the abuse of American fighting forces and the undermining of the United States Constitution:

a. The United Nations Organization is the product of internationalists whose objective is Soviet-style control over the world's people and resources.

b. A prime requisite for the achievement of one-world government under the U.N. flag is United Nations command of U.S. military forces.

c. Technique for achieving U.N. Command of the U.S. military establishment include U.N. manipulation of United States government agencies, establishment of interlocking propaganda media, and the employment of politically oriented agents who are in sympathy with one-world government policy.

The purpose of the disclosure is two-fold; first, to indict publicly the United Nations Organization and, second, to illustrate the importance of immediate action to resolve this condition of dire peril.

A major objective of the work is the presentation of a Constitution-centered citizen action plan which will lead to the reestablishment of the United States Constitution as the "Supreme Law of the Land." The concluding portion of the book will, therefore, be concerned with a proposal to insure that the limits of the U.S. Constitution are respected within the borders of the sovereign states.

It will be shown that Americans can act to avert terminal passage of our Christian nation into a Soviet twilight zone under the United Nations banner.

Of course, the Planners tell us that the United Nations is the hope of the world.

But we know that the United Nations is not what U.N. propagandists say it is.

We know that the United Nations is not what U.N. supporters think it is.

The United Nations is what the articles of the U.N. Charter say it is:

The United Nations is an agency for imposing

a one-world government on the nations of the world; by peaceful means if possible; by force and violence if necessary.

The law of self-preservation demands that Americans learn as much as possible about this international organization; an agency which is geared for a take-over of the United States. We must know its origins; we must study its charter, and we must examine its effect on our national policy.

Our study will be a candid examination of a new dimension in warfare. It will show that the weapons employed by our enemy are duplicity, subversion, and treason.

However, before exploring the events which placed our soldiers under U.N. command, it may be pertinent to explain why many army men have elected to become personally involved in this psycho-political war. Perhaps the most direct means of defining our position is to present the oath each officer takes upon being commissioned into the United States Army.

This was, and is the military creed:

"I, . . . , do solemnly swear that I will support and defend the Constitution of the United States against all enemies, foreign and domestic; That I will bear true faith and allegiance to the same; That I take this obligation freely, without any mental reservation or purpose of evasion, and that I will well and faithfully discharge the duties of the office on which I am about to enter. So help me, God."

A personal reason for resistance to a United Nations take-over lies in the fact that my ancestors helped to establish in this bountiful land, "the best form of government ever devised by the hand of man."

We must not relinquish the heritage of freedom so dearly won by the sweat and blood of our forefathers.

And, because resistance to collectivism is not a popular posture in America today, I offer my credentials of citizenship.

My great-great-great-great grandfather was William Roberts of North Carolina. William initiated our family tradition of army service during the American War for Independence.

Private Roberts, who was born in Connecticut, enlisted in Sharp's Company, Tenth Regiment of North Carolina in November 10, 1778, and served throughout the remainder of the Revolutionary War.

This Colonial farmer, Continental soldier, and American pioneer now lies buried in Washington Presbyterian Church Cemetery near Knoxville, Tennessee.

Another lineal ancestor, John Brown (sire to my great-great grandmother, Alice) also served in the army of General George Washington. Records of the Tennessee Society, Daughters of the American Revolution, show that John was a Private First Class in Captain Shelby's Company of North Carolina Volunteers.

A collateral ancestor, Josiah Roberts, saw service in the War of 1812. Josiah enlisted from St. Clair County, Illinois in 1811 and marched with the famous Tom Benton Regiment. He was in many engagements, including Horseshoe Bend and Tippecanoe.

This United States soldier now lies in Robert's Cemetery, Honey Bend (formerly Robert's Landing), Illinois.

My great-grandfather, John Corwin Roberts, was a veteran of both the Mexican War and the Civil War.

John, who was born in Marion County, Tennessee, migrated to Montgomery County, Illinois in 1842. He enlisted for the Mexican War on August 11, 1847 at Hillsboro, Illinois when seventeen years old and served with Troop H, U.S. Regiment of Mounted Rifles.

John was wounded at Chapultepec, Mexico and was subsequently discharged at Jefferson Barracks, Missouri on August 26, 1848 in the grade of sergeant.

Recalled to active duty on August 8, 1862, John served as First Sergeant, Company F, 126th Regiment of Illinois Volunteers throughout the Civil War. He was discharged at Pine Bluff, Arkansas on July 12, 1865.

John Corwin Roberts, soldier, farmer, preacher, now rests in Hopewell Cemetery, Litchfield, Illinois.

The father of my grandmother Anna was less fortunate in the War Between the States. Charles E. Lancaster, a private in Company E 118th Regiment of Pennsylvania Volunteers, was captured by Confederate forces at Gainsville, Georgia on June 2, 1864. He died the following October at Andersonville Prison and is buried in Plot Number 10548, Andersonville National Cemetery.

To bring this military lineage quickly to the present, I will conclude the Roberts's service record with that of my brother, the late Major Richard A. Roberts, United States Air Force, Reserve.

Richard volunteered for the Army Air Corps shortly after Pearl Harbor. Upon graduation from pilot training he elected to fly combat missions with General Chennault's Flying Tigers in China.

Lieutenant Roberts' P-40 was shot down by Japanese Zero fire over Japanese-held China on his twenty-third mission. Weeks later Chinese partisans carried him back to his base at Chun King on a litter.

He was discharged in the rank of captain upon termination of hostilities — sole survivor of his original volunteer group.

This personal data may serve to identify the origins of my political convictions . . . One hundred eighty-five years of army service is firm evidence that members of my family are motivated by no "ism" . . . except Americanism. This family motivation also explains my compelling reason to examine an international organization which directly threatens the principles to which generations of Americans have dedicated their lives, their fortunes, and their sacred honor.

The U.N. Charter is such a fantastic document that it must be of first concern to establish a criterion for credibility. Perhaps this can best be done by identifying the founding fathers of this improbable organization.

Many prominent members of U.S. government departments were involved in the preparation of the United Nations Charter. To mention a few:

Dean Acheson, Secretary of State. Acheson, on December 22, 1941, became one of fourteen "intellectual elite" selected by Secretary of State Cordell Hull to serve on a Presidential Advisory Committee on Post-War Foreign Policy which was organized to prepare for effective participation in the solution of "vast and complicated problems of international relations which will confront" the United States and the world after "the final defeat of the forces of aggression."

In a letter to President Franklin D. Roosevelt explaining the responsibilities of this United Nations Planning Commission, Hull said, "It (the Committee) will, accordingly, work in the inseparably interrelated fields of general security, limitation of armaments, sound international economic relationships, and other phases of international cooperation, the implementation of which is essential to enduring world peace and to economic progress."

All research, interdepartmental government agency coordination, and international cooperation was set up in the Department of State "or under its leadership."

In addition to himself as chairman, Cordell Hull listed the following members for his supra-government "brain trust":

Mr. Sumner Welles (Under-Secretary of State) Vice Chairman

Mr. Norman H. Davis (President of Council on Foreign Relations and Chairman American Red Cross)

Mr. Myron C. Taylor

Mr. Dean Acheson (Assistant Secretary of State)

Mr. Hamilton Fish Armstrong (Editor, Foreign Affairs)

Mr. Adolf A. Berle, Jr. (Assistant Secretary of State)

Mr. Isaiah Bowman (President, John Hopkins University)

Mr. Benjamin V. Cohen (General Counsel, National Power Policy Committee)

Mr. Herbert Feis (Department of State Advisor on International Economic Relations)

Mr. Green N. Hackworth (Department of State Legal Advisor)

Mr. Harry C. Hopkins (Chief of the Department of State Division of Commercial Policy)

Mrs. Anne O'Hare McCormick (Editorial Staff, *The New York Times*)

Mr. Leo Pasvolsky (Special Assistant to the Secretary of State and Chief of the Department's Division of Special Research) [1]

On or about December 28, 1941, the President wrote on this letter: "I heartily approve. F.D.R."

Mr. Adolf A. Berle, Jr. told the House Committee on Un-American Activities on August 30, 1948, that Acheson was, ". . . head of the pro-Russian group in the State Department." Acheson is credited with making important contributions to the plans for the United Nations, and, "in 1945 worked successfully for Congressional approval of the Bretton Woods Monetary Agreement." Major General Patrick Hurley, former Ambassador to China, linked Acheson, in December, 1945, with a group in the "State Department which wanted to arm the Chinese Communists and bring about the defeat of Chiang Kai-shek." Because he had been associated with Alger Hiss, accused of Communist affiliations by Whittaker Chambers, Acheson was obligated to undergo

[1] "Postwar Foreign Policy Preparation 1939-1945," *Department of State Publication #3580*, General Foreign Policy Series 15, Released February 1950, pages 63-64.

questioning by the Senate Foreign Relations Committee as to his connections with Donald and Alger Hiss and his law firm's activity in the international field." Alger Hiss was the principal assistant to Dean Acheson, who came to the firm defense of Hiss during Hiss's trial for espionage.[2]

Harry Dexter White, Assistant Secretary of the Treasury. Records of the Federal Bureau of Investigation show that White was a member of the Perlo Communist cell in Washington, D.C. and an espionage agent for the Soviets. White represented the Treasury Department on eighteen inter-departmental and international bodies.[3] He was the chief architect of the U.N. International Monetary Fund at Bretton Woods and at San Francisco. White, identified by Whittaker Chambers as a Soviet espionage agent, is cited extensively in many U.S. Senate investigations and reports dealing with Communist activity and subversion in the United States.

Harold Glasser, Treasury Department. This Soviet Agent was set by espionage leader Bykov to "control" Harry Dexter White.[4] Glasser was the Treasury Department spokesman on the affairs of UNRRA* "throughout its whole life" and he had a "predominant voice" in determining which countries should receive aid and which should not. Glasser was a constant consultant to Dean Acheson on UNRRA problems [5] and was a mem-

[2] *Current Biography,* 1949, pages 3-5.
[3] *The U.N. Record,* Chesly Manly, page 106.
[4] *Witness,* by Whittaker Chambers, page 430.
* UNRRA (United Nations Relief and Rehabilitation Administration).
[5] Report, USS Internal Security Subcommittee, April 14, 1953.

ber of the Perlo Communist cell in Washington.

Nathan Gregory Silvermaster, Treasury Department,
Elizabeth Bentley, for years a top courier for the Russian
Secret Police in America, identified Silvermaster as the
head of the "Silvermaster Soviet spy ring in Washington,
D.C." He was associated with Harry Dexter White at
Bretton Woods and is cited in the House Committee on
Un-American Acitvities hearings on Espionage. Silver-
master's testimony before the USS Internal Security Sub-
Committee regarding his espionage activities in the
United States comprises 175 pages of interrogation and
exhibits.[6]

Virginius Frank Coe, Treasury Department. Coe was
technical secretary at the Bretton Woods Conference
in 1944 and Secretary of the International Monetary
Fund established by Harry Dexter White. This former
Director of the Division of Monetary Research was
named in the original Berle notes from Chambers as
involved in the Communist underground. He was a
member of the Harold Ware Communist Cell. Coe was
Secretary of the International Monetary Fund from 1946
to 1952. He, also, took refuge in the Fifth Amendment
under questioning.

Victor Perlo, Treasury Department. A "Ware" Communist cell member, Perlo later headed the "Perlo"
Communist cell in Washington. He entered the Government in 1938 via the Department of Commerce. His
job was to accumulate and present facts for basic eco-

[6] "Interlocking Subversion in Government Departments," USS ISS,
Part 3, April 16, 1953.

nomic decisions by Secretary of Commerce Harry Hopkins. Perlo later transferred to the Division of Monetary Research whose directors were Harry Dexter White, followed by V. Frank Coe and Harold Glasser. He left government service in 1947 and authored the book, *American Imperialism.*

William L. Ullman, Treasury Department. Ullman was a member of the American Delegation at the U.N.-spawning San Francisco meeting, as an "assistant to Mr. White." He had previously assisted Harry Dexter White at Bretton Woods. Ullman was a perennial houseguest of Nathan Gregory Silvermaster and was the chief photographer of stolen government documents for the Silvermaster espionage ring. Ullman, then a Major, Material and Service Division, Army Air Corps, Headquarters the Pentagon, passed date of D-Day through Elizabeth Bentley, to the Soviets.[7]

Irving Kaplan, Treasury Department. Kaplan was the chief advisor to the Military Government of Germany on financial and economic matters. He received an "E" rating from Harold Glasser. He was associated with both the Perlo and Silvermaster cells and was employed by David Weintraub in the United Nations Division of Economic Stability and Development from February, 1946 through November, 1952. The Federal Bureau of Investigation has submitted eighteen adverse reports on Kaplan.

Laurence Duggan, Department of State. Duggan was head of the Latin American Division of the State De-

[7] *Web of Subversion,* by James Burnham, page 172.

partment and was recruited into the Soviet espionage apparatus by Hede Massing.[8]

Noel Field. Department of State. Field headed the Western European Division, State Department. He, also, was recruited into Soviet espionage work by Hede Massing.[9] Field disappeared behind the Iron Curtain during the Alger Hiss trial.

Henry Julian Wadleigh, Department of State. Wadleigh was head of the Trades Agreement Division, Department of State. During the Hiss Trial he confessed to being a member of the Bykov-Chambers-Hiss Soviet espionage group.

John Carter Vincent, Department of State. Vincent was Chief of the Chinese Affairs Division. He was identified as a Communist in hearings conducted by the United States Senate Internal Security Subcommittee.[10] Vincent was a member of the American Delegation at San Francisco.

David Weintraub, Department of State. Weintraub was head of the Office of Foreign Relief and Rehabilitation Operations. He was a key figure in the 1952 Senate investigations of Communism in the United Nations.[11] Weintraub occupied a unique position in setting up the structure of Communist penetration in governmental agencies by individuals who have been identified by witnesses as underground agents of the Communist Party.

8 "Institute of Pacific Relations," USS ISS, page 403.
9 "IPR," USS ISS, pages 235-237.
10 "IPR," USS ISS, page 403.
11 "Activities of U.S. Citizens employed by the United Nations," ISS.

There are many more similar cases. All of these Government Department employees contributed to the authorship of the United Nations Charter. And, all were agents for International Communism.

No person, of course, has special access to the ultimate truth. It is impossible to know whether these individuals became agents for Communism because of moral weakness, greed, lust for power, or because of ideological conviction. And, it is unimportant — for this study is more concerned with presenting an indictment of the United Nations than in the motives of those who created it.

In compiling this sorry record of subversion and betrayal it can be readily seen that, in listing the founding fathers of the United Nations, we are actually writing a "Who's Who of Organized Treason in the United States." The case histories are depressingly monotonous.

Rather than examine in detail each of these shallow little men, let us, instead, select for study three U.N. Charter authors who claim a special notice for infamy. These typical records will provide a ready index to the political philosophy and moral concepts of the men who launched the United Nations.

Our first choice in this gallery of rogues must be Mr. Alger Hiss, Chief of Special Political Affairs, Department of State. Mr. Hiss was deputy to Mr. Leo Pasvolsky and had policy jurisdiction over all internal State Department organization and the logistic and policy support of our activities in international organizations. This responsibility specifically included the United Nations, the specialized agencies in the United Nations, and the American complement of personnel in the United Nations.

The origins of Hiss's relationship to the United Nations and its charter is told in the book, *Seeds of Treason*, by Ralph de Toledano. On page 110 of his book, Mr. de Toledano says:

> "In August, 1944, Hiss attended the Dumbarton Oaks Conference as executive secretary. When he returned, all matters pertaining to the proposed security organization came under his direct supervision. With Harry Hopkins, Cordell Hull and others, Hiss worked on the first draft of the United Nations Charter."

Hiss, of course, was approved by Stalin, Churchill and Roosevelt as the "General Secretary" of the San Francisco conference which spawned the United Nations on June 26, 1945.[12]

Three years later, on August 3, 1948, Whittaker Chambers, in testimony before the House Committee on Un-American Activities, identified Alger Hiss as a Soviet espionage agent and a member of the Harold Ware Communist cell in Washington. Hiss was subsequently convicted of perjury for denying, under oath, his Communist activities.[13]

Alger Hiss, principal author of the first draft of the United Nations Charter, is also cited extensively in over thirty Senate hearings and reports dealing with Soviet

[12] *Seeds of Treason*, by Ralph de Toledano, page 112.
[13] *Witness*, by Whittaker Chambers, pages 535, 542-543.

espionage and Communist activities in the United States.[14]

Our second choice of U.N. founding fathers is Mr. Leo Pasvolsky, an obscure but powerful State Department director. Pasvolsky died on May 5, 1953 and, in an obituary of May 18, *Time* magazine said:

> "Died: Leo Pasvolsky, 59, Russian-born architect of the United Nations Charter and economics expert, at Brookings Institution . . . A late 30's protege of Secretary of State Cordell Hull Economist Pasvolsky served as Hull's principal behind-the-scenes strategist at the Dumbarton Oaks and San Francisco conferences, (he) broke a Big Five deadlock at San Francisco by 'reinterpreting' the veto question and rewriting the U.N. Charter." [15]

The *Time* magazine revelation that Pasvolsky, a Russian-born State Department chief, was the "architect" of the U.N. Charter may explain why much of the Charter is copied directly from the Soviet Constitution. One can place these two documents side by side and identify the material which has been taken from one and placed in the other.

In fact, the shadowy Pasvolsky provides such significant insight into the intricacies of our government that I feel you will be interested in further detail concerning his amazing accomplishments.

Pasvolsky was born in Russia of parents who were communist revolutionaries.

---

[14] "Cumulative Index to Published Hearings and Reports of the Subcommittee to Investigate the Administration of the Internal Security Act and Other Internal Security Laws." Committee on the Judiciary, USS, 1951-1955, pages 341, 342; and "Cumulative Index," 1956-1960, page 184.

[15] *Time* Magazine, May 18, 1953, page 99.

He penetrated our government in 1934 as an "economist" connected with the Bureau of Foreign and Domestic Commerce. One year later he transferred to the State Department under the title of "Special Assistant to the Secretary."

The 1945 edition of *Current Biography* explains the assignment in this fashion:

> "Politically, Leo Pasvolsky's early record placed him well to the left. The reason for his title of 'Special Assistant' was to spare the White House possible wrangling in Congress over a Russian-born expert with a political past as varied as a zebra's stripes." [16]

The true objective of the strangely talented Mr. Pasvolsky was revealed by Mr. L. V. Horner in a speech which he delivered in Oklahoma City on June 17, 1963.

> "One of the first acts of Mr. Pasvolsky upon entering our State Department," said Mr. Horner, "was to issue a memorandum in which he boldly stated that the objective and function of the Department of which he was named director would be, 'To survey the basic principles which should underlie a desirable world order to be evolved after the termination of present hostilities . . . and to devise means of limitation of national sovereignty'." [17]

I would say that the articles of the United Nations Charter meet Pasvolsky's requirements — particularly in limiting the national sovereignty of the United States of America.

[16] *Current Biography*, 1945, pages 448-449.
[17] *The United Nations a Threat to our Security*, by L. V. Horner, June 17, 1963, page 4.

The third and final character in this evil chorus of U.N. founding fathers is Mr. Phillip C. Jessup. Jessup was Assistant Secretary General of the UNRRA Conference in 1943; he was Assistant Secretary General of the Bretton Woods Conference in 1944, and he was a member of the American Delegation at the San Francisco Conference in 1945.

It is highly significant to know that Phillip C. Jessup is a former head of the Institute of Pacific Relations.[18] The Institute of Pacific Relations was investigated by the Senate Internal Security Subcommittee, which found it to be, ". . . a vehicle used by the Communists to orient American Far Eastern Policy toward Communist objectives."[19]

Many authorities on interlocking subversion in government departments have claimed that the activities of IPR were a primary cause for the loss of China to the Communists following World War II.

Jessup, perhaps predictably, is now the U.S. representative on the U.N. World Court.

Jessup would have been the United States Ambassador to the United Nations except for the fact that the U.S. Senate refused to confirm his appointment because of extensive subversive associations revealed by investigation into his background.

Jessup is cited in many Senate investigations on subversion, including the following hearings:

— Institute of Pacific Relations,

[18] *Current Biography*, 1948, page 316.
[19] "Institute of Pacific Relations," *Senate Report #2050*, July 2, 1952, pages 223-226.

— Activities of United States Citizens Employed in
  the U.N.,
   — Interlocking Subversion in Government Depart-
     ments,
— Strategy and Tactics of World Communism, and
— Scope of Soviet Activity in the United States.

The identification of these authors of the United Nations Charter, and the political persuasion with which
they are associated, will aid in comprehending the
concealed objectives of this strange organization.

On June 26, 1945, President Harry S. Truman addressed the closing session of the San Francisco Conference, approved the draft Charter, and attended its
signing on the same date. United States Delegates who
signed the Charter were:

The Secretary of State.

The two Democratic and Republican leaders of the
   Foreign Relations Committee of the Senate.

The two Democratic and Republican leaders of the
   Foreign Affairs Committee of the House of Representatives, and

Two Delegates from the general public.

The seal of approval was placed on the extraordinary
Treaty when the consent of the Senate to ratification was
granted on July 28, 1945 by vote of 89 in favor with
2 against.[20]

The Honorable William Langer, one of two Senators
opposing ratification (the other being Senator Styles
Bridges of New Hampshire), said on the floor of the
Senate this fateful day:

[20] *Postwar Foreign Policy Preparation 1939-1945*, page 450.

"Practically all members of this body have indicated that they will vote for the Charter. Under my oath, Mr. President, and under my conscience, I cannot so vote. If I did, I would feel that I was betraying the hundreds of thousands who have died in this war for the United States, and the hundreds of thousands who have sacrificed their loved ones and their treasure.

"I feel from the bottom of my heart," said Senator Langer, "that the adoption of the Charter — and make no mistake, we are going to implement it — will mean perpetuating war. I feel that it will mean the enslavement of millions of people from Poland to India, from Korea to Java, as well as people in many other places on this earth." [21]

Senator Langer's prophesy was to be confirmed in blood and agony, as we shall see.

[21] *Congressional Record*, July 28, 1945, pages 8188-8189.

CHAPTER III

WHO COMMANDS
U.N. MILITARY FORCES?

"It (the U.N. Charter) was patterned to some extent upon the Constitution of the Soviet Republic,
frequently paraphrasing the wording of that document. . . A perusal of articles 43 to 51, inclusive, will
reveal the fact that it was designed as an instrument
of force."
— Hon. John T. Wood of Idaho before U.S. Flag
Committee, New York, October 10, 1951

The expanding power of a U.N. military dictatorship
is obvious. Many people have become aware of this
threat to life and liberty — yet Americans are gripped
by a paralysis of indecision which inhibits effective action to defeat the surrender program of the Planners.

Intent of the surrender program becomes shockingly
apparent in a study of the office of the U.N. Undersecretary for Political and Security Affairs.

It is highly important to remember that the occupant
of this critical U.N. military post is also the Executive
Officer of the Security Council. He heads the armed
forces of the United Nations including those in Korea
and Viet Nam, for example.

The U.N. military post of Political and Security Affairs
is consistently awarded to a Soviet Communist.

Although Americans appear to be unmoved by the fact that their sons serve under the command of a Soviet Communist, this complacency is not due to lack of information. In fact, the *New York Times,* in an article headed, "Russian Named to High U.N. Post," dated May 22, 1963, put it this way:

> "The post for political and security council affairs traditionally has been held by a Soviet national. The undersecretary," said the *Times,* "is a senior advisor to the Secretary General." [1]

This U.N. undersecretary certainly is a "Senior Advisor:" —. He is the Commander-in-Chief of the U.N. Army.

The year books of the United Nations from 1946 through 1951 confirm the *New York Times* article. And, to keep the record straight, we will list the appointees to this position since the beginning of the United Nations. Here they are:

1946–1949	Arkady Alexandrovich Sobolev	USSR
1949–1953	Constantine E. Zinchenko	USSR
1953–1954	Ilya S. Tchernychev	USSR
1955–1957	Dragoslav Protich	Yugoslavia
1958–1959	Anatoly Dobrynin	USSR
1960–1962	Georgy Petrovich Arkadev	USSR
1962–1963	Eugeney D. Kiselev	USSR
1963–	Vladimir Pavlovich Suslov	USSR

Many leading Americans have voiced anxiety and horror at the constant appointment of Communists to

[1] "Russian Named to High U.N. Post," *New York Times,* May 22, 1963.

ill the U.N. military post of Undersecretary for Political and Security Affairs. All have expressed great alarm over the power which this undersecretary exercises over our armed forces.

One who clearly recognized the concealed purposes of the United Nations Security Council was the late Congressman Usher L. Burdick, of North Dakota.

On January 17, 1957, Representative Burdick delivered a penetrating speech on the floor of the House which he titled, "The Russians are and will continue to be on the Inside of any Military Action taken by the Security Council of the United Nations." In this important talk, Mr. Burdick said:

> "This means that since the Security Council was organized, the Russians, through the Secretary, have had close touch with all military plans. The directives to MacArthur and the reports coming from him," said the congressman, "passed through the hands of this secretary. Now can you realize what MacArthur was up against in trying to win the Korean War?" [2]

Since 1957, when Congressman Burdick warned of this danger, the United Nations has accelerated its usurpation of military power for subversive purposes. Today the United Nations Security Council is a prime instrumentality for global conquest.

This war-making capability is, of course, exactly what the authors of the United Nations Charter intended.

[2] "The Russians are and will continue to be on the Inside of any Military Action taken by the Security Council of the United Nations," Honorable Usher L. Burdick, *Congressional Record*, January 17, 1957, pages 795-796.

We need not speculate on how the Soviet gained con
trol of the U.N. Army for fortunately there is a record
of events which set the policy for a Communist being
consistently appointed as Undersecretary for Political
and Security Affairs. On page 45 of his book, *In the
Cause of Peace,* Mr. Trygve Lie, first Secretary General
of the United Nations said:

> "Mr. Vyshinsky did not delay in this approach. He
> was the first to inform me of an understanding
> which the Big Five had reached in London on the
> appointment of a Soviet national as Assistant Secre-
> tary-General for Political and Security Affairs." [8]

Further proof of the international collusion which
placed a Communist in supreme command of the
United Nations Armed Forces is contained in a letter
written by Mr. Wallace Irwin, Jr., Director of Public
Services, United Nations. In responding to an inquiry
concerning Soviet control of U.S. military forces by Ad
miral de la Houssaye, Sons of the American Revolution
Mr. Irwin said in a letter dated April 7, 1961:

> "...both Mr. Stettinius and the French stressed that
> their agreement to the Soviet Post was a limited one,
> designed to get the Secretariat off to a good start. It
> was not understood," Mr. Irwin declared, "that a
> permanent lien on the office of the Assistant Secre-
> tary for Security Council Affairs was granted to the
> Soviet Union."

Then Mr. Irwin went on to say:

> "As far as practice is concerned, it is true that from
> the beginning this particular Assistant Secretary
> General...has been a Soviet national."

[8] *In the Cause of Peace,* by Trygve Lie, page 45.

Thus, in his amazing letter, Mr. Irwin admits that he Commander-in-Chief of all United Nations Armed Forces, including ours, has always been a Communist.

In a concluding thrust, Irwin attempted to justify this shocking situation with these words:

> "This (the selection of a succession of Communists to fill the Undersecretary post) is a matter entirely within the authority of the Secretary General, whose basic guidance in the selection of the staff and in the determination of the conditions of service shall be the necessity of securing the highest standards of efficiency, competence, and integrity." [4]

Well — it may be that by U.N. standards only Soviet nationals have the efficiency, competence, and integrity to take charge of the military of all nations, including ours. But, their standards are not our standards and I denounce the men and the system which has forced our whole military establishment into this intolerable position.

The Undersecretary, of course, draws his authority from the articles of the United Nations Charter. Therefore, if we are to understand the power and importance of this office, we must now turn to the U.N. Charter.

Incidentally, a pocket-sized copy of the U.N. Charter is available from the United Nations Headquarters in New York City. Do get a copy of this document — and study it. Your life may depend upon it!

Now, the provisions for applying force and violence in achieving the concealed objectives of the United Nations are contained in Chapter VII of the Charter

[4] Letter, Wallace Irwin, Jr., Director of Public Services, U.S. Mission to the United Nations, April 7, 1961.

under the heading, "Actions with Respect to Threats to
the Peace, Breaches of the Peace, and Acts of Aggres
sion."

For example, Article 47 under Chapter VII states:

> "There shall be established a Military Staff Commit-
> tee to advise and assist the security Council on all
> questions relating to the maintenance of interna-
> tional peace and security."

And. . . .

> "The Military Staff Committee shall be responsible
> under the Security Council for the Strategic direc-
> tion of any armed forces placed at the disposal of
> the Security Council." [5]

This is certainly strange language for a "peace" organization. So, what does it mean. . .what does it really
mean?

This legalistic language simply means of course that
the Security Council of the United Nations has the authority to declare "peace" — and to go on shooting — as
was the case in Katanga.

It must also be noted that, contrary to the provisions
of the U.N. Charter itself, there is no properly constituted Military Staff Committee in the United Nations
There is merely a rotating chairman representing the
five original signatories to the Charter. The Military Staff
Committee concept was inserted into the charter to fool
the American people. Proof of this fraud is contained in
Mr. Lie's book, *In the Cause of Peace*. On page 431,
Lie says:

[5] U.N. Charter, Chapter VII, Article 47.

"The Military Staff Committee, covered under Article 47, so far has been stillborn."

The critical point here is that (because the Military Staff Committee was "stillborn") the power and authority covered under Article 47 is placed directly in the office of the Undersecretary for Political and Security Affairs.

Further — Article 46 states:

"Plans for the applications of armed force shall be made by the Security Council with the assistance of the Military Staff Committee."

Well — as there is no Military Staff Committee, this "assistance" is provided by the undersecretary whose "plans" have included the American defeat in Korea, the rape of Katanga, and our military and economic hemorrhage in Viet Nam.

Article 47 also reveals that the Congress of the United States have abdicated their constitutional responsibility. The U.S. Constitution, in section eight, Article I, directs that, ". . . Congress shall have the power to declare war." Yet the United States Senate has officially admitted that the U.S. Constitution was ignored in the Korean action.

On page 3605 of the General MacArthur hearings (about which we will have more to say later) a joint Senate Committee, comprising members of the Armed Services and Foreign Relations Committees, said:

"The United States should never again become involved in a war without the consent of Congress . . . For the first time in the history of our nation the Constitutional authority of the Congress to declare war has been bypassed." [6]

Korea, alas, has become not the exception but the precedent for U.N. jurisdiction in committing American soldiers to battle all over the world.

It is perfectly obvious that the Security Council of the United Nations, not the Congress of the United States, is now the supreme authority which, as in the case of Korea and of all the campaigns which have followed, sends our troops and equipment everywhere in the world to "maintain international peace and security."

At this very moment, America's sons at the direction and plan of Communists in the United Nations, give their lives and blood to further the concealed objectives of the United Nations Charter.

Another "loaded" Charter provision is found in paragraph 3, Article 47 which states:

> "Questions relating to the command of such forces (the U.N. international army) shall be worked out subsequently."

Now — I believe that the word "subsequently" means after the promoters of the United Nations had succeeded in having the U.N. Charter ratified by the United States Senate. There is little question but that the provision of "command" of the United Nations army was actually "worked out" far in advance of the San Francisco meeting.

[6] *Military Situation in the Far East and the Facts surrounding the Relief of General of the Army, Douglas MacArthur,* May 3 through August 17, 1951, page 3605.

In any event, it is a matter of historical record that the "strategic direction" of U.N. armed forces has been under a succession of Communists — the seven Soviets and one Yugoslav who have held the U.N. military post of Undersecretary for Political and Security Affairs.

This conspiratorial situation will not surprise those who know that the U.N. Charter was written by Communists and traitors; among whom are prominently listed Alger Hiss, Leo Pasvolsky, and Phillip Jessup.

Fellow Americans, we cannot escape the consequence of this grim situation, nor can we evade our responsibility for permitting it to continue.

The Communist-dominated U.N. Security Council was the military command structure under which Americans died in Korea.

The Communist-dominated U.N. Security Council was the policy-making organization which imposed a "substitute for victory" in the Far East.

The Communist-dominated U.N. Security Council is the supreme military headquarters which even now directs a "limited war" in Viet Nam.

And, the Communist-dominated U.N. Security Council is the international war council which manipulates U.S. armed forces in "no-win" military adventures all over the globe.

I respectfully submit that the real enemy in Korea was not the illiterate Chinese peasant who crossed the Yalu with a bag of rice and a Russian rifle. Our real enemy crouches in the chambers of the United Nations where he remains concealed to this very day.

This concealed enemy directs the destiny of America

unfettered by moral, religious, or political restriction. Neither have the protective guarantees of the United States Constitution been brought to bear to restrain and thwart his machinations. In fact, many of our judges have been led to believe that the U.N. Charter has superceded the U.S. Constitution as the "Supreme Law of the Land."

Should you doubt this statement, please permit me to quote from Senate Document Number 87 titled, "Review of the United Nations Charter," dated January 7, 1954. On page 239 there appears this decision of the California Court of Appeals in the case of Sei Fujii v. California, 1950:

> "The Charter (of the United Nations) has become 'the Supreme Law of the Land; and the Judges in every State shall be bound thereby, any Thing in the Constitution or laws of any State to the contrary notwithstanding,' U.S. Constitution, Article VI, section 2." [7]

In civil case after civil case the courts of this nation have ruled in favor of U.N. Charter "treaty law" over U.S. Constitutional Law.

In the case of Perez v. Lippold, the California Supreme Court purported to rule in favor of the U.N. Charter over domestic law by finding that, "The Charter represents a moral commitment of the foremost importance."

On June 16, 1952, Judge Preston Thatcher, of the Sixth Circuit Court, declared that the U.N. Charter took

---

[7] "Review of the United Nations Charter," USS Document #87, dated January 7, 1954, page 289.

precedence over Idaho law and that, therefore, aliens could legally own land in the state.

And the late John Foster Dulles, former Secretary of State, expounded the same theory of power of "treaty law" in an address before the American Bar Association in Louisville, Kentucky on April 12, 1952.

> "Treaties," said Mr. Dulles, "make international law and also they make domestic law. Under our Constitution, treaties become the supreme law of the land. They are indeed more supreme than ordinary laws, for congressional laws are invalid if they do not conform to the Constitution, whereas treaty law can over-ride the Constitution."

Then Mr. Dulles spelled out the new legal posture which members of the American Bar Association would be expected to assume in future interpretation of the United Nations Charter as the "Supreme Law of the Land."

> "Treaties," he said, "can take powers away from the Congress and give them to the President; they can take powers from the state and give them to the federal government or to some international body, and they can cut across the rights given the people by the Constitutional Bill of Rights." [8]

These statements, so ominous in their import and so devastating in their consequences if they are allowed to supplant our Constitution and our form of government, represent a bold challenge which the citizens of this

[8] "Is the Danger Facing this Country from the Power Granted the United Nations to be Feared?" Honorable Usher L. Burdick, *Congressional Record*, House, March 3, 1953, pages A1034-A1035.

country must prepare themselves to meet. It is the purpose of the concluding chapters of this book to show how this challenge can be met and how the constitutional heretics who would subvert our law can be made to comply with it.

I hope that we have now exposed the fiction that the United Nations is merely an international "debating society."

The United Nations is not a debating society. The United Nations is an instrumentality for global conquest. Its objective is to overthrow the government of the United States and of the several states, by peaceful means if possible; by force and violence if necessary.

It is a chilling tribute to the efficiency of our enemy that U.N. circumvention of our Constitution has been accompanied by a deliberate program designed to redirect the allegiance of our men in uniform so as to immobilize U.S. military resistance to the United Nations take-over.

Information concerning the re-molding of the role and mission of our armed forces has, of course, been withheld from the public through the technique of managed news. Nevertheless, current events prove that there is in progress within our military establishment a covert plan to debase and destroy the concept of "Honor-Duty-Country." This now "outmoded" army philosophy, which has motivated our soldiers since the American Revolution, is on the way out. The U.N. aim is to redefine U.S. military attitudes for "international responsibilities."

Today our men in service are being brainwashed to accept mercenary service in a United Nations army led by Communists.

A typical achievement of this policy is the creation of "Military Government Reserve Units." In army centers across the nation, considerable numbers of American soldiers are now in training as specialized elements in so-called "Logistical Commands." The real purpose of such training was first exposed in 1951 and reported by Dr. V. Orval Watts in his book, *The United Nations — Planned Tyranny*.

Describing the on-the-job training of these military government units, Dr. Watts said,

> "Their first sally took place . . . July . . . 1951, when they simulated an invasion and seizure of nine California cities: Compton, Culver City, Inglewood, Hawthorne, Huntington Park, Long Beach, Redondo Beach, South Gate and Torrence. The invading forces, however, did not fly the American Flag," Watts reports, "they came in under the flag of the United Nations and their officers stated that they represented the United Nations." [9]

On July 16, 1951 the Culver City *Evening Star News* reported that these forces arrested the mayors and police chiefs of the "liberated" cities for "refusing to collaborate with the occupying forces."

> "The simulated occupation of the city by troops of the Military Government, United States Army, marks the first time that the combined Military Government reserve units of an army area embracing six western states have ever been employed in a single field exercise.

[9] *The United Nations — Planned Tyranny*, by Dr. V. Orval Watts, page 7.

"It also gave the public an opportunity to see the little-known Military Government units in action," said the *Star News*.

"The enemy flag was raised over the city with Military Government officers directing the ceremony. Starting at 10:30 a.m.," continues this report, "the force of the M.G. began a systematic investigation into all phases of the operation of the city. They 'took over' the newspapers, the city's public utility companies and made a detailed study of the industrial capacity of the community.

"It is the aim of this field exercise," concluded the article, "to be able to completely take over Culver City and operate it in an efficient manner." [10]

The *Los Angeles Times* of July 17 printed a picture of Culver City's Mayor Klotz being hustled from City Hall as a "suspected collaborator." Pictures also appeared in the newspapers showing these heads of local government in jail.

"Under practical conditions," Lt. Col. (Thomas M.) Mullen explained, "the military government troops remove civil and business leaders from their positions, keep them incarcerated, and eventually try them on charges of collaborating with the enemy which has been in power." [11]

Local newspapers reported that the "Commanding General" of the occupying forces issued a manifesto reading, ". . . by virtue of the authority vested in me by the United Nations Security Council . . ."

[10] "Culver 'Liberated' Early Today," *Evening Star News*, Culver City, California, Monday, July 16, 1951.
[11] "Sham Army Rule put on Culver City," *Los Angeles Times*, Tuesday, July 17, 1951.

"Military government 'occupancy' of Huntington Park," said the *Bulletin,* aroused indignation from many responsible sources and many local people expressed misgiving over such a development.

"All concerned were outspoken regarding the *Bulletin's* coverage of the so-called occupation and it is believed that this newspaper was the only one . . . to feature the 'seizure' proclamation." [12]

The "seizure" proclamation titled, "United Nations Forces Military Government of Agressi, Proclamation Number 1," is highly significant in view of current U.N. Security Council employment of U.S. armed forces in international military adventures.

"Whereas, in prosecuting the war against Agressi," states Proclamation Number 1, "it has become necessary for the armed forces of the United Nations under my command, to occupy this town, adjacent areas and other portions of Agressi, and

"Whereas, it is the policy of the armed forces of the United Nations not to make war upon the civilian inhabitants of the occupied territory but to protect them in the peaceful exercise of their legitimate pursuits, insofar as the exigencies of war and their own behaviour will permit, and

"Whereas, in order to preserve law and order and to provide for the safety and welfare both of the forces under my command and of yourselves, it is necessary to establish Military Government in the occupied territory.

[12] "United Nations" Force . . . or Farce?," *Bulletin,* Huntington Park, California, July 26, 1951.

"Now, therefore, I, Jones Smithman, General, United States Army Commanding United States Forces Oceania, and Military Governor of Agressi, by virtue of the authority vested in me by the United Nations Security Council, do hereby proclaim as follows:"

The entire proclamation is reproduced in the exhibits section of this book.[B]

"At Huntington Park," said Watts, "they held a flag-raising ceremony, taking down the American Flag and running up in its place the United Nations banner."

This display was an arrogant notice to the American people that the U.S. Military establishment is no longer an extension of their will. With brutal force the Security Council revealed that the U.S. Army is now a coercive weapon of the United Nations, and is to be employed in consonance with the concealed objectives of the United Nations Charter.

We have, of course, subsequently witnessed many California-type U.N. "simulated" invasions of American cities, including those in Lampasa, Texas on April 3, 1952 and Watertown, New York on August 20 of the same year.

We have seen our military forces institute a program of counter-insurgency training — training which is practical only in the event of another civil war in America.

We have experienced the military invasions of Little Rock, Arkansas and Oxford, Mississippi.

[B] Exhibit — United Nations Forces Military Government of Agressi, PROCLAMATION NUMBER I

We have observed several joint U.N. army exercises on the order of "Operation Water Moccasin." [13]

And, we behold American soldiers employed in U.N. military operations all over the world. These military actions are not unrelated.

I would further invite your attention to highly significant testimony given during the Senate Hearings on "Military Muzzling" which bears on the issue of U.N. control of our military forces. The Report is headed, "Military Cold War Education and Speech Review Policies." On page 109 there is a statement by Dr. Robert E. Beerstecher, a professional witness:

> "The Communist theory of revolution," said Dr. Beerstecher, "holds that the power of the state rests upon the military, so that in order to achieve the Communist take-over they feel it is essential to destroy the military establishment and replace it by one of their own manufacture." [14]

The Senate "muzzling" investigations clearly emphasize an obvious and shocking parallel between the Communist theory of "Revolutionary Anti-Militarism" and the internationalizing of our military establishment.

"Secrecy and duplicity are keystones of the United Nations," said Mrs. Mary Davison in a Council for Statehood release. "They could not exist otherwise. So, during the Korean War they feared that the highly intelligent commanders in the field would become aware of the

[13] "The Water Moccasin Bites," editorial page, *The Richmond News Leader,* Richmond, Virginia, March 7, 1963.

[14] "Majority Report—Military Cold War Education and Speech Review Policies," Hearings before the Special Preparedness Subcommittee, Committee on Armed Service, USS (Committee Print), October 19, 1962.

Top Command back in the U.N. headquarters, and in order to conceal the position and performance of Mr. Zinchenko (U.N. Undersecretary for Political and Security Affairs), Trygve Lie, who himself had spent much time in the Soviet Union and was rumored to have served on the Presidium, established a three-man committee known as the Executive Military Authority which would have great powers — under Zinchenko, of course — including the right to fire the Commander-in-Chief which was the U.N. title conferred upon General MacArthur and to replace him. Details of this performance," said Mrs. Davison, "are recorded in the famous *Senate Document Number 87*, pages 569 to 653." [15]

The answer to our question, "Who Commands U.N. Military Forces?" is confirmed in *Senate Document Number 87*, "Review of the United Nations Charter," USS, dated January 7, 1954.[16]

Beginning on page 646 of this Senate Document there appears a report on "Military Measures" to be taken under authority of the United Nations Security Council, submitted to the Security Council and the General Assembly by the Collective Measures Committee as United Nations Document A/1891, dated 1951.

"In carrying out its responsibilities to study the military aspects of methods 'which might be used to maintain and strengthen internal peace and security,' the Committee," states this report in Chapter IV, "has been

[15] *Open Letter Number 53*, Council for Statehood.
[16] *Senate Document Number 87*, January 7, 1954, page 646-659.

guided by the principles set forth in the preamble to the 'Uniting for Peace' resolution. This preamble states the General Assembly's desire to ensure that, pending the conclusion of the agreements provided in Article 43 of the Charter (contribution of armed forces and equipment), the United Nations has at its disposal the means for maintaining international peace and security."

Command of these U.N. military forces is defined under subtitle, "Appointment of the executive military authority:

"Under the arrangements contemplated under Chapter VII of the Charter, the organization of United Nations armed forces is to be undertaken by the Security Council with the advice and assistance of the Military Staff Committee, which is to assume responsibility for their strategic direction."

It will be remembered that Trygve Lie, first Secretary General of the United Nations, stated that the Military Staff Committee was "stillborn." The organization and "strategic direction" of the United Nations armed forces, therefore, comes under the authority of the Undersecretary for Security Council Affairs, Vladimir Pavlovich Suslov, a Soviet Communist.

"The Security Council or the General Assembly," continues this Collectives Measures Committee report, "when it resolves to employ measures involving the collective use of armed force, will formulate the objectives and general policy of the United Nations. Within the framework so defined, or as developed subsequently by the appropriate United Nations body, the executive military authority should be responsible for the coordination and direction of the military operations."

"In the theatre of operations the executive military authority should have full responsibility for the coordination and strategic direction and control of the United Nations forces . . ."

To avoid any possible misunderstanding regarding the supreme authority of the Security Council in the conduct of United Nations military operations in "limited wars of liberation," the U.N. Executive Military Authority is further defined:

"In accordance with its responsibility, the executive military authority should be authorized to designate the Commander-in-Chief of the United Nations forces and to replace him."

". . . you will see," said Mrs. Davison, "that President Truman did not 'fire' MacArthur. He could not 'fire' the Commander-in-Chief of the United Nations armed forces (in Korea). The executive military authority under Zinchenko (Undersecretary 1949-1953) had the sole authority to do this. They dared not let the American people know this — as they dare not let us know who is running the war in Viet Nam — so after the decision was made (to replace General MacArthur) they (the United Nations) had Mr. Truman speak for them!

"Who is Commander-in-Chief of the United Nations armed forces?" asks Mrs. Davison. "The Red Herrings chasing their tails around Washington have absolutely no authority over the Viet Nam War. The Russian Suslov has ultimate authority there. He is the man through whom all contemplated action must be cleared. He knows how many of our troops are deployed and where. He will know every move we make — and he will relay all information in advance to the Communists."

As one American soldier, I bitterly resent the unconstitutional and illegal acts which are transforming our military forces into agencies of aggression for a United Nations take-over. You, too, should be alarmed by this prelude to conquest.

Certainly there can be small confidence in military and political leadership which would surrender American soldiers to exploitation by a United Nations authority — the same authority which cost us 157,350 casualties and a "no-win" stalemate in Korea.

CHAPTER IV

PERPETUAL WAR
FOR PERPETUAL PEACE

"The Soviet international organization has carried on
a successful and important penetration of the United
States Government and this penetration has not
been fully exposed."
— Report, "Interlocking Subversion in Government
Departments," USS, July 30, 1953, page 49

Our supine acquiescence to false leadership has
reaped a grisly harvest — as the bloody battlegrounds of
Korea mutely testify. The tally of the Korean War is
staggering evidence of the harsh consequence of permitting the U.N. Security Council to direct Americans in
combat.

Today, this same control with identical results is mani-
fest in Viet Nam and wherever Americans are sent to
fight "limited wars of liberation."

Our agony in Korea has been related in appalling
detail. Much of it by senior military commanders who
were called to testify before Congress on the conduct of
the war. Some of the most sobering of these hearings are
included in a series of Senate investigations titled, "Interlocking Subversion in Government Departments." A
part of the Korean War testimony was released on

January 21, 1955 under the title, "The Korean War and Related Matters." In it are recorded the first-hand experiences of General Mark Clark, United Nations Commander in Korea; Lieutenant General George E. Stratemeyer, Commander, Far East Air Force; General James A. Van Fleet, Commander, Eighth Army; Lieutenant General Edmond M. Almond, Commander X Corps; and Admiral Charles Turner Joy, Naval Commander, Far East.

These top military leaders revealed the stunned incomprehension of combat commanders who were directed by their civilian superiors to accept a "substitute for victory," in the Korean War.

General Clark, for example, fully supported General MacArthur. He believed that we should have won, that we could have won, and that we missed an opportunity by failing to act when the Chinese Communists intervened.

On page six of the "Korean War . . ." report, General Clark said:

> "I think that that was the crucial day in American history in 1950 when thousands upon thousands of Chinese ostensibly picked up individual rifles because they were individually mad at the United States and came across the Yalu and killed our men. I think," said the General, "at that time we should have indicated that we were at war with Red China and should have retaliated with everything we had at our disposal." [1]

Senator William E. Jenner, Chairman of the hearings, asked General Clark this question:

[1] "The Korean War and Related Matters," USS Report, ISS, Committee on Judiciary, January 21, 1955, page 6.

"General, many people favor our withdrawal from the United Nations. I would like to know what your opinion is in regard to that matter."

"Well, sir," replied General Clark, "here goes another honest answer. I have not had much respect for the United Nations. I believe that to permit the Soviet Union to have its large number of spies and saboteurs over here spawning in our country is wrong."[2]

American soldiers fought the Korean War against a background of treason and subversion. Proof of this treason is revealed in the incredible United Nations/State Department directives which forbade the bombing of Chinese troop assembly areas and supply points north of the Yalu.

Here is what General Stratemeyer, our air commander in Korea, had to say about these murderous orders:

> "It is contrary to everything that every military commander that I have been associated with or from all of your history — he has never been in a position where he could not win the war he started out to win. That is not American. And who did it — I don't know. I know that General MacArthur's hands were tied, I am sure, not by the Joint Chiefs of Staff, but by the, then, State Department."[3]

General Mark Clark has well expressed the horror with which professional soldiers view the mounting subversion in government departments. In his book, *From the Danube to the Yalu*, General Clark stated:

> "The nagging fear was that perhaps Communists had wormed their way so deeply into our govern-

[2] ibid, page 8.
[3] ibid, page 10.

ment on both the working and planning levels that they were able to exercise an inordinate degree of power in shaping the course of America in the dangerous postwar era. I could not help wondering and worrying whether we were faced with open enemies across the conference table and hidden enemies who sat with us in our most secret councils." [4]

We know that these fears were given form and substance in Korea.

The catastrophe in Korea is testimony to the fact that concealed policy-makers in the United Nations, and in the U.S. Department of State, did intervene to assure a badly extended and highly vulnerable Red Chinese field commander that there would be no danger to his forces by an American thrust into Manchuria — by ground or air. His assembly areas, logistic complex, and air-fields north of the Yalu were protected by international agreement.

General Van Fleet explicitly confirmed the sell-out of our combat forces in his reply to a question by Mr. Alva C. Carpenter, Chief Counsel in the Korean War hearings. "Do you believe," asked Mr. Carpenter, "that the Chinese Communists would have crossed the Yalu without assurance that our military action would be limited?"

"No," replied General Van Fleet, "he would not have entered Korea if he did not feel safe from attack in North China and Manchuria." [5]

The record of mis-direction, of deliberate and planned defeat for American forces in Korea, was succinctly

[4] ibid, page 5.
[5] ibid, page 14.

ummarized during the course of the "Korean War . . ."
earings by Senator Robert C. Hendrickson.

"We believe," he said, "as I know you believe, as
millions of Americans believe, that there have been and
till are hostile forces working tirelessly to corrupt, to
misdirect, and to destroy us from within.

"We believe," said the Senator, "that the most skillful
nd the most menacing of these forces are engaged in
rying to subvert our political and military policy." [6]

Well — as Senator Hendrickson knew when he made
hese statements, and as an increasing number of Amer-
cans know today, the spoor of anti-Americanism in the
Jnited Nations and in the U.S. Department of State is
 well-defined trail of subversion and corruption. The
xtent of organized treason in government departments
vas dramatically revealed during the General Mac-
Arthur hearings in 1951. During the period May 3
hrough August 17, over two million words of testimony
vere taken from thirteen witnesses who appeared be-
ore a joint Armed Services-Foreign Relations Senate
Committee.

In the concluding portion of the report, titled *The
Military Situation in the Far East and the Facts Sur-
ounding the Relief of General of the Army, Douglas
MacArthur,* our senators gave many warnings to the
American people.

On page 3590, for example, the committee stated:
"The testimony revealed only one positive plan for
ictory in the Korean War, the plan advocated by Gen-

ibid, page 3.

eral MacArthur . . . the appealing aspect of the Mac-Arthur program was that it aimed for victory . . . It is apparent that those with military responsibility for the Korean planning rejected this aim." [7] And on page 3591, the committee identified the policy-makers who set the stage for our defeat.

"The victory won by our Armed Forces in the Pacific has been squandered by our diplomats," said the senators, ". . . our diplomats gave away our victory in secret agreements, so that in the year 1951, our foreign policy in the Far East stands revealed as a complete failure." [8]

Responsibility for the sabotage of our combat forces in Korea was laid at the door of the State Department on page 3599 of the MacArthur hearings.

"It is common knowledge," said the committee members, "that efforts toward Communist infiltration of the State Department have been persistent over the years . . . It is obvious that a serious situation of Communist infiltration has existed and still endangers our national security." [9]

It is also apparent that the State Department and the United Nations synchronize their actions so as to achieve mutually desired intermediate goals which will further the long-range objectives of one-world government.

---

[7] *The Military Situation in the Far East and the Facts Surrounding the Relief of General of the Army, Douglas MacArthur*, Report Armed Services and Foreign Relations Committee, USS, June 27 1951, page 3590.
[8] ibid, page 3591.
[9] ibid, page 3599.

The thrust for world control, generated by those who manipulate U.N. policy, did not terminate with the release of Senate Report, "The Korean War and Related Matters."

Subversion has today's dateline.

U.N. propagation of stage-managed "wars of liberation" (wars in which American soldiers are exploited to further the objectives of one-world government) has, in fact, accelerated since the Korean betrayal.

A new facet of this incredible program of U.N.-sponsored "perpetual war for perpetual peace" came to public attention with the publication of the book, *Apartheid and United Nations Collective Measures,* prepared by the Carnegie Endowment for International Peace.

"Western delegations to the United Nations are expressing incredulity and shock over publication by the Carnegie Endowment for International Peace of a battle mapping out a U.N. invasion of South Africa," reported William Fulton, United Nations Correspondent for the *Chicago Tribune.*[10]

Circulated among the 114 member nation missions in the U.N., the tax-exempt foundation book, in 170 pages, sets out in elaborate detail military measures to be taken by ground troops and naval and air units in a war to crush British and Portuguese influence in South Africa and to turn these areas over to non-whites; presumably under a United Nations International Trustee System.[11]

[10] "U.N. Plan to Invade South Africa Shocks Western Delegates," *Chicago Tribune,* Saturday, July 24, 1965.
[11] U.N. Charter Chapter XII, "International Trustee System."

"A total of 93,000 ground troops with support from air and sea would cost $94,537,000 for a thirty-day blitzkrieg," said Fulton. "The idea would be to bring the government to heel for its apartheid (racial separation) policy."

The Carnegie Foundation book has the approval of U Thant of Burma, self-admitted Marxist U.N. Secretary General, and Alex Quaison-Sackey of Ghana, former President of the General Assembly. Quaison-Sackey, it will be remembered, opposed the air lift rescue of white hostages from U.N.-inspired anarchy in the Congo.

Inspiration for the U.N. "Collective Measures" war plan was credited to U Thant. Under U Thant's personal direction, members of the special U.N. Committee on Colonialism met with African nationalists and underground leaders in Southwest Africa. In these private sessions, a reliable source has reported, they obtained "evidence" and "freedom petitions" to present to the General Assembly to support the proposals drafted by U Thant calling for military action against South Africa.

The three key diplomats of the special U.N. mission to the South African nations were:

Jacob Malik, deputy foreign minister and Russia's principal representative at the U.N.; violent critic of U.S.-British policies in Africa;

D. Malachera, Tanzania's U.N. representative and close friend of Communist Chinese leaders. He is the chief advocate of U.N. military intervention in Southwest Africa;

Dr. Diza Gonzales, Venezuela's representative to the U.N. and vigorous opponent of U.S. intervention in the Dominican Republic, who strongly supports sending a U.N. police force to that strife-torn island.

These three United Nations diplomats stressed that U Thant will use force to throw out the Portuguese and British and to end South Africa's control over Southwest Africa.

The Carnegie Endowment study clearly indicates that any military action against South Africa will need U.S. support to be successful.

"If and how this would be obtained is not spelled out," said Robert S. Allen and Paul Scott in an article which appeared in the Manchester, New Hampshire, *Union Leader*.[12] "It is suggested," continues this report, "that if the International Court of Justice at The Hague rules that South Africa give up its League of Nations mandate over Southwest Africa, the U.S. probably would support U.N. action enforcing the ruling."

It will be remembered that Phillip Jessup, controversial former State Department official, is the U.S. representative on the international tribunal.

"Many U.S. intelligence experts," say Allen and Scott, "believe these developments will lead to a major crisis in Africa and commitment of large numbers of U.S. troops."

It is also expected that civil rights leaders will unleash giant demonstrations in New York, following the

12 "U.N. Pushes South African War," *Union Leader*, Manchester, New Hampshire, July 2, 1965.

anticipated World Court ruling demanding U.N. military intervention in South Africa.

Whether the Carnegie plan for a U.N. war in South Africa is an isolated incident or part of a pattern for international conquest is of transcending importance to the American people. If such a pattern of planned U.N. aggression can be illustrated and documented, then we must assume that the entire United Nations program is a gigantic fraud. The Carnegie Endowment War Plan would then be revealed to be a blueprint for the destruction and impoverishment of South Africa as complete as the destruction and impoverishment of the Dominican Republic, Katanga, and Viet Nam. The special U.N. Committee on Colonialism, in that case, would be exposed as a propaganda apparatus for misleading the American people and it would be clear that nobody in the United Nations cares about the welfare of any black man — or any other man.

Is there such corroborating evidence? Indeed there is!

In the spring of 1965, an employee of North American Aviation in California had the courage to spread the alarm concerning a fantastic contract NAA had received from the United States Government. This fifty-four page document titled, "Factors Operative in a Post-Arms Control Situation," (Contract Number AF 49(638)-1411), dated April, 1965 is addressed, "North American Aviation, Inc., Space and Information Systems Division, Operations Analysis Department." [c]

The paper, written in highly technical language, is

[c] Exhibit C — "Factors Operative in a Post-Arms Control Situation."

nothing less than an outline of a "war plan" for creating certain incidents with foreign powers; having those foreign powers react, then having the United States respond in such a manner as to create a socio-political climate favorable to surrender, by 1976, of the United States to a one-world government. The plan is a scenario for gradual disarmament and lists the wars which are to be fought between now and 1976, the world leaders to be assassinated, the governments to be overthrown — also scheduling the date-time sequence in which these events are to occur.

Before commenting further on this amazing study we must establish its authenticity. The background is told by the Reverend Robert Wells, Pastor, Central Baptist Church, Anaheim, California in a letter to me dated July 26, 1965.

"Briefly, the story of the document ('Factors Operative in a Post-Arms Control Situation') is that a Mr. William Manahan, who is a member of our church and a teacher of one of our adult classes, heard about the document and inquired as to the possibility of acquiring one. It seems," said Dr. Wells, "that there was no hesitancy in making a copy available; as a matter of fact, they were distributed rather freely. There was no suggestion that there would be any restriction on its use and there were no markings on the document of any kind whatever to indicate that it would be considered secret or classified.

"Because of his concern," Pastor Wells continued, "he (Manahan) brought the document to me and asked for my advice. I felt it should immediately be made available to the public; but, we should cover ourselves properly by sending copies immediately to congressmen and senators and other public representatives who are dedicated patriots before making it public locally via my pulpit and radio programs, and so forth. We followed this pattern and then I announced in the newspapers that I would be speaking on the subject and had a turn-away crowd. The reaction was tremendous. We decided then to print copies of five of the pertinent sheets from the document and make them available to the people.

"I was contacted by a representative of North American," Dr. Wells writes, "suggesting that maybe I had my hands on a classified document and requesting me to get it back to them into their vault immediately and not to say anything more about it, and so on. I refused to do this and have continued to promote it, and the only other reaction on the part of North American has been their dismissal of Mr. Manahan.

"We have heard from some key people on the inside of the company that in the top echelons there is considerable unrest and that the company is very much upset and has been in hot water with the Department of Defense because of this document.

"Some newspaper representatives contacted the North American Public Relations Department and were told that all of this was to be considered in the realm of sheer speculation; these were 'speculative projections,' not actual predictions.

"It is interesting to note," Dr. Wells concluded, "some of the things 'speculatively projected' have already been fulfilled, or are in process of fulfillment according to predictions made in recent newspaper articles such as the anticipated bombing of Red China's nuclear plants."

The document which cost William Manahan his job at North American is an outline of a proposal to bring about the total disarmament of our nation and to transfer U.S. sovereignty to a supra-national world government. It incorporates three major charts:

"Nuclear Free Zone Chronology" [C-1]

"Chronology of Scenario for Bi-lateral U.S.-USSR Agreement for Exchange of Military Missions" [C-2]

"Chronology for Partial Disarmament and Final General Disarmament Treaties" [C-3]

Thus, under the first heading for 1965 is found the following information:

"Increased cooperation in arms control — Additional US-UK-USSR agreements to curtail the spread of fissionable material for weapons."

Thereafter is listed, "Communist China Tests four small and medium nuclear devices" and "Indonesia explodes nuclear device."

Next in the predictions is, "USSR withdraws economic support from Cuba," and "U.S. and USSR agreement for destruction of obsolete bomber aircraft." This information has already been released to the press as "news."

[C-1] Exhibit — "Nuclear Free Zone Chronology," chart
[C-2] Exhibit — "Chronology of Scenario for Bilateral U.S.-USSR Agreement for Exchange of Military Missions" chart
[C-3] Exhibit — "Chronology for Partial Disarmament and Final General Disarmament Treaties," chart

Under the second heading, "Military Developments," is found the following:

"U.S. Fights Punitive Limited War vs. North Vietnam and Communist China including Destruction of Nuclear Plants."

In the next column, 1966, is the prediction, "Communist China admitted to the United Nations."

In the Chart headed, "Nuclear Free Zone Chronology," under 1965 and in a position on the chart that would suggest about the ninth month, is the following:

"Communist Chinese Government Leaders Commit Suicide."

Not only have the Planners scheduled admission of the Communist Chinese Government into the United Nations, but they have conveniently scheduled the liquidation of the more objectionable personalities so as to facilitate entry of bloody Communist China into the "respectable" U.N. Organization.

As the deadly play unfolds, we learn of "Aggressive Acts by Communist China and North Viet Nam against U.S. and SEATO" in 1965. Right on schedule the "USSR Abrogates USSR China Mutual Defense Treaty" by mid-1965, followed by "U.S. Punitive War vs. Communist China and North Viet Nam" in late 1965.

U.S. casualty lists certainly confirm this phase of the plan. North American planners might have written today's headline stories.

But there is more to this phony "peace and prosperity" program. Americans are to be brainwashed into believing that the USSR is "mellowing." The next item is supposed to lead the gullible public into believing it:

"Cuban Revolution," states the predictions under chart number two, "The Guevara Government Overthrown," which is to take place about June, 1966. The U.S. press, of course, has already reported the "disappearance" of Guevara himself.

The scenario projects defeat of Indonesian guerillas by Maylaysia in 1967; deterioration of Indonesia's military posture in 1968, and the growth of France's nuclear power through 1968. The year 1971 is given as the "effective date for a general armament reduction treaty," and the year 1973 as the year for "completion of execution of partial disarmament treaty," "Completion of execution of final phase of the disarmament treaty" is set for 1976.

There are even some diversionary incidents planned including a breach of security at the U.S. Naval War College in 1966 and in July of the same year, a security leak from the USSR Mission, United States Pacific Command.

Mr. Richard Cotten, radio commentator and publisher of *Conservative Viewpoint*, prepared an extensive summary on "Factors Operative in a Post-Arms Control Situation," which has received wide distribution in the United States.[13]

It is perfectly clear that present day "history" doesn't just happen — it is planned under contract by industrial "think factories." It isn't every day that the average citizen can secure a blueprint ahead of time and watch the drama unfold.

[13] "We Planned it That Way," *Conservative Viewpoint*, June 16, 1965.

Obviously, state legislators must obtain these files.

Mr. Manahan states he was informed that the North American contract was "prepared in cooperation with the Arms Control and Disarmament Agency, United States Government." [14] It dove-tails exactly with the surrender program directed in *State Department Bulletin* 7277, "Freedom from War: The United States Program for General and Complete Disarmament in a Peaceful World," with Public Law 87-297, "Arms Control and Disarmament Act," and of course with the articles of the United Nations Charter.

It is up to North American Aviation Company to explain to the American people who wrote this strange and terrifying "scenario," a plan that proposes to make all men slave "actors" on a world stage under the direction of Marxists in the United Nations' one-world government.

U.S. military leaders, too, have a grave responsibility in exposing and defeating the take-over program of the Planners.

Mr. Edward Hunter, author of many books on the techniques of "brainwashing" practiced on American troops by Communist jailors in Korea, states, "Our career military officers and men understand the decisive role of the new battlefield weaponry in the nuclear age. What they have not been able to grasp is the way politics, too, has become weaponry, and to this extent is their business, as well as the politician's. This is the essence of

[14] Transcribed telephone conversation, Mr. William Manahan and Dr. Billy James Hargis, June 12, 1965.

psychological warfare," says Mr. Hunter. "Lines are blurred or are erased. In the past, politics controlled decisions on policy matters, while not intruding into the choice of weapons and their use in combat. Nowadays, politicians are pre-empting decision-making in this area also. Some deep thought is required to straighten out this situation.

"In the past, the tradition of our military has been to keep strictly out of politics. To this day, this tradition is being maintained by them. Yet the type of warfare being imposed upon us by the enemy is psychological, in which a political deed is as much a weapon as a hand grenade. This gives the military nowadays as distinct a role in politics and in policy formulation as the civilian official has in military matters." [15]

[15] "Physical Courage is Not Enough," *Tactics,* December 20, 1964.

CHAPTER V

THE PLAN TO SURRENDER AMERICA

"None of the funds appropriated in this title shall be used to pay the United States contribution to any international organization which engages in the direct or indirect promotion of the principle of one-world government or one-world citizenship."
— Public Law 495, Section 112, 82d Congress

At this point in our study we have, I believe, clearly defined the terrifying war-making functions of the United Nations Security Council. Now, let us learn something about the international sleight-of-hand which has transferred our soldiers to the United Nations army.

For this part of our search we must turn again to the military articles of the United Nations Charter. Under Article 43, Chapter VII is found the basic "treaty law" for establishing an "Armed United Nations."

"All members of the United Nations," states Article 43, "in order to contribute to the maintenance of international peace and security, undertake to make available to the Security Council, on its call and in accordance with a special agreement, or agreements, armed forces, assistance, and facilities, including

rights of passage, necessary for the purpose of maintaining international peace and security." [1]

The most cursory examination of Article 43 permits
only one conclusion: It is the intent of this article to
provide the United Nations with unlimited war-making
powers.

Article 43 will wipe national boundaries off the map.
It will create an irresistible international army. And it
will chain the people of the world to the wheel of a
military juggernaut.

We have now arrived at the concealed objective of the
United Nations Charter.

Absolute, monolithic world military power is the concealed objective of the United Nations.

However, this monstrous goal cannot be achieved by
raw force alone. Force must be preceded by brainwashing, which will condition the population to accept a
world military dictatorship. Therefore, the Planners employ Fabian * Socialist techniques to accomplish their
purpose.

The internationalists, by gradualism and indirection,
have made collectivism an acceptable political philosophy. And, through the media of mass propaganda, they
have conferred legal status upon illegal acts.

In illustration of this technique, we might recall that
on September 1, 1961, the United States Government

---

[1] United Nations Charter, Chapter VII, "Actions with respect to
Threats to the Peace, Breaches of the Peace, and Acts of Aggression, Article 43.

* FABIAN . . . In the manner of the Roman general Quintas
Fabius Maximus, surnamed Cunctator (delayer) who avoided
decisive contests against Hannibal; hence cautious, indirect activities.

filed with the U.N. Secretary General a plan for the transfer of our entire military establishment to the United Nations.

Yet — there was no cry of outrage from the American people.

The policy document for surrender is *State Department Publication Number 7277*, titled "Freedom From War: The United States Program for General and Complete Disarmament in a Peaceful World." D

In it, our State Department calls for ". . . progressive reduction of the war-making capability of the nations and the simultaneous strengthening of international institutions to settle disputes and maintain the peace . . ." Which means, of course, the disarming of the United States and the establishment of a United Nations Army.

Our government now states that we must pluck the deterrent to Communist aggression from the control of American citizens and place our defense forces in the hands of the Communist-dominated U.N. Security Council.

Allegedly acting in the name of the American people, and for the "nations of the world," the U.S. State Department set forth the objectives of their program of general and complete disarmament in a "Declaration on Disarmament" in a world where adjustment to change "takes place in accordance with the principles of the United Nations."

D Exhibit—"FREEDOM FROM WAR: The United States Program for General and Complete Disarmament in a Peaceful World," *State Department Publication Number 7277*, September, 1961.

"The Nations of the world," says our State Department, "declare their goal to be the disbanding of all national armed forces and the prohibition of their reestablishment in any form whatsoever, other than those required to preserve internal order and for contributions to a United Nations Peace Force."

"The Nations of the world," says our State Department, are determined to eliminate all armaments, including weapons of mass destruction, "other than those required for a United Nations Peace Force."

"The Nations of the world," says our State Department, will establish an effective International Disarmament Organization within the framework of the United Nations, "to ensure compliance at all times with all disarmament obligations."

"The Nations of the world," says our State Department, will institute effective means for the enforcement of international agreements, for the settlement of disputes, and for the maintenance of peace, "in accordance with the principles of the United Nations." [2]

Under this plan, the United States will finance and man a totalitarian U.N. military complex. We, of course, will exercise no control over this international army.

The State Department proposes that the disarmament of the United States and the concurrent build-up of the United Nations army be accomplished in the following three stages:

[2] "Freedom from War . . . ," *USS Department of State Publication* 7277, page 11.

Stage One: "The States shall develop arrangements in Stage One for the establishment in Stage Two of a U.N. Peace Force."

Stage Two: "During Stage Two, States shall develop further peace-keeping process of the United Nations to the end that the United Nations can effectively in Stage Three deter or suppress any threat or use of force in violation of the purposes and principles of the United Nations."

Stage Three: "In Stage Three, progressive controlled disarmament and continuously developing principles and procedures of international law would proceed to a point where no state would have the military power to challenge the progressively strengthened U.N. Peace Force."

And there you have it — neatly spelled out by the U.S. State Department: a totalitarian, one-world government — its edicts enforced by an international army.

To implement the U.N. take-over, of course, it is necessary to go through the motions of translating the policy of *State Department Publication 7277* into so-called law and to assure brainwashed Americans that this "law" is in their own best interest.

This is the way it was worked.

In the same month that the State Department presented its "Freedom from War" plan to the U.N., the U.S. Congress was pressured into passing Public Law 87-297, "The Arms Control and Disarmament Act" . . . This Public Law, dated September 26, 1961 established the United State Arms Control and Disarmament Agency.[E]

Among the functions of this agency are the following:

"The preparation for and management of United States participation in international negotiations in the arms control and disarmament field.

"The dissemination and coordination of public information concerning arms control and disarmament."

And . . .

"The preparation for, operation of, or as appropriate, direction of United States participation in such control systems as may become part of United States control and disarmament activities."

Stripped of its deliberately confusing and evasive semantics, the "Arms Control and Disarmament Act" purports to confer upon socialistic bureaucrats the authority to destroy our sovereignty in secret international agreements; to propagandize the American people into accepting these felonious acts as being in the best interest of the United States, and to transfer the Armed Forces of America into the United Nations "Control System."

"The so-called Disarmament Act," stated Congressman James B. Utt, "sets up a super-agency with power greater than the power of Congress, which delegated it. The law was almost a duplication, word for word, of a disarmament proposal by the Kremlin in 1959, and so we find ourselves again advancing the Moscow policy. As an example of the power, Section 43 (of the Disarmament Act) provided that the President may, in advance, exempt actions of the Director (U.S. Disarmament

[E] Exhibit — "The Arms Control and Disarmament Act," Public Law 87-297, 87th Congress, September 26, 1961.

Agency) from the provisions of law relating to contracts or expenditures of Government funds whenever he determines that such action is essential in the interest of United States arms control and disarmament and security policy.

"The Disarmament legislation," continued Congressman Utt, "was passed for the purpose of implementing the *Department of State Publication 7277*, entitled 'Freedom from War — The United States Program for General and Complete Disarmament in a Peaceful World.' This little gem from the State Department," he said, "laid out the program for complete disarmament on a three-stage basis, the purpose of which was to reduce the armaments of every nation to almost the zero point, including our own National Guard and to concurrently augment an international peace force under the benevolent guidance of the Communist-dominated United Nations, whose recent, murderous actions in Katanga should make every American shudder at the thought of the U.N. blue helmets enforcing the edicts of U Thant in this Republic. The idea was to reduce our military capability to zero with the exception of a small federal army trained in counterinsurgency to put down civil strife within this country.

"One of the first steps of the Arms Control Agency," said Mr. Utt, "was to recommend the repeal of the Connally Amendment and to make this country completely subservient to the International Court of Justice. The International Court of Justice is about as un-American as possible. It is true that the World Court is not supposed to act on domestic matters, but so does the U.N.

Charter provide that the U.N. should not inject itself into domestic matters. Yet, the Congo is living proof that they have no intention of living by the Charter. There is every intention," said Congressman Utt in conclusion, "on the part of the Disarmament Agency to destroy the sovereignty of this nation and put us under the control of international tyranny, and they are moving rapidly in this direction." [3]

Significantly, the U.S. Arms Control and Disarmament Agency published an "Outline of Basic Provisions of a Treaty on General and Complete Disarmament in a Peaceful World" which faithfully reflects *State Department Publication 7277.* Headlined, "Blueprint for the Peace Race," dated May, 1962, the newly formed Disarmament Agency declared that a United Nations "Peace Force" would be established which would be equipped with "agreed types of armaments" and would be supplied "agreed manpower." [4]

"Blueprint" was to become a major weapon in re-orienting the allegiance of United States military personnel to the U.N. banner.

Six months after initial publication the Disarmament Agency "Blueprint" appeared, word for word, in a Department of Defense "Armed Forces Information and Education" publication titled, *For Commanders — This Changing World.*

For Commanders is designed to provide military leaders and their information staffs with "official" policy

---

[3] *Washington Report,* Congressman James B. Utt, February 14, 1963.

[4] *Blueprint for the Peace Race,* U.S. Arms Control and Disarmament Agency, May, 1962, page 3.

and is expected to influence officer and enlisted education programs within the armed forces.

"States," the Department of Defense told U.S. armed forces personnel, "should retain at their disposal only those minimum forces and non-nuclear armaments required for the maintenance of internal order and the protection of the personal security of citizens. While disarmament was being carried out (under the U.S. Control and Disarmament Agency), states should contribute agreed man power and arms to a U.N. peace force to 'deter or suppress any threat or use of arms in violation of the purposes of the United Nations'."

U.S. conformity with the provisions of *State Department Publication 7277*, and with Article 43, United Nations Charter, was thus "legalized" by the U.S. Congress and by the Department of Defense.

The enormity of this subversion is nearly incomprehensible — as is the failure of the American people to protest the criminal abrogation of the United States Constitution.

As one American soldier I bitterly resent being turned over to an organization whose every precept and very existence contravenes the Constitution I have sworn to uphold.

I reject the illegal agreements which would place me under a foreign flag and an enemy commander-in-chief.

And I deny the right of anybody in my government or anywhere else to enlist me in a United Nations army.

Redirecting the allegiance of American fighting men toward the United Nations banner and reshaping the role and mission of United States military forces for global responsibility in a one-world government is, of course, prerequisite to the success of the Planners. The importance of capturing U.S. military forces for enforcing the edicts of a one-world government is suggested by the thrust of the infamous *Reuther Memorandum,* authored by Victor Reuther.

It will be remembered that the brothers Reuther, Victor and Walter, wrote to friends in the U.S. from their factory jobs in Soviet Russia during the 1920's, urging unstinting efforts for the creation of a "Soviet America."

In the fall of 1961, Victor and Walter Reuther visited Attorney General Robert Kennedy to discuss their views on the so-called "right-wing" in America with particular attention given to "The Radical Right Inside The Armed Services." They had, they said, some specific suggestions that might be considered for a campaign to silence the growing voice of conservatism. These suggestions were put in written form at the suggestion of Mr. Kennedy and subsequently were sent to the Attorney General as a twenty-four page document on December 19, 1961.[5]

"The problem of radical right influences inside the Armed Services," said Victor Reuther, "is an immediate one made all the more so by the up-coming hearings of the Senate Armed Services Subcommittee (on military 'muzzling').

"It has been widely reported," the *Reuther Memorandum* continues, "that General Walker's (Major General Edwin A. Walker) radical right viewpoint is shared by a substantial number of his colleagues. One observer,

[5] *The Reuther Memorandum,* by Victor Reuther, Office of the Attorney General, Washington, D.C.

Louis J. Nalle, has reported that Walker's position 'represents the publicly unexpressed but privately outspoken views of an important part of our American officer corps in all three services.' [6] Drew Pearson has twice reported without contradiction that a Lieutenant General has leaked secret information to Senator Thurmond in support of the Walker position. The 'Americanism Seminars' espousing radical right wing doctrine and sponsored or co-sponsored by the Armed Services in various places could only have been accomplished by radical right officer personnel with the armed forces," said Messers Reuther.

"It also appears," continues this amazing report, "to have been widespread pressure from right-wing Generals and Admirals in the Pentagon which brought about the recall to duty of General Van Fleet . . . All that the recall has accomplished is to embarrass the Administration when Van Fleet irresponsibly attacked the Administration's Ambassador to the United Nations."

The brothers Reuther then exposed the real reason for their report to the Attorney General:

"An alternative to getting Senator (Richard B.) Russell to broaden the hearings would be for Secretary McNamara to start his own investigation of radical right Generals and Admirals."

The report then states with gross impertinence: "This might have the effect of causing the resignation of some of these Generals and Admirals which would certainly be in the national interest. At any rate, political activity

[6] *New Republic*, November 20, 1961.

after such warnings would be grounds for dismissal from the service."

A major objective of the take-over crowd is, of course, the silencing of articulate anti-Communists within the military services. This one mission has, and continues to receive, high priority. The success of the Planners in imposing one-world government on the nations of the world is dependent upon eradication of resistance or possible resistance, by the United States military establishment.

It will be recalled that Secretary of Defense Robert S. McNamara immediately implemented a similarly motivated *Fulbright Memorandum* and precipitated a witch hunt in the American army in 1961. On July 31 of that year, *Army News Service* released a Pentagon Directive giving full responsibility to Mr. Arthur Sylvester, Secretary of Defense for Public Affairs, for "providing policy guidance not only for all public affairs activities of the Department and its entities, but also for the conduct of any informational programs directed in whole or in part to the general public." [7]

"Defense Secretary Robert S. McNamara has ordered the Joint Chiefs of Staff to revise a directive that permits military men to instruct civilians in anti-communism," said the *Chicago Sun-Times* in an article covering the Secretary's action.[8]

The importance of this anti-anti-Communist victory

[7] Release Number 47, *Army News Service,* July 13, 1961.
[8] "Curb Military Anti-Red Crusaders," *Chicago Sun-Times,* July 13, 1961.

over conservatives in uniform is succinctly presented in an article by Gus Hall, General Secretary, Communist Party, U.S.A. Writing for *The Worker* three days following the McNamara crack-down on military anti-communists, Hall said:

> "In the opinion of the Communist Party there can be no question but that the threat from the extreme Right is serious . . . Another pronounced characteristic of this growing fascist movement is its spreading influence among the higher military personnel. The case of General Walker was only a symptom of a much deeper affliction. Even the Pentagon had to admit recently that it was 'worried' over the extent of Birchite and similar influences among the ranking officers of the military services." [9]

Following the pattern of the now well-publicized *Fulbright Memorandum*, the Reuthers, in continuation of their recommendations to the Attorney General, state with ill-concealed hysteria:

"The strong posture against radical right Generals and Admirals suggested in this memorandum would go far to answer Soviet propaganda that American foreign policy is not in responsible hands and that there is a substantial 'preventative war' group in the Pentagon which may ultimately get the upper hand. This strong posture would not only reassure our own allies," says Reuther in the logic of the anti-anti-Communist, "but might give support to factions within the Soviet Union that strive for a more flexible position on the Soviet's part."

[9] "The Ultra-Right, Kennedy, and the Rise of the Progressives," by Gus Hall, *The Worker*, July 16, 1961.

The validity of the Reuther rationale may be judged by the comments of Lieutenant Colonel O. Aleksandrovsky who wrote in the July 18 edition of *Red Star* (official Soviet Army newspaper):

> "No matter what happens, this scandalous story of the business of General Walker and the Birch Society clearly shows that the Pentagon is teeming with generals and admirals who openly profess fascism and are attempting to drag the country down the road to unleashing the Third World War." [10]

The intemperate charges placed against General Walker and his troop education program in the 24th Infantry Division by Reuther, Hall, Aleksandrovsky, and other like-minded individuals, were part of the witch hunt in the American army.

A top source for hard facts with which to confront these professional internationalists is found in United States Senate Report, "Military Cold War Education and Speech Review Policies," a Committee summary of the findings made by the Special Preparedness Subcommittee, Committee on Armed Services during the course of the 'Military Muzzling' hearings.

"It is well," states this Senate report, "to comment on the popular misconception that General Walker was disciplined because of his troop indoctrination activities in connection with the 'pro-Blue' program. This is incorrect. The army investigating officer specifically found that the division information and education program conducted by General Walker under the name of 'pro-Blue' was

[10] "Reds make Hay out of Rebuke to General Walker," *New York Journal American*, August 15, 1961.

'basically sound' and he consequently recommended that it 'continue to be implemented in the 24th Infantry Division'." [11]

Nevertheless, the pro-Blue program brought down upon the head of General Walker the concentrated fury of pro-Communists and anti-anti-Communists in the United States and overseas. It resulted in Walker's being relieved of his command by order of the President. And, it ultimately inspired a Senate investigation of military cold war education and speech review policies.

The strange case of General Walker sheds revealing light upon the concealed conflict within the U.S. military establishment. It has, therefore, an important place in this study of the conspiracy to transfer American sovereignty to the United Nations one-world government.

The General Walker case began with a midnight telephone call from Heidelberg, Germany in late April, 1961, to my residence at Fort Hamilton, New York.

[11] Committee Print, USS, Committee on Armed Services Report, October 19, 1962, page 31.

CHAPTER VI

IS PRO-BLUE TROOP TRAINING UN-AMERICAN?

"Freedom can only be won . . . The warfare is continuous and each generation comes to the front to fight for it as though the battle had just been joined." — *The Bulwarks of* Freedom, by Bishop R. A. Brown

On Thanksgiving Day, 1960, my family and I arrived in New York harbor aboard the USS Simon B. Buckner army transport, ending a two and a half year duty tour in Germany.

My new assignment was Special Projects Officer, New York Office, Chief of Information, Department of the Army.

This title, by strange coincidence, was identical to the one I had held in the 24th Infantry Division when writing and implementing the Pro-Blue Troop Information program for Major General Edwin A. Walker.

Much mis-information, deliberate and otherwise, has been published about the Pro-Blue program. To show why it came under attack by anti-anti-Communists it will be helpful to sketch in the background of this plan.

The Pro-Blue program was presented to troop audiences under the title, "Citizenship in Service." It was prepared in consonance with Department of Defense directive, "Collateral Cold War Activity," published by the National Security Council in 1958.[1]

This NSC Directive was subsequently disseminated to army commands in Europe in the form of USAREUR Circular 350-50 (Secret), and Seventh Army Special Plan 308-61.[2]

Tough-minded General Walker initiated this program upon assuming command of the 24th Infantry Division in the fall of 1959.

He assigned to me the task of creating a program which would reflect his troop training desires and which would be based on Army Regulation 515-1 (Confidential), Army Regulation 355-6, and other appropriate army directives. Under this guidance, I prepared a troop information plan, wrote the instructor scripts, designed the training aids, coached a staff, acted as senior instructor, and prepared all reports and after-action studies.

The resulting "Citizenship in Service" program, a six-hour theatre production dealt with democracy, freedom and personal morality, through a series of hard-punching lectures, skits and special effects.

The instructor group comprised fifteen officers and men of the "Taro-Leaf" division who employed giant training aids, costumed actors, lighting and sound to dramatize their instruction.

The first lecture of the series set the theme for the entire project with the statement, "The common de-

[1] "Collateral Cold War Activity," National Security Council, (Top Secret), 1958, Number 5906-1.
[2] "Collateral Cold War Activity," U.S. Seventh Army, Special Plan 308-61, 1960.

nominator of American Democracy is the sensitive conscientious action of the individual."

In retrospect it is difficult to imagine a more naive program for Americans in uniform.

"Citizenship in Service" stressed Christian spiritual values and resisted atheistic statism.

"Citizenship in Service" promoted patriotism and exposed the thrust for a Communist world.

"Citizenship in Service" taught individual responsibility and rejected the rationale of state omnipotence.

"Citizenship in Service" generated a love for freedom and the liberties guaranteed by the U.S. Constitution — and demanded preservation of this document "against all enemies, foreign and domestic."

The "Citizenship in Service" program was, in fact, in direct conflict with the aims and purposes of the United Nations Charter. The planners who created the United Nations organization, and who manipulate U.S. military policy through its Security Council, would never permit resistance to U.N. objectives to prosper within the army.

"We here in the United States," said the late Congressman Usher L. Burdick, "believe in the Christian religion as the very basis of all our strength in government, opportunities of the individual, our educational and cultural systems, while the Russians reject the story of Jesus Christ and scoff at the Christian religion. Yet UNESCO (United Nations Educational, Scientific, and Cultural Organization) undertakes to harmonize these religious views and present to the world one harmonious group of people under a one-world government.

"To bring this country into line to accept world government," said Congressman Burdick, "many things must be done by the United Nations and her agencies, such as UNESCO. First of all, love of country on the part of the people of the United States is found by these conspirators to be very deep and hard to destroy. Here, UNESCO comes into play and out it goes among the school children of the United States with specially trained teachers from Columbia University who teach those children that love of country — like that we have in the United States — interferes with a loyalty to a world organization; that they must be fitted, educationally, and temperamentally, to forget love of their own country and transfer their loyalty to the world organization.

"Of course," he said, "this world organization cannot afford to leave in the hands of the people the rights of free speech, a free press, and free religion, because the exercise of these precious rights will have the power to prevent what these conspirators want." [3]

It was not until we launched an investigation into the untouchable *Overseas Weekly* and traced the source of its power that we discerned interlocking subversion in government departments. No effective anti-Communist-pro-American program, we learned, will ever be permitted to thrive in the United States military establishment until U.N. authority over the army is repudiated.

Quite innocently, the "Citizenship in Service" program became a counter-revolution within the armed services. This troop education effort soon threatened the careful

[3] "UNESCO: A State Department Agency created to put the United States into a World Government," Honorable Usher L. Burdick, *Congressional Record*, August 3, 1953, page 13186.

"brainwashing" of U.S. troops by U.N. agencies and became an embarrassment to those who had master-minded a silent revolution in America.

Therefore, an elaborate but camouflaged campaign was set in motion to destroy the "Citizenship in Service" program and to stamp out any further threat to U.N. ambitions which might be inspired by the 24th Infantry Division Pro-Blue plan.

To paraphrase Whittaker Chambers, I aimed my dart at Communism but struck the hidden power behind Communism.

The part which *Overseas Weekly* played in this attack on the Pro-Blue program will be revealed in further chapters.

On December 13, 1961, I was called before a closed session Special Committee, Senate Armed Services Committee, to testify on the 24th Division Pro-Blue Program. Present were Mr. James T. Kindell, Chief Counsel; Mr. Robert M. Neal, professional staff member; Mr. Gunther E. Martel, professional staff member; Mr. Alfred Consello, professional staff member, and Lieutenant Colonel Hayden J. Price, Army Congressional Liaison Officer.

Upon opening this meeting, Mr. Kindell advised me that Committee members would direct questions to me and that they would "query me on any matters pertinent to this investigation."

Extracts from this hearing which bear on the origins of the Pro-Blue program began with my description of the events leading to initial organization of the project:

"The action which was to culminate in the preparation of the 24th Infantry Division 'Pro-Blue' program," I said, "leading to the relief of Major General Edwin A. Walker and to a subsequent investigation by this Committee of

Military Muzzling charges brought by the Honorable
Strom Thurmond, began in October, 1959 at Augsburg,
Germany, headquarters of the 24th Infantry Division.

"About the middle of the month, I was called to the
office of the Division Surgeon, Major Arthur Grant, and
told that the Assistant Chief of Staff, G1, Lieutenant
Colonel E. C. Vogelsang, wanted to talk to me about setting up a special training program in the Division.

"The instruction under consideration, Colonel Vogel-
sang said, was a project desired by General Walker who
had recently assumed command of the Division.

"It was also noted that initial planning would be based
on three prime points listed by the General; namely, an
emphasis on 'espirit' and combat readiness factors under
the general headings of Body, Mind, and Spirit.

"Methods, techniques, and procedures were to be presented in the form of recommendations to the Chief of
Staff, Colonel James H. Skeldon."

Mr. Neal

"Why were you chosen for this job? Did you have any
special training or experience for this sort of thing?"

Major Roberts

"I suppose that several facts prompted this decision;
among these might have been entries in my "201" file,
which show that I'm a graduate of the Army Information
School and the Command and General Staff College.
This record would also reveal that I had had repeated
assignments in the Army Information Career Field since
1949; Information Officer of the 3rd Infantry Division,
101st Airborne Division, 11th Airborne Division and
187th Airborne Regimental Combat Team, and Associate
Editor of the Army Information Digest were among these
assignments. I had also operated a small advertising

agency in Denver, Colorado, between World War II and the Korean Conflict.

"Further, the recent arrival of two senior officers in the Medical Battalion moved me from battalion commander to assistant executive officer — a rather pointless job.

"All of these conditions," I pointed out, "made me a pretty reasonable choice for a special duty assignment with little attendant dislocation."

Subsequent talks with the Chief of Staff, the G1, and the Division Surgeon established some guidelines for the project.

General Walker, they said, was determined that the men of the 24th Division would not shatter under stress as some U.S. soldiers had done in Korea. Taro-Leaf men were to be physically and mentally toughened. They would also be indoctrinated with information about American origins, the Constitution, and the Code of Conduct so that the principles of "Honor, Duty, Country" would inspire pride in service.

Command problems, too, were to be considered in drawing up a schedule of instruction. Low re-enlistment rates, high incident rates, soaring sick-call, and mounting courts-martial figures were important areas demanding attention.

And finally the commander wanted a realistic implementation of army anti-Communist directives so that members of the command might recognize the face of the enemy and understand his methods of attack on the social, economic, and military fronts.

All of these troop training objectives are, of course, directed under the authority of Army Regulation 3556-6, the primary guidelines of which may be summarized as follows:

   a. To further develop in each soldier his belief in the principles of American democracy, his sense of responsibility as a citizen, his awareness to the threat of Communism, his determination to fight to preserve his heritage, his will to resist against military odds, and his endurance under stress.

   b. To convince each soldier he is of importance to the army, his duties are essential, his unit is vital, and military service is a patriotic duty.

   c. To explain to each soldier the mission of the army, the mission of his unit, his service obligations, policies which affect him, his civilian relationship, and national and international events which affect him as an individual.

My job was to dig out the appropriate directives and references and to build a troop information program for the 24th Infantry Division.

Subsequent research in fulfilling this mission included review of films and written material used in troop training, information and education programs, produced and made available to the services by the Office of Armed Forces Information and Education, Office of the Secretary of Defense. The areas covered included world affairs, citizenship, nature of our government and of foreign governments, area orientation, and Code of Conduct. The material researched comprised unnumbered pamphlets, Department of Defense pamphlets, Department of Defense Fact Sheets, films, and other recommended reference works.

"I spent the next several weeks searching out appropriate directives and devising a plan of instruction which would effectively meet the requirements given me," I said during the Washington interview.

The resulting memorandum outlining a professionally staged, dramatic approach to troop education was submitted to the Division Personnel Officer, Colonel Vogel-sang. This study was subsequently circulated as an action paper to the Division Surgeon, the Chaplain, and to the Chief of Staff for concurrences and to the Commanding General for approval.

This paper was titled, "Citizenship in Service", dated November 27, 1959, and called for. . ."instruction in 'responsibilities of Citizenship,' " and stated in part:

"The Commanding General desires that a program of instruction be prepared on the subject, 'Citizenship in Service.' "

"The project was handled by a steering committee," I told Senate investigators, "whose primary mission would be to develop, plan, implement, and supervise the program." The following persons were on this committee:

Colonel Paul Hert, Deputy Brigade Commander,

Major Archibald E. Roberts, 24th Med. Bn.,

M/Sgt. Richard T. Flynn, 19th Infantry.

On December 3, 1959, I was transferred to Division Headquarters to continue development of the "Citizenship in Service" program.

It is important to note that throughout the development phase of this program each proposal and every instructor script was reviewed and approved by appropriate general or special staff members.

For example, on January 2, our committee chairman, Colonel Hert, circulated a directive for the attention of the following "reviewing officers": Division Personnel Officer, Plans and Training Officer, Staff Judge Advocate, Chaplain, Provost Marshal, Surgeon, Information Officer, and the Inspector General. The directive had as enclosures the staff study on "Citizenship in Service," and the draft, "Training Directive."

"By the middle of January, 1960," my testimony continued, "I had completed the preparation of the instructor scripts. I wrote all of these except the hour of instruction entitled, 'Communism and the Soldier's Code,' which was prepared by Master Sergeant Richard T. Flynn, who had, himself, been a prisoner of the Chinese Communists in Korea."

Some of this instruction on Communism incorporated certain findings by Lieutenant Colonel William E. Mayer, Army Medical Corps, who, as the medical member of the Japan Joint Intelligence Processing Board, made an exhaustive study of all conditions surrounding Americans who were held prisoner by the Communist Chinese and to study their reaction to the special new conditions of captivity during the Korean War.[4]

"On January 18," I continued, "we published an action paper, with the concurrences of G1, G3, SJA, Chaplain, Provost Marshal, Surgeon, and Information Officer, advising the Commanding General that instructor training and training aids manufacture were completed and that we were prepared to stage a fifty-minute audition of the 'Citizenship in Service' program before an audience composed of major unit commanders and general and special staff members. Attached to this memorandum were final copies of the proposed curriculum, training directive draft, proposed training schedule and the lesson plans and instructor scripts for all six hours of instruction."

[4] "Military Cold War Education and Speech Review Policies," Hearings before the Special Preparedness Subcommittee, Senate Committee on Armed Services, Part 3, March 8, 9, 14, 15, and April 3, 1962, page 1151.

The entire "Citizenship in Service" program has been entered in the *Congressional Record*, issue of August 30, 1961, by Senator Tower of Texas, under the heading "Senators Thurmond and Tower present case for Major General Edwin A. Walker, including Text of his Pro-Blue program."

Upon placing the "Citizenship" scripts and allied material in the record, Senator Tower stated, "It is very important that the Senate have available to it the program which provided the basis for the charges against General Walker; namely, the citizenship-in-service program, sometimes referred to as the Pro-Blue program, of the 24th Infantry Division. I therefore ask unanimous consent that it be printed in the *Record* at the conclusion of my remarks, along with five editorials on the subject."[5]

The *Congressional Record* has failed to reflect the list of references upon which these training scripts were based. An example of the source and authority for the instruction is provided by the references used in preparation of the first hour, "Citizenship in Service and Getting Along in Germany." Material used included: *"The Constitution of the United States*, Norton Committee," *"Militant Liberty*, Secretary of Defense, 1955," *"Time* magazine, January 11, 1960," *"The Bulwarks of Freedom*," by Bishop R.A. Brown, 1959," *"U.S. Economic Almanac*, 1956," *"Statistical Abstracts of the United States, Germany and Western Defense*, USAREUR Information Bulletin Number 14-6," *"Problems and Policies*, USAREUR

---

[5] "Senators Thurmond and Tower present case for Major General Edwin A. Walker, including text of his Pro-Blue Program," *Congressional Record*, August 30, 1961.

Fact Sheet Number 36," and "*Agreements on Status of Forces,* Germany, Bonn Convention, May, 1956."

"When and where was the first 'Citizenship' program presented?" *Mr. Hartel* then asked me.

Major Roberts

"The final training plan created an instructor group of fifteen officers and men of the 24th Infantry Division who comprised a traveling 'show', something like a theatrical troup," I replied. "Our first presentation was made in Garrett Theatre, Reese Kaserne, Augsburg, Germany on Monday, April 25, 1960 before approximately six hundred men and officers of the 19th Infantry and 724th Ordnance Battalion, 24th Infantry Division.

"The training program was to continue three days a week, two hours each Monday, Wednesday, and Friday afternoon for eleven weeks. During this period, ending July 29, 1960, we presented the 'Citizenship' troop information program to about five thousand commissioned and enlisted men of the command.

"Now, contrary to the impression created by some news reports, the 'Citizenship' program was never a 'secretly' conducted operation of the 24th Infantry Division," I assured the committee members. "I want to explode that myth right now by stating that throughout the course of the development and presentation of this instruction, we kept higher headquarters advised and forwarded reports and copies of the instructor scripts as the program progressed. In fact, after the *Overseas Weekly* attack on General Walker and the Pro-Blue program, I was called into the Pentagon from my duty station in New York for questioning and was able to pull from the files of the Chief of Troop Information, Office of the Chief of Information, Department of the Army, copies of reports and instructor scripts so forwarded. I will speak more on this matter later."

Mr. Kindell

"Has there been any assessment of the effect or value of the program, good or bad, on the men or any check on practical results?"

Major Roberts

"Well, we conducted end-of-course tests for about one-third of the number attending (est: 5,333). The average division percentile score came out to 84.72 per cent, indicating a satisfactory comprehension of the material presented. A questionnaire was given to a test proportion of three classes (1,107) which provided an index as to audience reaction to the program. Of these, 66.4 per cent recorded 'favorable' comments about the program.

"Also," I continued, "we requested major unit commanders to comment on the program at the end of the first eleven-week schedule to see if we were gaining our objective. Some of the typical comments were as follows:

> *CO, 19th Infantry:* 'The course was well presented, was interesting and was well received. Of particular value was the information made available to junior leaders, both officer and NCO, for influencing their subordinates through counseling.'
> *CO, 34th Infantry:* 'The program of instruction and the instruction itself was superior throughout. Subjects were presented in such a manner that student interest was maintained.'
> *CO, 13th Artillery:* 'The program was one that is vitally needed in all troop units on a world-wide

basis. The personnel whom I queried on an informal basis all agreed that it was a highly educational and inspiring program. It definitely left a good taste in the mouths of the troops.'

CO, 24th Infantry Division Trains: 'Based on the evaluation of the unit commanders of Division Trains, the program seems to be very effective. There seems to be a definite need for additional presentation.'

"Comments were solicited from higher commands to which we had forwarded 'Citizenship' reports," I told the Senate group. "The replies included the following sample remarks:

Information Officer, Seventh Army: 'The program identifies an area of need within the army and fulfills that need in an excellent manner. It also serves as an outstanding vehicle in completing the requirements of Section I, of Seventh Army Circular 355-5, and of Circular 600-515.'

Commandant, U. S. Army Special Warfare School: 'Conscious of the psychological implications of our actions overseas by civilians and military alike, we are deeply pleased to note the interest and positive steps manifested by you and your staff to instill in members of the military an awareness of their national responsibilities.'

Chief, USAREUR Training Aids Center: 'Would it be possible to receive two more copies of your script, "Citizenship in Service" to be used in devising a "smaller scale" program in kit form?'

"All of this material," I noted, "and much additional evidence in support of the program, was contained in an 'After-Action Report' which I prepared for the Commanding General, dated September 21, 1960. This report was forwarded to all intervening headquarters and to the Department of the Army." [6]

After the Pro-Blue program became a national issue, several independent writers revealed that morale and combat readiness factors in the 24th Infantry Division had, indeed, improved as a result of this troop information effort. They reported that church attendence was up eight hundred per cent, that incidents with German nationals were down, that re-enlistments in the Division were up, and that the men and officers of the 24th Infantry Division exhibited a remarkable sense of unit pride and fierce "Americanism." Mr. Hanson Baldwin, for example, reporting in the *New York Times* of September 21, 1961, said: "Under General Walker's leadership the 24th Division was judged variously by superiors as the best, or one of the two best divisions in the European Theatre and perhaps in the army." [7]

You can't do much better than that.

And yet, as early as August 6, 1960, the "Citizenship" program had drawn the fire of a peculiar brand of news reporter who didn't like this kind of "Americanism" being taught to 24th Division troops. The *American Weekend* of this date carried an article titled, "GI Hatred of Communism being taught in Augsburg." This transparent attack on the aims and purposes of the program said in part, "Soldiers of the 24th Infantry Division are currently

[6] "After-Action Report," 24th Infantry Division Citizenship in Service Program, period April 25 through July 30, 1960; September 21, 1960.

[7] "Army's Handling of General Walker Case Disturbs Troops in Europe," by Hanson W. Baldwin, *New York Times*, September 21, 1961.

being taught to hate Communism and love God in a series of skits, plays and lectures. Called "Citizenship in Service," the six-hour program is designed to wake soldiers up to the horrors of Communism, according to Major Arch E. Roberts, author of the script and director of the show." [8]

There was more to come.

[8] "GI Hatred of Communism Being Taught in Augsburg," *American Weekend*, August 6, 1960.

CHAPTER VII

PRESS ATTACKS
PRO-BLUE PROGRAM

"The State Department is right now supporting UNESCO through its United States National Commission for UNESCO, and its propaganda is designed to hide the truth from the people."
— Honorable Usher L. Burdick, *Congressional Record*, August 3, 1954, page 13186

At the conclusion of the initial instruction tour of eleven weeks, General Walker directed an expansion of the "Citizenship in Service" program in line with a directive received from Seventh Army Headquarters titled, "Collateral Cold War Activities." This directive was Circular Number 308 and was based on the 1958 policy directive published by the National Security Council. The NSC directive authorized the use of military personnel, facilities, and equipment to acquaint military and civilian public with the world-wide Communist effort to control populations and productive capacities of nations. When introducing this expanded project, General Walker called together all major unit commanders and staff members for a briefing on the aims and purposes of this effort. During the course of this presentation, the Division Intelligence Section illustrated the growth of Communist imperialism since World War

II, by graphically depicting the inroads of Soviet armies and Communist agents through the use of a world map. The Communist and Satellite countries were shown in red and the remaining Western countries were marked in blue.

"At this point a young officer stood up," I told Senate investigators, "and remarked that, since the over-all program was to educate soldiers to the dangers of international Communism, we might call the program in our command the 24th Infantry Division 'Anti-Red program.'

"General Walker said no, this was a negative thought. We didn't want to be against something. We wanted to be for something. He said then that if it was necessary to have some kind of identification for the program, keeping in mind that we were in fact fighting Communism, that we could call it the 'Pro-Blue program,' and he pointed to the blue portion of the map."

During the course of the Pro-Blue briefing, it developed that the new program was to include the establishment of special "Anti-Communism" libraries in each of the ninety-six companies in the division. We would also have visiting authorities speak to military personnel and dependents on the techniques of Communism. Articles on Communism would be prepared for the division newspaper and every means would be employed to emphasize the American heritage and the responsibilities of citizenship throughout the command. The "Citizenship in Service" program would continue to be the central vehicle for this effort and would be "beefed up" in compliance with "Cold War" directives.

"At General Walker's order," I told the Committee, "I secured a copy of the Seventh Army 'Collateral Cold War Activity' circular and prepared a plan for the expanded 24th Infantry Division 'Pro-Blue program.' This plan, dated October 28, 1960, stated in part: '(The objectives of this program are) to orient military personnel and their dependents in the scope of world Communism by studying the philosophy, objectives, and imperialistic expansion of Communism following World War II. To educate military personnel and their dependents in the para-military technique of Communist infiltration, subversion, and propaganda, in influencing legal government, seizing power, then ruling through brutality and fear. To instruct military personnel and their dependents in the recognition of overt and covert Communist methodology in their attempt to subvert military morals, espirit, prestige and leadership.'

"This plan further outlined the methods and techniques through which the subject matter was to be disseminated and suggested the organization structure which could accomplish the mission."

Mr. Neal

"What about the book, *The Life of John Birch* and other John Birch Society material distributed to members to the 24th Infantry Division? Was this included in your program?"

Major Roberts

"This is another falsehood perpetrated by irresponsible members of the press. Let's kill that lie here.

"The books for the company libraries were as follows: *Masters of Deceit*, by J. Edgar Hoover; *A Guide to Anti-Communist Action*, by Anthony T. Bouscaren; *The Techniques of Soviet Propaganda*, by Committee on the Judiciary, U.S. Senate; *Techniques of Communism*, by Louis F. Budenz; *In Every War But One*, by Eugene Kinkead; *The Life of John Birch*, by Robert H. Welch,

Jr.; *The Pentagon Case,* by Colonel Victor J. Fox; *The Story of Mary Liu,* by Edward Hunter.

"It should be noted that *The Life of John Birch* was written two years before the formation of the John Birch Society and that it says nothing at all about the John Birch Society. The book is the story of the murder of an American officer by the Chinese Communists after the end of World War II and is an illustration of the immediate change of face of the Chinese 'Agrarian Reformers' once the threat of Japan was removed."

Mr. Neal

"Who made up this list of reading material? Did you?"

Major Roberts

"No. I did not prepare the reading list. However, I believe that the list was prepared by Master Sergeant Flynn, based on 'recommended reading' lists from the Pentagon. I do know that Flynn had installed an extensive 'Anti-Communist' reference library in his office which was separate from my own. In fact, I used some of this material in the writing of the original 'Citizenship in Service' program. I might also add that I was informed that the reading list was forwarded to Seventh Army with a request for funds to purchase the books. The request was returned, I was told, with the notation that there were no Seventh Army funds available for this purpose and that the purchase would have to be made out of 24th Infantry Division funds. The Headquarters fund, I believe."

Mr. Hartel

"What about the book, *The Pentagon Case?* Do you think that this is a good book for troops?"

Major Roberts

"I understand that this book is based on an actual case

of an American Naval Officer who, because of his strong anti-Communist views, was harassed by certain anti-anti-Communist elements in the Pentagon and finally resigned his commission."

Mr. Hartel

"Did you know that the book, *The Pentagon Case*, is on an 'approved' army reading list?"

Major Roberts

"No, I did not.

"I subsequently cleared the new Pro-Blue program through G1, G2 and G3 and the Information Officer and gave it to the Chief of Staff, Colonel Skeldon, on October 28, 1960," I said in continuing testimony.

"A few days later the manuscript was returned with General Walker's approval. The plan was then turned over to the Division Plans Officer, Lieutenant Colonel Avery, for final make-up and publication.

"The division did subsequently publish Circular Number 350-20, *24th Infantry Division Pro-Blue Program* dated January 4, 1961, which incorporated the material included in my draft of October 28, 1960."

Shortly thereafter, on November 15, 1960, I departed Germany and arrived in New York on November 25 for assignment to the Office of the Chief of Information, New York Branch, at 663 Fifth Avenue.

Three and a half months later on February 25, 1961, The *People's World*, Communist mouthpiece in San Francisco, triggered a blast against the John Birch Society. This shrill attack immediately repeated in left-leaning press across the nation, was to have far-reaching effect upon the 24th Infantry Division Pro-Blue program, although I did not understand the significance of this Communist move at that time.

On April 16, 1961, about five months after my assignment to New York, *Overseas Weekly* published their attack on General Walker and the Pro-Blue program. This feature treatment carried banner headlines on the front cover, "What's Going On at the 24th Infantry Division?" On page three of this issue there appeared three articles, one of which was headed, "Military Channels used to Push Birch Ideas." This article was written by Bob Jones, S.W. Naujocks, and John Dornberg.[1]

The character of these three writers can be judged by the fact that Naujocks, born in Danzig, Poland — who claims that he worked for the Propaganda Ministry of the Nazis during World War II — was convicted in a German court on three counts of slander against General Walker;[2] that Jones, a reputed alcoholic, was barred from Seventh Army Support Command in August, 1960 for taking unauthorized photographs; and that Dornberg is the author of a book, *Schizophrenic Germany*, which has created much ill-will for the U.S.A. in Germany.[3]

Dornberg attempted to intimidate General Walker after the General barred Naujocks from the 24th Infantry Division. Dornberg threatened to write an attack against Walker in *Overseas Weekly*. He was to later claim "credit" for "exposing" Walker.

Also on page three of the April 16th issue of *Overseas Weekly* (a publication termed "repulsive" by Secretary of Defense Robert S. McNamara) there appears a double

[1] "Military Channels used to Push Birch Ideas," *Overseas Weekly*, Sunday, April 16, 1961.
[2] "Writer Guilty of Slandering General Walker," *U.P.I.*, Augsburg, Germany, September 26, 1960.
[3] "'Book Ad' Strikes Blow at our Ally," These Days, by George E. Sokolsky, *New York Journal American*, June 13, 1961.

column of "proof by association" purporting to show similarities between the 24th Infantry Division Pro-Blue program and the John Birch Society Program.[4]

In this carefully contrived smear, the John Birch "side" is allegedly stated. Opposing each such statement for the John Birch "side," *Overseas Weekly* thoughtfully asked their readers to note the comparison with the 24th Infantry Division "side."

Samples of this strange "indictment" included:

> "The name of the John Birch Society's book of principles is the Blue Book . . . The name of the 24th Infantry Division's pro-freedom educational program is 'Pro-Blue'."
>
> "Charles W. Pavey, an official of the John Birch Society in Ohio, said on April 1, 1961 that the 'Communist influence is in everything you can mention — visible and invisible.' Welch maintains that Communism is being slipped over on the American people so gradually and insidiously that before long 'they can no longer resist the Communist conspiracy . . .', . . . General Walker said that Communism has infiltrated every institution in the U.S. in an open attempt to overthrow our way of life. Pro-Blue is designed to acquaint every man in the command with the Communist threat and the vital role each man must play in its defeat . . . The Communists and fellow travelers . . . are all around us working for our destruction."

This is the type of "proof" offered by *Overseas Weekly*. It was sufficient cause for the late President John F. Kennedy to summarily remove General Walker from command of the 24th Infantry Division — without a hearing and with no charges being placed against him.

[4] "John Birch vs. 24th Infantry Division," *Overseas Weekly*, April 16, 1961.

"Whatever one thinks of the John Birch Society," I stated to the Senate Armed Services Subcommittee, "the fact is that I had never heard of the John Birch Society when I prepared the 'Citizenship in Service' program. Furthermore, subsequent investigation of the Pro-Blue plan by Lieutenant General Frederick J. Brown, Commanding General, V Corps in Germany, disclosed that the Pro-Blue program was not attributable to the program of the John Birch Society." [5]

There is little question that the liberal press attack on the John Birch Society was a smear technique for mounting a campaign against the 24th Division Pro-Blue program to destroy it and thereby discourage all pro-American, anti-Communist, military education programs.

Supporting evidence lies in the fact that Sidney Gruson, reporter for the *New York Times*, wrote a smear story against General Walker and the Pro-Blue program using as a basis the *Overseas Weekly* material. However, Gruson's story appeared in the *Times* on April 14th — two days before *Overseas Weekly* came out with their own issue on the Pro-Blue program.

Mr. Neal

"Did the army take any action regarding your interest in the Pro-Blue program at this time?"

Major Roberts

"Oh, yes! The army called me into the Pentagon on April 17, for questioning.

"A Colonel Alexander Musyk, Chief of Army Troop Information, was the principal interrogator. I covered much the same material as has been presented here today

---

[5] ARL 681, Chief of Information, Department of the Army, TWX Number 89, June 12, 1961.

and further, secured from his files the reports and copies of the instructor scripts, after-action report, and other papers which I had forwarded to his office many months previously.

"At that time I reiterated the facts which created the 'Citizenship' and 'Pro-Blue' programs; noted the authority and directives which formed the basis for the actions (including the Seventh Army 'Collateral Cold War' circular), and suggested that rather than investigate General Walker, the army might do well to investigate the *Overseas Weekly* which is distributed through *Stars and Stripes* facilities — a government sponsored newspaper.[6]

"In fact, on April 23, 1961 I sent a letter to Colonel Muzyk summarizing our talks and suggested that '. . . it is clear that the U.S. Military — with its disciplined organization, training methods, and civilian contacts through ROTC, Reserves, and industry — can and must help others to wage non-military warfare. The enemy has all of his conflict managers on the board. The Free World needs guidance from its own professional students of strategy, tactics, and conflict!"

"I had no response from this letter."

On May 2, I wrote to (among others) Lieutenant General Walter L. Weible, U.S.A. (ret), Executive Vice President, Association of United States Army, saying in part:

"The directors of the Association of the United States Army know well the long-enduring support

6 Letter to Mrs. Marion von Rospach, The *Overseas Weekly,* Frankfurt Press Center, 12 am Leonhardsbrunn, Frankfurt, Main, from Arthur L. Jergenson, Lt. Col., Editor-in-Chief, *Stars and Stripes,* dated August 13, 1953.

rendered to AUSA by one of its most aggressive champions, Major General Edwin A. Walker.

"In appreciation of your keen awareness of the conspiracy which has now launched an attempted career-assassination of one of the army's most respected combat leaders now on active duty, I felt that you would welcome a factual rebuttal of the contrived charges fabricated by the salacious *Overseas Weekly*."

In outline I then described the background of the Pro-Blue program and my part in it and suggested that AUSA add the decisive prestige and authoritative voice of the Association of the United States Army to this campaign, "in defense of General Walker."

A similar letter was addressed to General Lucius Clay, President, Continental Can Company and others, requesting that they help secure a fair investigation of the General Walker case.

Not long after this, Lieutenant Colonel William V. Schmitt, my immediate superior in the New York office, OCINFO, called me to his office to say that the Pentagon had received complaints from general officers to the effect that I had sent out letters over my signature and rank requesting aid for General Walker. The Pentagon, he said, did not want me involved in the Walker case.

During later sessions, Colonel Schmitt "counseled" me in the same manner adding that I was "jeopardizing my career and my family" by activity in behalf of General Walker. These warnings were repeated at several similar "talks."

On September 11, 1961, Colonel Schmitt notified me that on orders from the Office of the Chief of Information I was to be relieved from assignment in the Information

Career field and reassigned to a medical unit in Fort Lee, Virginia. The reason given was that OCINFO had determined that I was "not suitable" for continued duty in the Army Information Career Field.

A form letter prepared by the Chief of Information and sent to persons asking about my transfer stated in part, "Major Roberts has associated himself with written criticism of the army in admonishing Major General Edwin A. Walker. He circulated packets of critical material in envelopes bearing his name and military title. These actions disqualify him to represent the army as an Information Officer."

"This letter of explanation further stated that I was reassigned . . . 'because of personal actions which placed him at variance with established positions of the Department of the Army.' " [7]

Mr. Hartel

"Did the army ever show any interest in investigating *Overseas Weekly?*" the Senate Armed Services Committee Counsel asked during my interrogation concerning the Pro-Blue Program.

Major Roberts

"Not to my knowledge, sir."

Mr. Kindell

"Major Roberts, I have here a copy of the *Petersburg Progress Index* of November 19 which carries a story by Mr. Jimmy Ezzell, which purports to be an interview conducted with you. In the story you are quoted as saying that 'subversive elements have infiltrated the service and government,' that you know whose these people are,

[7] "Believes Aid to General Walker Halts Career," by Willard Edwards, *Chicago Tribune*, October 3, 1961.

and that when the subcommittee begins its investigation 'they will be fingered.'

"Is this story essentially correct?"

Major Roberts

"Yes sir, the story is essentially correct, but needs some clarification. In the first place, this *Progress Index* story is a matter of treatment. For example, here is another story which appeared on the same date in the *Richmond Times-Dispatch,* written by Mr. Robert Gordon, with no mention of these charges attributed to me. Yet both Mr. Ezzell and Mr. Gordon were in my home at the same time and I talked to both of them at the same time.

"Next, I believe that I have shown that there are, indeed, personnel, such as those employed by *Overseas Weekly,* who are certainly highly suspect as 'subversive infiltrators.'"

Mr. Kindell

"Well, I don't mean these people. What about persons in government? Will you give me the names of people in our government whom you classify as 'subversive infiltrators.'"

Major Roberts

"Sir, you will note that in the *Index* story the comment is reported as, 'We know who these people are . . .' Now the term, 'we' was used in the team sense. There are persons very well qualified to make a professional observation of this kind who are now on the 'team' working to expose subversion in our government. One of these is Mr. Edward Hunter. In hearings before the Senate Internal Security Subcommittee, Mr. Hunter said, 'Moscow simply acquired agents who mingled with the new, intellectual elite at the top on terms of equality; were sometimes members of it themselves. They infiltrated the White House and other topmost government offices.'

"Mr. Hunter also noted in this hearing that, 'a growing grassroots movement has developed in the United States . . . ,' and this movement is opposed by a '. . . Red anti-anti-Communist drive that was openly initiated under orders issued to the Communist forces of the world, especially to those in the United States, through the Red manifesto of December 5, 1960.'

"He then said, 'The primary target as it is developing is the Pentagon; specifically the program to train and alert our troops and our people to the Red techniques and the inherent evil in Communism. The Reds have seen that this program and the directives issued to implement it — in spite of sabotage — do make the big difference. Unless this program can be destroyed, the anti-Communist movement cannot be liquidated. So the forces are joined between the enforcement of the Red manifesto and the implementation of the training program that came out of the Korean war.' [8]

"Much of this testimony was subsequently inserted in the *Congressional Record* and reprinted as extracts by the Honorable Strom Thurmond on August 25, 1961," I said.

The *Associated Press* wire service also carried news stories of this hearing, and articles appearing in the *New York Sunday News*, August 27, and *New York Journal*

[8] "The New Drive against the Anti-Communist Program," testimony of Mr. Edward Hunter before Senate Internal Security Sub-Committee, July 11, 1961.

American of the same date, reflect the charge that Moscow agents 'infiltrated the White House.' [9]

Mr. Kindell

"Major Roberts, I have here a copy of a letter in which you suggest that 'Fabian-Socialists' have infiltrated our government. Aren't you concerned that if you continue in this sort of activity the army might cashier you?"

Major Roberts

"The army has not ordered me to stop my personal anti-Communist activity and I will continue to contribute whatever I can to this fight as long as possible, including speeches such as the one I made on November 30 in Washington, D.C. before the Young Americans for Freedom." [10]

Thus concluded my testimony before the Senate Armed Services Special Committee concerning the origins of the 24th Infantry Division Pro-Blue program.

The New York Council of the Veterans of Foreign Wars charged, on August 12, 1961, that removal of Major General Edwin A. Walker as commander of the 24th Infantry Division "was not the main objective of the smear experts. Their real aim was to wreck the Pro-Blue program.

"This objective has been reached," says this report. "The Pro-Blue program has been completely washed out. The enemy has scored a tremendous victory." [11]

[9] "Charges Soviet Agents Infiltrated White House," *New York Journal American*, August 27, 1961.

[10] "Ex-Aide of General Walker Defends Pro-Blue Plan," *Richmond Times Dispatch*, December 1, 1961.

[11] "Real Target of Smear was 'Pro-Blue' Program," *Brooklyn Tablet*, August 12, 1961.

The conditions which gave the enemy a "tremendous victory" became visible during our subsequent investigation of the personnel and policy of the "repulsive" *Overseas Weekly*.

We will see how *Overseas Weekly* promotes the objectives of the United Nations Organization and International Communism.

CHAPTER VIII

WHAT POWER
PROTECTS
OVERSEAS WEEKLY?

"We don't think much of the *Overseas Weekly*. Called the 'over-sexed Weekly' by the troops, it has been termed 'subversive to the command' by an admitted adherent of General Walker 'since it carries news calculated to destroy unit loyalty, smear non-commissioned leaders, and assist anti-American forces in their campaign to disunite NATO by portraying the American soldier as rowdy, disorderly, dishonest, and immoral'."
— "The Walker Case", *Army Times*, May 6, 1961

Immediately following my April 17 Pentagon talk with Colonel Muzyk, Chief of Army Troop Information, I wrote to Sergeant Tom Flynn, senior NCO, Special Projects Office, 24th Infantry Division, pointing out the urgency for exposing the fictitious charges against the Pro-Blue program being published by *Overseas Weekly* and other anti-anti-Communist papers. I further suggested that he advise me of General Walker's current address so that we might have his approval for coordinating counter-action which, at that time, we hoped would be generated by concerned Department of Army officials and senior commanders in the service.

This ill-founded optimism stemmed from a January, 1961 conference with Mr. Frank B. Barnett, Associate Program Chairman, The Richardson Foundation. The Richardson Foundation has a long association with "psywar" programs at the Army War College and with Army Reserve "cold-war" training programs. Mr. Barnett made it a point to meet me in New York on January 9, about two months after my arrival from Germany, so that he might have a complete briefing on the 24th Infantry Division troop information effort. During the course of ensuing conferences, he received complete background information on Pro-Blue operations and copies of the training scripts. These, he said, were to be used as a guide in preparing a similar project under the sponsorship of the Richardson Foundation.

I was particularly flattered by Mr. Barnett's confidence that he planned to 'approach' General Layman Lemnitzer, Chairman, Joint Chiefs, and General George Decker, Army Chief of Staff, urging adoption of the 24th Infantry Division Pro-Blue plan for Army-Navy-Air Force troop information programs.

My conference notes pertaining to these meetings with Barnett were transmitted to General Walker on January 18 and to the Chief of Information, Department of the Army.

Needless to say, General Walker was not impressed by this attention and was to quickly correct my illusions concerning hoped-for support from higher command in warding off the *Overseas Weekly* attack.

At midnight, April 22, 1961, General Walker telephoned me from USAREUR Headquarters, Heidelberg, where he had been transferred in panting haste as a result of the brazen falsehoods published by the *Overseas Weekly*.

Rather than depend upon the dubious interest of army compatriots, he advised, it would prove more practicable to enlist public sympathy by revealing the questionable objectives of *Overseas Weekly* and the subversive inclinations of its staff. I could begin, he suggested, by contacting his uncle, Mr. Frank de Ganahl, in New York City; his attorney, Brigadier General Clyde J. Watts, Oklahoma City; and a brother, Mr. George P. Walker, Jr., Center Point, Texas.

Thus was organized in very loose fashion, "The Friends of General Walker" which was to quickly expand into a nationwide network of workers and supporters.

By April 29 I was able to report to General Walker through the efforts of a former associate, Brigadier General John R. Beishline (then a professor at New York University) we had conferred with Mr. William Ward, a leading Democratic Party figure in New York. Through Mr. Ward we reached Mr. Robert Kennedy, then U.S. Attorney-General.

The Attorney-General, said Mr. Ward, had transmitted our material on the Pro-Blue program and *Overseas Weekly* articles to the Federal Bureau of Investigation for study.

I also talked at length with Mr. John G. Keenan, publisher of *Counter-Attack* (an anti-Communist periodical), an attorney and former FBI investigator. Keenan was to prove highly effective in establishing the apparatus which unearthed much damaging evidence during our subsequent investigation of *Overseas Weekly* and its ramified operations.

By this date also, we had enlisted the aid of the late Merwin K. Hart, National Economic Council; the late

George E. Sokolsky, nationally syndicated columnist; Senator Barry Goldwater; and the Honorable O.C. Fisher, Congressman from Texas. It was, in fact, Mr. Fisher who employed the initial fruits of our *Overseas Weekly* investigation in a report to the Congress on May 24, 1961.[1]

"From inquiries and documented evidence, I am convinced," said Congressman Fisher, "that the (*Overseas Weekly*) charges are unfounded, and actually constitute a bold and brazen attempt by a salacious tabloid newspaper to smear one of our most respected combat officers.

"The army has recently published a position paper on cold-war intelligence, Classified Army Regulation 515-1, titled, 'Collateral Activities, Army Cold War Activities,' (U) dated March 29, 1961," Congressman Fisher continued in his address on the House Floor. "This AR defines troop information objectives and actions to be achieved in instructing American troops in cold war principles. And this regulation very strongly reinforces the principles contained in the 24th Infantry Division Pro-Blue program.

"Major Arch E. Roberts drafted the original plan," said Mr. Fisher. "I have sought and obtained information from him regarding it."

Quoting the official 24th Infantry Division directive which established the Pro-Blue program, Congressman Fisher then noted, "While this highly laudable program was in effect and apparently functioning successfully,

[1] "Notorious *Overseas Weekly* Attacks Anti-Communist Pro-Blue Americanism Program of General Edwin A. Walker," Congressman O. C. Fisher, *Congressional Record*, May 24, 1961.

it was suddenly attacked by the *Overseas Weekly*. Thanks to the fertility of its imagination, the *Weekly* decided the Pro-Blue program was nothing but a John Birch Society indoctrination plan. . . .

"Mr. Speaker, the fact that the (Mrs. Marion) Rospach charges are apparently spurious and phony gives rise to a question of the 'character and policies' of the *Overseas Weekly*," said Congressman Fisher.

This was our question too. And so we began a study of the "character and policies" of *Overseas Weekly* which lead into some amazing channels.

A collateral need of the "Friends of General Walker" was to arouse public support for an official congressional investigation of anti-anti-Communist Pentagon policies. This public relations campaign was launched largely through the devotion of Mrs. Mark Byron, New York City. Because of Mrs. Byron, "The Friends of General Walker" soon had a national telephone-telegraph network which could — and did — generate thousands of letters to newspapers, radio, and television stations across the country and to congressmen and senators in Washington.

"About one hundred people were contacted Thursday night," I wrote General Walker on April 29, "to start the ball rolling — including: Kent Courtney (*Independent American*), New Orleans, Louisiana; Mr. Frank Hanighen (*Human Events*), Washington, D.C.; Fulton Lewis, Jr.; Dean Manion, the President General, Daughters of the American Revolution; Society of New England Women; Catholic War Veterans; American Legion; Federated Women's Clubs; and Mr. McCormick of the *Dallas* (Texas) *News*."

The flood of news articles prompted by "The Friends of General Walker" campaign is familiar to every American family and needs no repetition.

Sufficient to say that within a matter of weeks the late Senator Styles Bridges, Senator J. Strom Thurmond, and Senator John G. Tower became leading champions in the "Case of General Walker" and prepared the way for later Senate hearings on "Military Cold War Education and Speech Review Policies," which were to extend from September, 1961 through June, 1962.

About the first of May, 1961 we inserted an agent into the New York office of *Overseas Weekly*. A professional, private investigator, this man was also an accomplished journalist. This background was ideally suited to his "cover" as a liberal writer seeking original material which would support a series of laudatory articles he proposed to write about *Overseas Weekly* and its sterling part in exposing a "John Birch" general.

Starting with the lead information which Mrs. Marion von Rospach had conveniently supplied in her letter to Colonel Jorgenson of *Stars and Stripes* on August 13, 1953 in which she identified herself as "President, International Media Company" (we thought this rather promising), we proceeded, bit by bit, to uncover the *Overseas Weekly* interlock with other subversive publications.[2] This information was collated with intelligence received from European sources and other American contacts and published in a series of reports numbered one through five. These reports formed the basis for a sequence of news releases. Our intelligence reports were forwarded

[2] Letter from Mrs. Rospach to Lt. Col. Jorgenson, *Stars and Stripes*, August 13, 1953; "Defense Secretary McNamara on Senate Resolution 191"; Hearings before the Committee on Armed Services, September 6 and 7, 1961, page 234.

to key persons involved in the "Friends of General Walker" program. The News releases were disseminated to the press.

Within a week we had our first report, "Inside *Overseas Weekly*."

At about the same time, a liaison officer from the Pentagon arrived at the New York office, OCINFO, to warn me that should I become involved in organizing a "pro-Walker campaign," I would be jeopardizing my family. Because of my known involvement in the 24th Infantry Division Pro-Blue program, he said, I might have already seriously compromised my military career.

By this time, I was neither surprised nor shocked by such overt military protection being afforded the salacious *Overseas Weekly*.

"It appears," I wrote General Walker, "that the anti-morality, anti-religious, and anti-American crowd has a pretty strong union in Washington."

Our side, too, was growing in stature, as evidenced by a telephone call from Mr. Ward on May 19, who advised me that the FBI was then conducting a field investigation of *Overseas Weekly* in Germany.

Overseas Weekly, began our first report, "is a privately owned newspaper which is read by English speaking members of the Armed Forces stationed in Europe. It has bureaus in London, Paris, and Munich and a New York Office which handles American advertising. The main European office is in Frankfurt, Germany. Marion Rospach is the publisher and executive editor and John Dornberg is the news editor."

The first and last pages of the paper, we found, almost always carry pictures of semi-nude females. Leads to stories in the paper carried on the first page are lurid; "Armed GI Holds Family of Five in Hour of Terror," "Model Won't Rest on her Laurels," "Attacker of Girl still at Large." (June 14, 1959 issue). Stories and headings throughout every issue of this paper are similarly prurient or violent in their appeal to the reader. Crime, usually violent, and sex — usually in terms of rape or prostitution — are the main themes followed in the pages of the *Overseas Weekly*.

Also the paper provides an unusual "service" to its GI readers. The July 28, 1960 issue carried a full story on publication of a "Ladies Directory," listing "Play-for-Pay gals" by name and address in the Soho district in London. The *Weekly* hinged its story on the court proceedings which occurred after issuance of the Directory. No detail was lacking, including the price of the book, its publisher, and where it could be bought.

The October 9, 1960 issue of the paper (page 16) gratuitously provided its readers with the information that one Martha Watts had written a 235 page book on "The Men in my Life," published in London. GI's were informed in detail of the contents of the book, including the "news" that its author had been convicted four hundred times for soliciting as a prostitute and that her busiest day had been on VE Day in 1945 when she entertained forty-nine GI's.

There is another side to the *Overseas Weekly*, we learned, which is reflected in its "Editor's Notebook" written by Marion Rospach. Her editorials are usually very "serious" in content. For example, the September 18, 1960 issue contains one of her editorials (page 4) which is entitled "Censorship" with the subheading, "Policemen of the Nation's Morality."

The column is devoted entirely to a review and commentary on two books, *The First Freedom*, edited by Robert B. Downs, and *Comstockery in America*, by Robert W. Haney, a Unitarian minister. Marion Rospach informs her readers that "Roger N. Baldwin, former director of the American Civil Liberties Union, reviews them in the *Saturday Review*." She does not, however, reveal to her readers that Roger Baldwin has one of the most extensive records of association with Communist and Communist-front enterprises of any man in the United States, reaching back to the year 1919, when he went to prison for refusal to register for military service in World War I. Baldwin raised the endowment and directed the notorious Garland Fund in the '20's. This Fund, in just six years, distributed $1,600,000 to direct Communist and Socialist movements, including a whole cluster of Communist newspapers, publishing houses and schools. There are hundreds of references to this man's activities on behalf of Communists and their allies in the various hearings and reports on subversive activities which have been formed in this country from 1919 to date.

The First Freedom, which is reviewed so admiringly by Roger Baldwin and by Marion Rospach, is a book which came about because of an agreement entered into by its publishers and the Fund for the Republic organization which has been the subject of an intensive investigation by the House Committee on Un-American Activities. Hearings on various aspects of the Fund's activities and publications, relating to their pro-Communist character, have been printed and published by the House Committee in recent years.

The First Freedom, consists of the writing of various "experts" on censorship. As Marion Rospach writes, "The volume is therefore an argument against all current legal bans on alleged obscenity, incitements in print to juvenile delinquency, political subversion, race libel, sacrilege, blasphemy."

Authors whose writings appear in *The First Freedom* include Walter Gellhorn, Elmer Rice, John Haynes Holmes, Morris Ernst (a review of his book, *"To the Pure"*), Paul Blanshard (a notorious anti-Catholic writer), Max Lerner (of the *New York Post*), Henry Steele Commager, Harold D. Lasswell (on political subversion), John Steinbeck, James T. Farrell, Archibald MacLeish, Benjamin Fine (of the *New York Times*), Elmer Davis, and many others. Every one of these authors has a Communist-front record.

The second book *Comstockery in America* praised by Marion Rospach, is another attack on censorship of pornographic, obscene and other prurient material.

Marion Rospach's column in the March 21, 1960 issue of her paper is again titled, "Censorship." In it she quotes from a bulletin which deplores the banning of various books and films in the United States by parents groups. She singled out the action of one school group which warned students "against contaminating their minds by seeing the prize-winning film, *He Who Must Die*." She considered this "hysteria."

The film *He Who Must Die* is a straight Communist-line production which attacks basic Christian tenets in a particularly foul manner. Its directors were Jules Dassin and Ben Barzman. Both men have been identified as members of the Communist Party. Dassin left the United States to avoid a subpoena by the House Committee on Un-American Activities and started producing or directing films in Italy. The House Committee identified him as a member of the Party in its Annual Report issued on December 28, 1952 (page 44). Ben Barzman was similarly identified by the House Committee in its annual reports for 1952 and 1953.

The hard intelligence garnered by the investigative efforts in New York confirmed the vague information which my experiences with *Overseas Weekly* in Germany had raised. The vicious, anti-military editorial policy of *Overseas Weekly*, well-known to all Americans who have served in Germany, had not been previously correlated and documented to my knowledge. Our rapidly expanding dossier on *Overseas Weekly* and its personnel, therefore, constituted the first professional effort to properly label this destructive publication.

Our foreign contacts, too, were beginning to add fuel to the fire under Marion von Rospach. French and German press representatives, in addition to American journalists, started digging for facts about this civilian newspaper, which had such an amazing control over U.S. military circles in Europe and in Washington.

Our investigations soon began to reveal *Overseas Weekly* interlock with other subversive publications, the strange character of its writers and the thrust of its policies.

"The *Overseas Weekly's* New York City office," our investigator reported in a subsequent statement to me, "is located at 380 Lexington Avenue. The *Overseas Family*, which is another of Marion von Rospach's publications also is listed at the same address.

"The New York office handles most of the advertising which appears in the Rospach publications. In fact were it not for the New York office, *Overseas Weekly* and *Overseas Family* could not possibly obtain the lucrative advertising which fills their pages."

This office, we discovered, is not just a branch office of the *Weekly*. It is a firm called Pan American Publishers Representatives (PABCO). It has represented the *Overseas Weekly* throughout its publication history since 1950. Members of the firm engaged in an extraordinary amount of activity on behalf of the *Overseas Weekly* and its editor in the matter of the controversy which followed that paper's attack upon Major General Edwin A. Walker in its issue of April 16, 1961.

Our work revealed that PABCO also represents *Swank*. This is particularly significant in view of the reputation of Marion Rospach's newspaper, called the "Oversexed Weekly" by the troops in Europe.

Large piles of recent issues of *Swank* are openly displayed on shelves in the New York office of *Overseas Weekly* (PABCO) alongside of issues of the *Weekly* and the *Family*. The May, 1961 issue of *Swank* featured the writings of Norman Mailer, James T. Farrell, Bob Kaufman, and Laurence Ferlinghetti. A recent book written by Norman Mailer is *Advertisements for Myself*, a filthy, obscene volume. A typical Communist-front with which Mailer has been associated is the notorious Fair Play for Cuba Committee which he sponsored. (See "Fair Play for Cuba Committee", Hearings, Senate Internal Security Subcommittee, 1960-61, page 6.) This Committee was secretly financed by the Castro Government of Cuba (Hearings, page 87), and was identified by the Internal Security Subcommittee as a "Communist operation" (page 92).

The July, 1961 issue of *Swank* — in addition to its picture of nudes and semi-nudes — carried an excerpt from *Naked Lunch*, written by William S. Burroughs and described by him as a, "sexual inferno, a systematic desecration of the human image." (*Swank*, July, 1961, page 51). This excerpt was given to *Swank* by poet Allen Ginsberg. *Naked Lunch*, the ultimate in horrible filth, is described by a *Swank* writer (page 50) as having been written after, "twelve years of addiction to dope" and "after steeping himself in vice." Here is one of the milder statements in the Burroughs excerpt in *Swank*, represented by *Overseas Weekly's* New York office:

> "Gentle reader, we see God through our. . .in the flash bulb of the orgasm. . .The Word, gentle reader, will flay you down to laughing bones and the Author will do a strip-tease with his own intestines. Let it be, no holes barred. The Word is recommended for children and convent-trained. . .need it special to learn what every street boy knows: 'He who rims the Mother Superior is a success-minded brown nose and God will reward him on TV with a bang at Question 666'. . .I will issue a Bull on Immaculate Birth Control. . ."

No wonder Marion von Rospach is such a vociferous enemy of "censorship!"

The August 28, 1960 issue carried a Marion Rospach editorial (page 4) headed, "Fixed Beliefs Vulnerable" which is a particularly vicious example of slanted propaganda against patriotism. Its sub-heading was "Brainwashing Antidote Sought." It quoted an Air Force psychiatrist, Lt. Col. Paul Eggersten, although, significantly, no source was given for his statements. The column started out,

"How can ordinary Americans be preconditioned to withstand Communist brainwashing? . . . at the start it was assumed the real answer was an unshakeable faith in Americanism."

The psychiatrist was quoted as stating:

"Surprisingly we're finding that the more you train a guy to trust and believe implicitly in any political system — including our own — the more vulnerable you leave him to this type of coercion (brainwashing).

"The man who stands up best is the man with a healthy disrespect, and irreverence almost, for all authority."

This column was built around the question, "How effective is the six-point Soldier's Code of Conduct," drafted in 1955 by a six-man committee headed by retired Army General John E. Hull, which is posted in all armed forces installations.

The column ended with this observation:

"The most important point it seems to us, is that qualified doctors and observers believe a man who thinks and questions so-called facts is most likely to be true to his country and himself. This fact alone makes censorship, as it is being practiced by some schools and libraries at home, dangerous to the very foundation of the American system."

Such reasoning is almost as warped as that of the anti-censorship "experts" — so beloved by Marion Rospach — who claim that pornography is "must" reading for children and sex perverts! Children benefit by becoming *healthy*-minded from reading pornography; sex perverts tend to *not* commit depredations against children if they read pornography because the material gives them a release! Marion Rospach is saying, in so many words, to the American soldier, spit on your flag and country;

then if the Communists capture you, you can't be brain-washed. She neglects the obvious corollary to such a situation: the Communists would not have to brainwash such a soldier — there would be no need to waste the energy.

The character and policy of *Overseas Weekly* as revealed by Marion Rospach's columns and by her promotion of prurient sex, offers a startling parallel to the *Communist Rules for Revolution*.

"Corrupt the young," is the first precept; "get them away from religion. Get them interested in sex. Make them superficial, destroy their ruggedness."

"By specious argument," directs rule seven of *Communist Rules for Revolution*, "cause the breakdown of the old moral virtues, honesty, sobriety, continence, faith in the pledged word, ruggedness." [3]

The similarity between the objectives of *Overseas Weekly* and *Communist Rules for Revolution* is not accidental.

In fact, our initial investigations revealed that *Overseas Weekly* is not "A bit of home away from home," as its masthead proclaims. *Overseas Weekly*, we found, is an instrument used to propagate international ideologies and to compromise U.S. Army combat readiness. We also became aware that *Overseas Weekly* was but one element in an international transmission belt employing public information media of varied persuasion, from *The Worker* to the *New York Times*, and many foreign publications, all of which are aligned to further the same international objectives.

It was at this point that we established substantial

[3] *"Communist Rules for Revolution,"* Dusseldorf, May, 1919.

elements of proof that policy and editorial control over *Overseas Weekly* does not terminate at 380 Lexington Avenue.

How we traced these reins to other pro-Communist media, to U.S. government agencies and to an invisible world empire, will be told in succeeding chapters.

CHAPTER IX

... AND
SUBVERSIVE
MOVEMENTS

"More and more, the world is being dominated and controlled by the organized forces of Godlessness... The Godless army is following a perfectly mapped out strategy. It holds almost complete sway in international organizations, financial circles, and the press, cinema, radio, and television."
— The Very Reverend Pedro Arrupe, S.J., Superior General of the Jesuit Order, Vatican Council debate, September 27, 1965

Mention should be made of certain aspects of the first attack on General Walker in the April 16, 1961 issue of *Overseas Weekly*. It must be remembered that the *Weekly* publicized this matter long, long after the events described allegedly took place. Page 3 of this issue contained three stories on the controversy, two unsigned. The story headlined "John Birch Society Under Fire In U.S. Also Finds Support," which is presented as a straight news story, contained a number of remarkable statements including the widely quoted one that Robert Welch "has acknowledged adopting the Communist techniques of setting up 'front' organizations." Whatever the truth may be about the John Birch Society, use of this particular type of description is the same method so deplored by the "liberals" and Communists — guilt by association. In this case it is guilt by association of techniques without any mention of the significant fact that Communist-fronts are run under rigid, hidden discipline.

The lead story on Walker, headed "Military Channels Used To Push Birch Ideas," written by Bob Jones, S.W. Naujocks and John Dornberg, is accompanied by two editorial page cartoons. One is from the *New York Herald Tribune* and has the title, "Malice in Wonderland." It pictures a snake with a hood (KKK), a white rabbit (White Citizens Council), a rat (U.S. Nazi Party), and a caricature of Uncle Sam (John Birch Society). The other cartoon from the *Washington Post* depicts two rabid-looking men labeled Committee on Un-American Activities and John Birch Society. The heading over the cartoon is "They're all Communists except Thee and Me. . ." What effect are these cartoons intended to have on the minds of the readers of the story which follows, accompanied by a picture of Major General Edwin Walker (immediately below the cartoons)? By the technique of innuendo, it is implied that Walker is pushing Nazi, Fascist, and terroristic ideas and that anti-Communism (House Committee on Un-American Activities style) is per se evil. What Communist publication could have done a better job? Yet *Overseas Weekly* presents itself as anti-Communist!

This lead story on Walker contains a number of statements worthy of mention. One in particular is interesting: "In the February 25, 1961 issue of the *Taro-Leaf* Division newspaper," said *Overseas Weekly*. ". . . Captain Hyde put the entire division into a position of 'saluting' Admiral Arleigh Burke, Chief of Naval Operations, for his 'outspoken' anti-Communist stand." In a derogatory story of this nature the inference made is plain. Now there also appears in the *Worker*, May 7, 1961, page 8, a story, "Warriors Looking for a War," written by Mike Newberry, which attacks a long list of military men including Admiral Arleigh Burke (for his "warmongering speech"). The *Worker* did not like Burke's tough talk nor did the *Weekly*.

The third story, "John Birch versus 24th Infantry Division" links the Birch Society to promotion "of the controversial film 'Operation Abolition.'" It also seems to deplore the fact that the "Birch Society encourages members to write Congressmen and bring influence to bear." We had thought that all citizens in this country had the right of petition and redress of grievances. The *Weekly* takes another view. "Operation Abolition" was shown to officers of the 24th Division. The *Weekly* most certainly did not approve of this.

The John Dornberg story (page 2) on the Birch Society uses the quotation, "Subversion, whether of the left or the right, is still subversive." All statements used by Dornberg in his story were against the Society. This, however, is not the point because the effect of the story quotation was to implant in the readers' minds the idea that Walker and anyone else in the division involved in the Pro-Blue program were "subversive" just like the Communists.

Marion Rospach's editorial (page 4) on the controversy (which she initiated) is a propaganda device from start to finish. Among other things she says, "It is furthermore our responsibility to point out officials who propagate beliefs in direct opposition to those upheld by the duly elected leaders." This incredible statement completely ignores the nature of our government; ignores the Oath of Office of every officer in the Armed Forces, based on the Constitution; and ignores the attitude of millions of others — that followers, officers, and otherwise, of Hitler could not take refuge in the plea that they were only following orders when they supported the Nazi Government. This is not to say that the United States is such a country or that it has such a government. Nevertheless, duly elected leaders are fallible human beings and treason has been committed in the United States by "duly elected leaders" in the past. Marion Rospach quotes material from *The Life of John Birch* which she says, "viciously and blindly attacks the government the soldier has vowed to serve." One statement she considers in this light is that, "former Secretary of State Dean Acheson brought into office and surrounded himself with Communists and their sympathizers." Voluminous proof of this assertion has been established by numerous Congressional committees and some of the greatest leaders in America long, long before the John Birch Society was born.

John Dornberg wrote a long story in the *Overseas Family* of April 28, 1961, page 2, headed "Birch Society Methods May Aid, Not Hurt Reds." He wrote: "The Communist threat to America has been apparent to most Americans for nearly fifteen years . . . But far more dangerous is the fact that the John Birch Society poses, potentially, an equal if not greater threat to the American way of life.

"This threat lies . . . in its methods and its consistent attacks on American leaders and its policy of labeling as Communist everything which it opposes.

"In our society, still reeling from the extremist attacks popularized by the late Senator Joseph McCarthy, pinning the label of 'red' or 'pink' on anyone is a sure-fire way of ruining his reputation."

Dornberg noted that Hitler had cried "red." He felt

that the Birchist's, "methods and many of their beliefs are frighteningly akin to fascism." He again referred to Hitler, "Not long ago, in Germany, there was a man named Adolf Hitler who held and espoused very similar views."

And further, ". . . these attacks and others he (Welch) has made since the *Politician* was printed and revised a few years ago are strangely similar to the smear tactics to which German Government leaders were subjected during the Weimar Republic from 1918 to 1933." This last quotation is a revealing one, for any person conversant with the history of the Weimar Republic knows that some of the top Communist agents in the history of Communism were leading politicians in the Weimar Republic and that the Government was at times almost completely Marxist in its complexion.

Dornberg's attack on the Birch Society — non-existent in Europe — in this context could only have reinforced the view the paper wishes to propagate against General Walker: that he shares these views and that he is following the tactics of Hitler. The use of such articles against the Birch Society is a flagrant smoke screen to hide the *Weekly's* real purpose. This purpose grew starkly apparent as our investigations continued.

It was during this phase in our research on *Overseas Weekly* that we started to expose some of the political figures who had extended their prestige and authority protectively over Marion Rospach when her paper came under scrutiny by army commanders in Europe.

A Washington Bureau servicing the news media reported that the Pentagon officials who know of the *Overseas Weekly's* history over the years state that Marion Rospach appealed to Congressman Samuel Yorty of California for help at the Pentagon in 1953, after Major

General Charles Bolte had banned the *Overseas Weekly* from the army newsstands.

"Samuel William Yorty accompanied Marion Rospach when she appealed to the Pentagon for relief of the suspension, according to the report referred to above," stated this authority.

Sam Yorty, Mayor of Los Angeles, was to become the central issue of newspaper treatment concerning my talk before the Seventy-first Congress, National Society, Daughters of the American Revolution, on April 19, 1962.

My statement, "I can assure you that it is the responsibility of all Americans in and out of uniform when the Mayor of a great city in the United States has a Communist background," was alleged to be the reason for my dismissal from active duty assignment on order of the Secretary of the Army.

Because it represents the problem of pro-Communism in the Congress, full documentation on the Yorty matter will be introduced in a later chapter under the title, "Is Sam Yorty a Communist?"

A significant and highly interesting facet of our investigation of the *Overseas Weekly* is that part of its operations which relate to its parent publishing company, International Media Company.

The *Overseas Weekly* is published by International Media Company and has been since its establishment on May 14, 1950. It was incorporated in Wilmington, Delaware, February 20, 1952.

International Media Company, whose president is Marion von Rospach, is located at 380 Lexington Avenue, New York (the same as that for *Overseas Weekly*). Marion von Rospach is a co-owner of *Overseas Weekly*, which leaves no question of the interlocking directorate.

International Media Company is staffed by the same individuals who handle *Overseas Weekly* and PABCO affairs.

Among the publications which International Media represents, controls, or owns are: *Flugwelt* and *Flugcorper* (both in Germany), *Pourquoi Pas* (Belgium), *Le Matin* (daily newspaper in Haiti), and *Drum* (Africa).

The Tarrytown New York *Daily News* of May 1, 1961 carried a local feature news item which identified one Gene Bernald, 126 Millard Avenue, "Philipae Manor," as a "director" of International Media Company. The article also stated that Bernald is a "participant" in the operations of Radio Swan which is "privately owned and independently operated" for "commercial purposes" by "American business." [1]

Radio Swan is a very powerful transmitter which is located on Greater Swan Island, the larger of two islands in the Western Caribbean Sea, north of Honduras and which are owned by the United States. The same news item stated that Radio Swan had "opened up its far-reaching facilities to those who would fight 'isms', whether Castro or Trujillo-oriented."

The *New York Times* for September 9, 1960 carried an item which stated that Radio Swan had begun operations as a privately owned commercial radio station (fifty-thousand watts) in May, 1960. The Gibraltar Steamship Corporation (29 Broadway, New York City) was stated to be the owner of record, but as a "holding company" rather than as the real owner of the station. The State Department stated that as far as the Depart-

[1] "Bernald involved in two International Incidents," *Daily News*, Tarrytown, N.Y., May 1, 1961.

ment knew there was a "weather station" on Swan Island.

The *New York Times* item of September 9, 1960 also stated that Radio Swan's owners had negotiated a contract with Walter S. Lemon of World-Wide Broadcasting for taped programs.

The Tarrytown *Daily News* identified the news feature story on Gene Bernald and his relationship to International Media and Radio Swan as having emanated, as prepared copy, either directly from Gene Bernald or from his company. Mrs. Gene Bernald stated that her husband's office was in the International Media Company's offices which are — as has been mentioned earlier — those of the *Overseas Weekly*.

The significance of the relationship of Gene Bernald, International Media Company, *Overseas Weekly*, and other publications and companies in the complex which centers in the office at 380 Lexington Avenue, to Radio Swan, lies in the peculiar part this radio station played in the Cuban Invasion debacle.

The *New York Post* of May 24, 1961, page 5 carried a story headed "Cuba Underground: 'Invasion Betrayed Us,'" which was written by Robert Berrellez, an AP correspondent who had been arrested when the Cuban Invasion began and who had spent three and a half weeks in prison before he was released. He wrote, "A leader of the Cuban underground sat in a Havana prison, bitter and weeping.

"'If we overthrow Fidel we'll shoot the invaders as traitors,' he declared. 'They destroyed our counter-revolutionary organization by not telling us they were coming.'"

He was referring to the fact that Radio Swan was supposed to broadcast a signal in code to the Cuban underground which would announce the beginning of the invasion and the moment for the Cuban underground to rise up against Castro. This signal never came from Radio Swan. Consequently, while Castro knew every minute detail of the invasion plans, no part of the Cuban underground forces knew of the invasion until it was too late. The invaders were killed or imprisoned and the Cuban underground was nearly totally destroyed. Also it should be noted that the Cuban Revolutionary Leader, Miro Cardona, was supposed to have broadcast a message directly to the Cuban people at the time of the invasion, calling for an internal uprising. Radio Swan did not carry that message as agreed.

Robert Berrellez wrote further, "Thus did one of Fidel Castro's enemies vent his desperate anger on a band of a thousand invaders who came to save Cuba and, in the view of many underground fighters, betrayed their comrades.

"Many underground members were caught in the mass roundup of Cuban citizens in mid-April immediately after the pre-invasion bombing of the country's main airfields. The prisoner, a twenty-two year old Cuban and former student at Texas A&M, was a topranking officer in one of the many underground factions that might eventually overthrow Castro."

Two hundred and fifty-thousand Cubans were detained by Castro at the height of the invasion.

The prisoner said, "We weren't told when the invasion was coming. It now seems that American newspapermen knew the exact day and hour. But why weren't we told?" He was "arrested a month before the April invasion."

He bitterly blamed an anti-Castro radio station for his arrest. This station on Swan Island has had close links with the U.S. Central Intelligence Agency.

"This station paid tribute to me by name, for helping exiles get out of Cuba clandestinely," he said. "That tipped off G-2 and I was finally trapped."

The *New York Times* (April 18, 1961) described the invasion then taking place and commented (page 14, column 2) that "a possible location of the staging area" for the invaders "is the Swan Islands where there is an anti-Castro radio station."

The *New York Times* (April 21, 1961, page 4, column 5) stated that "Radio Swan, the anti-Castro station that has been in operation for many months from Swan Island in the Caribbean, is easily received throughout Cuba. But even anti-Government Cubans complain of that station's indiscriminate use of unconfirmed reports and rumors — a number of which have been quickly proved unreliable. That record was maintained by Radio Swan during this week's fighting, the Cubans complained." Also, "they specifically complained that the insurgents had not established any effective means of addressing the Cuban people." The *New York Times* (April 22, 1961, page 1, column 7 and page 2, columns 6, 7, and 8) carried a story headed "CIA Is Accused by Bitter Rebels." The last two paragraphs of this story stated that "one of the important criticisms of the landing operation was that it was not accompanied by broadcasts into Cuba urging the people to rise and informing them who was leading the attack. This," it was stressed, "left Cubans in a state of uncertainty and confusion compounded by broadcasts by Radio Swan, a CIA-operated propaganda station on Swan Island, claiming victories and uprisings that were not actually happening."

The data on Radio Swan and its mysterious connection with the parent company of *Overseas Weekly* should serve to underscore the vital need for an official investigation of this publication and its inter-locking firms.

Such a widespread network of communication media provides a ready-made apparatus for use by someone interested in such facilities, whether for intelligence purposes or for other reasons. The evidence would indicate that the *Overseas Weekly's* attitude towards what it sneeringly calls "pro-Americanism" is conclusive proof that the forces at work behind the scenes are not dedicated to the principles of American patriotism.

Background information on three *Overseas Weekly* employees confirms the pro-Communist policy of these hidden forces which manipulate International Media Company and its strange assemblage of international affiliates.

The first of these three is a co-owner of *Overseas Weekly,* Harold Melahn.

Harold Melahn, graduate of the University of Minnesota and a sergeant in World War II, is an owner of the *Overseas Weekly* according to Mrs. Marion von Rospach (*Dallas Morning News,* "The Strange Case of General Walker," by Harry McCormick, May 7, 1961). The masthead of the *Overseas Weekly* shows that for a number of years Harold Melahn was an associate editor of the paper.

"Communist Political Subversion," Part 2, Appendix to Hearings, House Committee on Un-American Activities, November to December 1956, page 7237, contains a reproduction of the official list of American delegates attending the World Youth Festival in Prague, Czechoslovakia in 1947 (booklet, *The Bright Face of Peace*). Among those delegates listed is "Harold Melahn, Columbia School of International Affairs, Minneapolis, Minn."

The significance which can be attached to this citation goes far beyond that which is accorded an ordinary Communist-front affiliation. *The Testimony of Walter S. Steele Regarding Communist Activities in the United States*, House Committee on Un-American Activities, July 21, 1957, contains extensive material on this particular Youth Festival.

"Officers of American Youth for a Free World and its delegates participated in the World Youth Congress held in Paris in 1945. The congress was almost completely dominated by Communists," said Mr. Steele. "On the occasion of the third meeting of the Soviet Youth Anti-Fascist Committee in Moscow, American Youth for a Free World presented a scroll of greetings from the American youth organization to the youth of the Soviet Union. It is an affiliate of the World Youth Council established at the International Youth Conference held in London in 1942 and also of the World Federation of Democratic Youth established at a youth congress held in London in November, 1945," (pages 78-79).

". . . the World Federation of Democratic Youth (was) later transferred to Paris in order that the group might establish closer relations with the two other Red internationals, the world Federation of Trade Unions and the International Democratic Women's Federation," (page 81).

"It has been announced that great preparations are

being made for a world youth festival to be held in Prague from July 20 to August 7 this year (1947). A student division of the United States Committee for the World Youth Festival has been set up with offices at the headquarters of American Youth for a Free World in New York City. The festival is sponsored by the World Federation of Democratic Youth with the cooperation of the International Union of Students, through the Czechoslovakian youth movement," (page 82) (See *Guide to Subversive Organizations and Publications,* HCUA, January 2, 1957, page 94 for citation of the World Federation of Democratic Youth — "a long-established Soviet-controlled international organization").

The Senate Internal Security Subcommittee held hearings in 1951-1952 on "Communist Tactics in Controlling Youth Organizations." This volume contains a detailed study of this youth festival and of subsequent youth festivals held in Budapest and Berlin.

Witnesses testified that the principle objects of the American Youth For a Free World were (a) To facilitate passage for Communist Party members and sympathizers to the festivals in Europe and (b) To serve as the courier agency between the Communist International and their youth representatives to the American Communist Youth movement in the interim years when they did not have the World Youth Festival. Witnesses stated that only those persons of whom the Communist Party approved were permitted to attend the Youth Festivals. Harold Melahn met the Communist Party requirements.

Case history number two is that of John Dornberg.

John Dornberg has been News Editor of the *Overseas Weekly* since 1958 and has been associated with the paper since his discharge from the army in Europe in 1954. He was born in Erfurt, Germany in 1931. His family fled Germany in 1939 and came to the United States. He is now a U.S. citizen. He was educated at the University of Denver and majored in journalism (three years). During his last year at College he worked as associate editor of the semi-weekly university paper, then as an associate in a Denver public relations firm. He left school and continued in public relations assuming the editorship of a regional trade magazine. He was drafted into the U.S. Army, assigned overseas as publicity and advertising director for the full-time professional 7th U.S. Army Symphony Orchestra in Stuttgart, Germany which played a schedule of one hundred and fifty concerts per year in all North Atlantic Treaty Organization countries. He has thus traveled extensively throughout Europe. He has written articles for *The Nation, The Roundup* (week-end feature section in the *Denver Post*), trade magazines and *The Reporter.*

The Nation (June 3, 1961, page 485) carried an advertisement of his book, *Schizophrenic Germany,* published by the Macmillan Company of New York, on May 22, 1961. The ad was headed, "Will there be a Fourth Reich?" It contained the following statements:

"Do you know that. . .over forty thousand German youths belong to para-military groups?. . .there may be an underground ring — operating with the tacit cooperation of German authorities — to help ex-Nazis escape trial and arrest. . .as many as 685 anti-Semitic incidents have been *officially recorded* in one month alone. . .These are the smoldering remains of Hitler's Germany that could ignite at the least provocation.

"*Schizophrenic Germany,* by John Dornberg, is a meticulously researched new book that reveals the growing Nazi and neo-Nazi influences in West German government, business, education, and communications. Mr. Dornberg, whose articles have appeared in *The Nation* and *The Reporter,* is News Editor of *Overseas Weekly.* He recently uncovered Major General Edwin A. Walker's alleged attempt to indoctrinate American troops in the principles of the John Birch Society."

The last sentence quoted from the ad pins the smear against General Walker directly to John Dornberg, who is, on the evidence of the ad, quite proud of his role in bringing about the suspension of the General. Macmillan's *Advance News of Books* release of May 3, 1961 also cited Dornberg's role in the suspension.

A third member of this strange staff is Johanna Prym.

Dornberg stated in his book that Johanna Prym, German Editor of *Overseas Weekly,* had rendered him invaluable aid in the preparation of the book.

An article by Johanna Prym was condensed and reprinted "Courtesy, *Overseas Weekly,*" in the publication, *Prevent World War III,* issued by the Society for the Prevention of World War III, Incorporated (New York City). It appeared on page 10 of Number 47, Winter Issue, 1955 and 1956.

The Society for the Prevention of World War III is officially cited as a Communist-front in the Second Report (1948) of the Washington State Joint Legislative Fact-Finding Committee on Un-American Activities (page 80).

Prevent World War III (Number 48, 1956, page 28) carried reprints of stories from *Overseas Weekly* of May 13, 1956 and of April 1, 1956 (page 48). *PWW III,* Issue Number 49, 1957, page 38 carried a reprint of a story by John Dornberg from the *Overseas Weekly* of November 18, 1956. Number 51, 1958, page 42 carried reprints of stories from *Overseas Weekly*, October 20, 1957 and November 3, 1957. Number 53, 1959, pages 23 and 41 carried reprints of stories by Sidney Gruson of the *New York Times* of April 14, 1961, page 1 (two days before publication in Germany). Material from *Nation* and *Reporter* (magazines in which John Dornberg's articles have appeared) is used many, many times in *Prevent World War III*. The line and data in this Communist-front publication appears to parallel that used in Dornberg's book.

John Dornberg acknowledges his appreciation of *The Nation's* courtesy in allowing him to incorporate an article he had written for that publication as Chapter 6 of his book. He also wrote an article for *The Nation*, December 8, 1956 entitled "Defying the Draft," (pages 494 through 497) which was essentially a plea for avoidance of the draft by young Germans.

The Editor of *The Nation* is Carey McWilliams. Appendix IX (1944) of the Special Committee on Un-American Activities lists over sixty subversive affiliations for Carey McWilliams. His record of association with such fronts had continued far beyond that date.

The Senate Subcommittee to Investigate the Administration of the Internal Security Act and Other Internal Security Laws of the Committee on the Judiciary held hearings on "Subversive Infiltration of Radio, TV and the Entertainment Industry," Part I, May 25, 1951. Vincent W. Hartnett testified under oath (page 15) that "there is a certain group functioning which I will call the Jack Goodman Group . . . This group of highly placed writers and publishers is in a position to exert a synchronized and powerful influence for Communist or pro-Communist causes throughout a large segment of the publishing field . . . One of the interests of this group is the column entitled 'The Observer,' a feature of the *Nation* Magazine. This column has faithfully and militantly echoed the Communist Party line, particularly with reference to counter-attacking any attempts to expose and to offset Communist infiltration in the literary and theatrical worlds."

The editorial interlock of International Media Company publications (*Overseas Weekly, Overseas Family, Swank,* etc) and its satellite media in Germany, Belgium, Haiti and Africa, with Communist and Socialist and Internationalist newspapers in America (such as *People's World, Prevent World War III, The Nation, The Reporter,* and the *New York Times*) comprise a significant and important opinion-forming combine for the propagation of international objectives and subversive movements. The professional coordination existent between the staff members of these and similarly oriented periodicals provides clear evidence of a centrally-directed propaganda campaign to undermine the morale and morals of the American soldier, to paralyze military resistance to subversion and to promote the concealed aims of a totalitarian one-world government.

Our investigation of *Overseas Weekly,* its character, policies and personnel, while not exhaustive, added impetus to the public demand for a Senate hearing on "military muzzling." We now had convincing proof of a conspiracy against the Pro-Blue program, the political orientation of our attackers and a record of subversion aimed at the American fighting man.

Preliminary questioning of Defense Secretary Robert S. McNamara in early September, 1961 by the Committee on Armed Services, set the stage for a subsequent full dress examination. A portion of an exchange between Secretary McNamara and Senator J. Strom Thurmond recorded during this preliminary hearing is particularly revealing in light of our previous findings concerning *Overseas Weekly* and its attack upon the morals and morale of U.S. military men.[2]

Senator Thurmond

"In answer to a question by Senator Beall, you stated that the *Stars and Stripes* serves as a distribution agency for *Overseas Weekly,* for which service *Stars and Stripes* receives forty percent of the sales price of this weekly.

"In view of the fact that *Overseas Weekly* is a malicious, sexy, cheap and dirty publication, its close association with *Stars and Stripes* seems to most people reprehensible.

"I hand you an issue of this paper of June 4, 1961 and ask you to look on the back of it at the naked women or women who are almost naked and ask you if you think it is very wholesome for that paper to be distributed with the *Stars and Stripes* to our boys overseas?"

Secretary McNamara

"I personally find it repulsive, Senator Thurmond. I think my view is shared by many of the responsible commanders in the European theatre. But I have read their recommendations on this subject, or I should say, the analysis and reports they have made on the basis of which they have concluded that they should not stop its

---

[2] Defense Secretary McNamara on Senate Resolution 191, Committee on Armed Services, USS, September 6 and 7, 1961, pages 43-47.

distribution, and I did not feel that this was an action that the Secretary of Defense should over-rule a local commander on.

"I think they agree with you — they feel as repulsed by it as I am — but they feel that within the limits of freedom of speech and freedom of the press it has a right to be distributed."

Senator Thurmond

"Mr. Secretary, I hand you an issue of this paper of July 23, 1961 that contains a picture of almost naked women and ask you if you think it is again wholesome for this type of issue to be going to our men overseas who are already lonesome?"

Secretary McNamara

"I would reply to this issue the same as I did the previous issue. I think it is repulsive and it is not just the pictures that are repulsive — it is the words in the issue that I find disgraceful."

Senator Thurmond

"I hand you an issue of *Overseas Weekly* dated Sunday, July 30, 1961 with poses of women in different positions with wording concerning this, and ask you to look at this and tell me if you, as Secretary of Defense, approve sending out papers of this kind with the *Stars and Stripes* to our servicemen overseas."

Secretary McNamara

"I should emphasize what I believe the committee knows, that this is a private corporation, privately owned, privately operated, in no way subsidized by the Department of Defense.

"It has a perfect right to be sold in the market place according to the laws of the country in which it is sold and according to our own laws — and the question is, therefore, one of possible extra action that should be taken by local commanders in connection therewith; and the local commanders today, I believe, have decided against it.

"I will be quite frank with you and say that if this were a major military matter that I would over-rule them on it. My own views are quite at variance with theirs on this particular subject."

Senator Thurmond

"Mr. Secretary, I hand you an issue of *Overseas Weekly* for Sunday, August 6, 1961 that also contains pictures of women who are almost naked and ask you to look at this and tell me whether you, as Secretary of Defense, approve of sending this kind of publication along with the official publication, *Stars and Stripes,* to our servicemen overseas?"

Secretary McNamara

"I want to emphasize, of course, that these decisions as to distribution of private print, printed matter, particularly periodicals and newspapers which this claims to be or allegedly is, are decisions made by the local commanders — in this case in the European theatre."

Senator Thurmond

"Mr. Secretary, if you were making the decision as to whether the issues of the *Overseas Weekly,* which I have just handed to you, should go with the *Stars and Stripes* for the men serving overseas, what would your decision be?"

Secretary McNamara

"I would say (a) I would not buy it as a periodical and as a private individual; (b) I would not recommend that it be bought by any associate of mine or any subordinate of mine; (c) I would recommend specifically that they not buy it; (d) I am not exactly certain what I would do specifically if you asked me if I would take steps to prevent its distribution."

Senator Thurmond

"Do you or not, have the power as Secretary of Defense to discontinue assuming responsibility for the distribution of this *Overseas Weekly* even if *Stars and Stripes* is getting forty percent, or one-hundred thousand dollars a year, as I understand they are getting?"

Secretary McNamara

"I believe that as a practical matter — whether as a legal matter or not I cannot say for sure — but as a practical matter I believe I have the power to make it very difficult for one of the members of the Armed Forces to obtain that paper at the same point of distribution at which they obtain *Stars and Stripes*."

Senator Thurmond

"Mr. Secretary, would you consult your records and tell us when General Walker recommended discontinuing distributing this paper?"

Secretary McNamara

"I will be very happy to do so, sir."

(Information subsequently furnished):

"On May 26, 1961, General Walker wrote General Bruce C. Clarke, Commander in Chief, U.S. Army, Europe, expressing his view that *Overseas Weekly* should be eliminated from army newsstands and requesting an investigation. On June 3, 1961 General Walker wrote to the Chief of Staff, U.S. Army, requesting that the *Overseas Weekly* be banned from army newsstands immediately. As far as the available records indicate, these are the only requests made by General Walker. It may be that other requests have been made within the European Command which were not forwarded by that command to Washington."

I would say that the McNamara testimony makes it perfectly obvious that military accommodation of subversion and perversion is possible only when higher echelon fails to exercise command control; when superiors encourage erosion of army morale and imperil combat readiness by omission or commission.

One of the concluding actions of the "Friends of General Walker" campaign was the preparation and distribution of a news release summarizing the results of our findings over the previous four months. Titled, *Why General Walker was Purged,* and authored by our New York investigator, this article traced the origin and explained the reason for the attack on General Walker and the Pro-Blue program. Of primary importance was the pattern of anti-anti-Communism, leading from news media through the Pentagon, to Congress, to the Central Intelligence Agency, to the Department of State and, finally, to the United Nations — all synchronized and interlocked, to paralyze or destroy military resistance to Socialist-Communist ambitions.

This release constituted one of the "packets of material" which "placed me at variance with established policy" regarding the General Walker case.

Material from the report, *Why General Walker was Purged,* is incorporated in the succeeding chapter.

CHAPTER X

WHY GENERAL
WALKER WAS PURGED

"It (antimilitarism) dates, insofar as the Soviet Union is concerned, from 1901. Since that time there has been a constant development of this doctrine and the means of its realization; that is, of subversion, propaganda, agitation, and infiltration against the military establishments of countries where the Soviets, the Communists, hoped to gain control."
— *Revolutionary Antimilitarism in Communist Theory and Practice,* Dr. Robert E. Beerstecher

The motivating influence behind the administration's wrecking operation against the 24th Infantry Division Pro-Blue troop indoctrination program; the attack against Major General Edwin A. Walker, ousted commander of the unit; and the drive to "curb" all anti-Communist officers in the Armed Forces of the United States was soon exposed to public view.

The *New York Times* of July 21 carried a front page story by Cabell Phillips headed "Right-Wing Talks by Officers Curbed."

Phillips finally revealed the truth about the source of material quoted during the previous month, beginning with his own article of June 18 and other items which appeared in left-wing and Communist sources.

Phillips confirmed the issuance of a "right-wing curb" directive by Robert S. McNamara, Secretary of Defense, and then informed his readers that "this action resulted from a critical memorandum from Senator J. W. Fulbright, Democrat of Arkansas, sent to the White House and to Secretary of Defense Robert S. McNamara." [1]

The "memo" was written a month ago, said Phillips.

Shortly after receipt of the Fulbright document (and after a subsequent conference between Fulbright and McNamara), Arthur Sylvester, Assistant Secretary of Defense for Public Affairs, was given authority over the information programs in the armed forces.

Another outgrowth of the memo was "the decision by the House Government Information Subcommittee, headed by Representative John E. Moss, Democrat of California, to open its own inquiry into the field," based upon a staff study of "right-wing propaganda by the military."

A spokesman for the committee said that "a field investigator would start on-the-scene studies next week covering a number of army and navy installations in this country."

Senator Strom Thurmond, Democrat of South Carolina, immediately denounced the memorandum as "a dastardly attempt to intimidate the commanders of the United States Armed Forces." He termed the memo an effort to prevent U.S. commanders from teaching their troops "the nature of the menace of world Communism."

"Suppression of the military's dissemination of this

---

[1] "Memorandum Submitted to Department of Defense on Propaganda Activities of Military Personnel," Senator J. W. Fulbright, *Congressional Record*, August 2, 1961, pages 14433-14439.

knowledge would be disastrous," he said. (*New York Times*, July 22).

Fulton Lewis, Jr. and the *New York Daily News* attacked the issuance of the memorandum on July 22 and July 23, respectively. *The New York Times* of July 24 editorially supported the memo.

To appreciate the full significance of this sinister development, the action must be examined with a knowledge of the position of the Communist Party vis-a-vis the General Walker issue.

The Worker, official voice of the Communist Party, U.S.A., on July 16 contained a major policy directive issued by Gus Hall, General Secretary of the Communist Party, U.S.A., which was titled, "The Ultra-Right, Kennedy, and Role of the Progressives."

This directive should be read in its entirety by every patriotic American who is interested in combatting Communist-aiding activities.

The policy directive was accompanied by a request for "reports of united front discussions and activities in left and progressive circles," which relate to the contents of the directive.

The first part of this revealing document is headed, "The Threat from the Ultra-Right," and states:

"In the opinion of the Communist Party, there can be no question that the threat from the extreme right is serious."

The article continues,

"...the present movement is taking the form of a membership organization, in conspiratorial action groups, including secret military formations...

"The fascist network. . .advocates the right of 'revolution'. . .that is, in fact, counter-revolution. It proclaims the aim of seizing political power. . .

"Another pronounced characteristic of this growing fascist movement is its spreading influence among the higher military personnel. The Case of General Walker was only a symptom of a much deeper affliction. Even the Pentagon had to admit recently that it was 'worried' over the extent of Birchite and similar influences among the ranking officers of the military service."

Hall named no other officer than General Walker in his directive. He attacked the "cold-war" directive of the Joint Chiefs of Staff and called for a united front against the ultra-right among all "progressives."

Mainstream, a major organ of the Communist Party, contains in its June, 1961 issue an article by P. A. Luce titled, "From Candy Bars to Anti-Communism," which contains this statement:

"Here is a group (the John Birch Society) whose avowed purposes and obvious racist connections can only be termed fascistic. Here is the organization that may well be used as the groundwork where any attempt (is) made by the right-wing to try a coup of the American government. This idea is not unrealistic but has instead basis in fact. Harrison Brown and James Real, in their book *Community of Fear* have expressed this same concern, as have Paul Sweezy and Carl Marzani."

The foregoing quotation from a Communist publication could be dismissed as a typical propaganda gambit were it not for the fact that the booklet, *Community of Fear*, does express such a fear. The Fund for the Republic has issued a series of studies on "The Free Society" through its Center for the Study of Democratic Institutions in Santa Barbara, California. The Brown-Real study of United States foreign and military policy was issued in September, 1960 with a foreword by Reinhold Niebuhr, considered to be the foremost theologian in the United States by the left-liberals. Niebuhr has a Communist-front record comprising nearly a half-a-hundred citations and has been associated with over fifty more Socialist, Pacifist, and Radical organizations and enterprises.

The Board of Directors of the Fund for the Republic include: as Honorary Chairman, Paul Hoffman, who as Director of the United Nations Special Fund originated the proposal to give substantial aid to Castro through the Special Fund; Charles W. Cole, Vice-President of the Rockefeller Foundation; and Arthur J. Goldberg (now U.S. Ambassador to the United Nations). Consultants to the Center include: A. A. Berle, Jr., Kennedy-appointed Latin-American "expert" who participated directly in the planning which led to the Cuban invasion fiasco; Henry R. Luce, Publisher of *Time, Life,* and *Fortune;* and others of similar prominence.

The Fund's publications are considered to be extremely important reflections of the beliefs and ideas of the left-liberal "elite" in this country.

Community of Fear contains a number of statements expressing the identical idea enunciated in the *Mainstream* article, namely:

> "It is conceivable that military officials in the US or in the USSR might bring about a coup and order an attack of their own without adequate approval . . .
>
> "Thus, if things continue the way they are going, the possibility of a coup by the United States military is real. The general assumption that the American soldier is automatically responsive to his civilian

masters might be rudely shaken were there a serious
and clearly visible retreat on the world front by the
American policy-makers. The same might be true
in the event of a disarmament agreement which the
military does not consider fool-proof."

Harrison Brown is the major source for the contents
of *Community of Fear*. He is an editor-at-large of the
extremely influential *Saturday Review of Literature* and
has been professor of geochemistry at the California Institute of Technology in California since 1951. Prior to
that he was associated with the University of Chicago,
University of California atomic projects. Both projects
were overrun with Soviet espionage agents and assorted
pro-Communists.

Brown, as early as 1939, was a contributor to the cited
Communist Institute of Pacific Relations publication,
Pacific Affairs. (IPR hearings, Part 14, 1952, Senate In-
ternal Security Subcommittee, page 5518.)

What have these writings by the *Mainstream* author,
by the Communists Paul Sweezy and Carl Marzani, and
by Harrison Brown and James Real, to do with the
General Walker case?

Everything! Their predictions reflect the objectives of
the very individuals who conspired to destroy General
Walker, the Pro-Blue program in the 24th Infantry Division, and all sincere anti-Communists within the armed
forces.

No other explanation fits the facts. The Communists
and the Fabian-Socialists have identical aims, namely:
The destruction of the American Republic and the establishment in its stead of a Socialist super-state.

Fabian-Socialists and their puppets are directing the
purge of anti-Communists in the military services. They

are doing so because they are afraid of patriotic personnel in the armed forces; afraid of their pro-American indoctrination programs for the troops; afraid of their possible future resistance against a treasonous sell-out of this country. These Fabian-Socialists presume that their plans for the complete socialization of America will succeed — and there will come a time when "right-wingers" in the military might constitute a danger to these plans.

This arrogance is based on the premise that the "masses" are too brainwashed to resist and that the legislature will accede to such plans.

There is not the slightest basis for a justification — on moral, ethical, or constitutional grounds — of the purge of pro-American officers and programs in the armed forces. Such a purge can only be rationalized on the basis of fear — fear that such persons are dangerous.

Dangerous to whom, and to what? Certainly not to the American people and their soldier sons. No! The answer lies in the statements quoted from the Communist press and Fabian-Socialist publications (always the avant-courier in spreading the "correct" line to the lower echelons of the Communist-Socialist conspiracy).

There is, of course, another factor involved which is not mentioned in these publications. And that is this: As pro-American officers and enlisted personnel are purged, a real danger to the American people arises. That danger is the growing possibility that a totalitarian dictatorship of the left will be established in America, headed by Fabian-Socialists.

Fabian-Socialists are imbued with doctrines which are avowedly treasonous. Naturally, they would like to wipe out all potential resistance to such a dictatorship as the first step in such a direction. Once the armed forces become willingly responsive to dictates from the Fabian-Socialist Politburo, the great American Republic will have passed away, forever.

Let us examine the chronological sequence of events and statements which occurred during the course of the Walker controversy, or which have a bearing on the case.

The spate of stories attacking the John Birch Society started with an article in the official Communist paper, The *People's World,* published in San Francisco, issue of February 25, 1961. *Time* magazine followed with a lengthy article in its March 10, 1961 issue. Then the whole left-liberal press opened up with attacks on the Society. This laid the groundwork for the attack on Walker. Then the *New York Times* of April 14, 1961 carried a story attacking General Walker under the by-line of Sidney Gruson, who has written many peculiarly motivated stories from Germany, Poland, and other central European countries in recent years — stories which quoted Communist propaganda handouts without evaluation as to their credibility.

Overseas Weekly's full-scale attack against General Walker appeared in its issue of April 16, 1961. Quite strangely, the *Overseas Weekly* story was the basis for the Gruson story which had appeared two days previously in the *New York Times.* John Dornberg, News Editor of the *Overseas Weekly,* supervised the preparation of the attack against General Walker, wrote some of the copy, and later took credit for initiating the attack.

Marion von Rospach editorialized in the same issue of *Overseas Weekly,* of which she is the executive editor, that it was her paper's "responsibility to point out officials who propagate beliefs in direct opposition to those upheld by the duly elected leaders."

Major General Edwin A. Walker was relieved of his command of the 24th Infantry Division by personal order of the late President Kennedy and transferred to the army's European headquarters in Heidelberg on April 17th, the day after the attack by the *Overseas Weekly* appeared! Who is there so naive as to believe that such a precipitous action on the part of a U.S. President — in the face of Walker's denial of the accusations made against him — was not pre-planned?

On April 23, 1961, the official Communist paper, *The Worker*, carried a story headed, "West German Agents and U.S. Hate Groups," written by Mike Newberry, which paralleled in many ways the line of John Dornberg's book, *Schizophrenic Germany*, issued the following month (May 22nd). The same issue of *The Worker* (page 4) carried an attack on an anti-Communist "military-industrial-educational conference" held in Chicago.

Then on May 8th, the same Communist paper carried a long article by Mike Newberry on "Warriors Looking for a Gun" (page 8) which was a full-scale development of the theme enunciated in *Community of Fear*. In fact, Newberry quoted from that source:

> "There is rather clearly a military elite emerging in the United States which is dedicated to a position of perpetual hostility toward the Soviet Union and which wields enormous political as well as military power. Indeed, the military elite is clearly in a position to assume political command over the U.S. striking forces if there are serious signs of 'weaknesses' in U.S. foreign relations."

Newberry calls this "the threat by 'the industrial-military complex,' of which former President Eisenhower warned in his Farewell Address." He centered his attack on retired officers such as *Major General Charles A. Willoughby,* Chief of Intelligence in Douglas MacArthur's command in the Pacific; *Lt. General Charles B. Stone,* Third Air Force; *General Alfred Wedemeyer,* former General Staff Officer on War Plans Division under the Joint Chiefs; *Lt. General John O'Daniel,* Military Attache, U. S. Embassy in Moscow, 1948 through 1950, Commander of the Army of Pacific, 1952 through 1954, Chief, U.S. Military Advisory Group in Viet Nam, 1954 through 1955; *Lt. General P. A. del Valle,* U. S. Marine Corps; *Rear Admiral Harley Cope;* and others of lesser rank.

Newberry cited *The John Franklin Letters,* published by The Bookmailer, as "a tactical guide" which has the "backing of top military brass" (named above). He called it a "manual of arms" for the future. Wrote Newberry: "Patriotic underground armies should be established, say the *Franklin Letters,* named the 'Rangers' who will train to assassinate, sabotage, and overthrow the 'Peoples Democracy'." He characterizes the contents of the book as "Hallucinations! Insanity! The ravings of madmen!", but then writes: "Wasn't Hitler once belittled as a madman?"

He attacked "the warmongering speech by Admiral Arleigh Burke, Chief of Naval Operations" which was suppressed by the late President Kennedy.

Then on May 31, 1961, the Pro-Blue program General Walker had put into effect was secretly shelved under instructions from the civilian heads of the Pentagon.

The Worker of June 4, 1961 attacked Major Edgar C. Bundy (who had been named in the "Warriors" article of May 7th and had been attacked by the *Overseas Weekly* in its April 16th issue) and carried a long article by Sam Kushner of Chicago headed "Military Discusses New Moves" which again attacked the Military-Industrial Conferences and such individuals as Admiral Burke and Major General Arthur D. Trudeau, Chief of Research and Development of the Army.

On June 9th, stories appeared in the press and in *Newsweek* of June 12th which predicted that General Walker would be rebuked (based on leaks from the Pentagon) three days prior to the official announcement.

The Worker of June 11th carried an attack on the National Strategy committee of the Chicago-based American Security Council and specifically its military members: *Rear Admiral Chester Ward, Lt. General Edward M. Almond, Admiral Arthur W. Radford, Admiral Felix A. Stomp, General Maxwell Taylor,* and *General A. C. Wedemeyer.*

On June 12th, the Secretary of the Army issued the announcement of the admonishment of General Walker and the cancellation of his orders to a post in Texas.

On June 14th, the Pentagon blandly informed the press that the Pro-Blue program had not been touched.

On June 18th, the *New York Times,* under the byline of Cabell Phillips, carried a fantastically revealing story headed "Right-Wing Officers Worrying Pentagon" based on confidential army files and reports leaked to the *Times* by faceless members of the civilian team running the Pentagon.

Phillips admitted that General Walker had operated his anti-Communist efforts under a three-year old policy of the National Security Council which called for a mobilization of all arms of government in the "cold-war" struggle; but, then he quoted "high officials at the

Pentagon" as stating that they hoped that the admonishment of General Walker would have "a restraining effect on other military men whose zeal in the same cause has been creating mounting embarrassment for them."

General Walker's activities could *only* have embarrassed the Communist conspirators and their Fabian-Socialist allies; therefore, this statement proves that Walker was made the scapegoat and was sacrificed on the altar of appeasement and abasement to atheistic Communism.

Arthur Sylvester, Assistant Secretary of Defense for Public Affairs, a Newark, New Jersey, newspaperman whose known hatred for General Walker places him high on the list of those involved in the planned purge of the General, was quoted as saying,

"It is no secret . . . that this sort of activity . . . has been a disturbing problem for us."

No further mention of any Pentagon civilian official by name is made throughout the eight-column spread story.

Cabell Phillips also wrote:

"The problem for the Pentagon arises from support by its higher ranking officers of so-called forums, schools, and seminars . . . preoccupied with radically right-wing political philosophies . . . a militant anti-Communism . . .

". . . Liberalism is equated with Socialism and Socialism with Communism . . . citizens often are urged to form their own groups to 'educate' others about the Communist menace and to be alert in discerning Communist influences in their neighborhoods, schools, newspapers, and local governing bodies."

A score of military bases have evolved programs of troop indoctrination which "have caused alarm among the new civilian team in the Pentagon." The team suspects, however, "that the trend is somewhat more widespread than their reports currently indicate. They are quietly trying to find out how widespread it is."

This faceless Pentagon informant then pulled some dossiers out for the privileged Mr. Phillips. It seems that Captain Robert T. Kieling, commanding officer of the Naval Air Station, Wold-Chamberlain Field, Minneapolis, had co-sponsored a military-civilian Project Action in April, 1961. At the two-day seminar, "several films were shown and literature was distributed purporting to explain the nature of Communist subversion with particular emphasis on its attack upon American morals." The informant then whipped out a letter from an unidentified newspaper editor who had complained that Project Action was "politically partisan . . . although the partisanship is not of the party label type." This statement can only be interpreted as meaning that the editor objected to pro-Americanism as being too partisan for his taste.

Captain Kenneth J. Sanger, commanding officer of the Sand Point Naval Air Station, Seattle, Washington was the next target. "His activities over the last year have aroused a storm of controversy." His crime was use of the two films, *Operation Abolition* and *Communism on the Map*. "Critics contend the film is distorted and misleading." (Phillips does not, of course, mention that the Communist Party initiated the criticism.)

A Pittsburgh seminar held on April 15 was supported by Lt. General Ridgely Gaither, Commanding General,

Second Army; Major General Ralph C. Cooper, Commanding General, Twenty-first Army Corps; and by Admiral Chester Ward, retired, who was reported as having said that "some of the advisers now surrounding the President have philosophies regarding foreign affairs that would chill the average American." And he had mentioned Adlai Stevenson and George F. Kennan by name!

"This sort of thing, if carried far enough among susceptible people, can breed a wave of vigilantism and witch-hunting," one Pentagon official said. The hackneyed Communist propaganda phraseology is familiar.

One of the civilian chiefs in the Pentagon is quoted as complaining that "these fellows" look "for spies under the bed or in the PTA;" whereupon he, too, whipped out a "guidance" directive from Secretary of Defense Robert S. McNamara which muzzles officers expressing any opposition whatsoever to the established policy laid down by the President or the heads of the Department of Defense.

The strange elevation of McNamara to his present position of power has never been adequately explained. His Harvard background and his support in Michigan of the Walter Reuther puppet and radical leftist, G. Mennan Williams, might have been contributory factors leading to his appointment. (*California Monthly,* University of California, June, 1961.)

Phillips cites certain dilemmas facing the new team. They don't want to be tagged "as being against anti-Communism." Also, they know that the Korean War proved that our soldiers are not as "tough" as they ought to be, that many lacked moral stamina and patriotic dedication. They also know that the "cold war policy" evolved by the National Security Council in 1958 cannot be shunted aside lightly. Yet, what have they done? They have begun screening all troop indoctrination material and have banned use of the film *Communism on the Map,* and have banned *Operation Abolition.*

Phillips's article ended with another statement from one of his informants: "Who is to tell a three-star general how right-wing — or how left-wing — his political outlook can be?

"Our best hope is that the extremists will begin to get the message themselves, as from General Walker."

This article is quoted only because it represents a clarion call to arms by the liberal-left community against the terrible forces of the right. The May 21st *Worker* did a much better job in the same vein.

The Communist Party seized upon Phillips's article as ammunition for its own purposes the day following its publication. Gus Hall, General Secretary of the Communist Party, issued a statement which was quoted in *The Worker* of June 25th (page 2):

"It is now confirmed, as has been charged frequently, that the John Birch and associated groups have been preparing overt action — including secret military training — to achieve their aims . . .

"Only yesterday it was revealed in the press that the Pentagon is harassed by the cropping up of Birchite and pro-fascist sentiment and activity in the officer corps. And yet only a polite reprimand was given General Walker for his espousal of Birchite doctrine within his military command . . .

"It is high time the American people take serious note of where the real danger to peace and democracy comes from, and who is working for a garrison state here. When you get a combination of military and civilian fascist groupings, then a real and pressing danger exists which cannot be hidden or averted by spreading the Big Lie of anti-Communism."

On July 13, the *Chicago Sun Times* (page 5) carried a story by Thomas B. Ross which was headed "Curb Military Anti-Red Crusaders" and which was filed from Washington. Ross revealed that Secretary McNamara had ordered the Joint Chiefs of Staff to revise the 1958 National Security Council "cold-war" directive. This revision was expected to take several weeks. Nevertheless, "the Glenview Naval Air Station (in Northern Illinois) has been ordered to stop its civilian instruction program and a high ranking defense department official warned that stern action would be taken to make the order stick," said the *Times*.

Ross wrote that a public information officer from the Great Lakes Naval Training Center near Glenview had said on July 12 that, "Navy enlisted men there have been discouraged from presenting anti-Communist programs to civilians since McNamara made a statement several weeks ago that he did 'not believe men in uniform should be making public statements on matters relating to foreign policy'." He also noted that, in the case of General Walker, "the Administration invoked President Kennedy's new order . . . that military men are not to dabble in politics and foreign policy." This casts an entirely new light on the circumstances surrounding the purge of General Walker.

Furthermore, "McNamara's instructions to the Joint

Chiefs were explained as an effort to stop the use of government property and tax-payers' money for the propagandizing of a minority political position."

The majority political position — with which McNamara has identified himself — was further explained by Sam Kushner in *The Worker* of July 23rd: "Will Government Act Against Military-Right-Wing Alliance?" Kushner, writing from Rockford, Illinois led off his story with a reference to McNamara's demand for a revision of the "cold-war" directive, based on "the embarrassment of the Kennedy Administration at the large number of self-styled military men who have donned the mantle of 'anti-Communist' crusaders." Kushner attacked Admiral Arthur W. Radford, who in 1955 as Chairman of the JCS, promulgated the original order which led to the directive.

> "One outgrowth of the Radford fostered policy was the recent scandalous revelation concerning Major General Edwin Walker in Germany, who was charged by *Overseas Weekly* with purveying John Birch material to his troops and to the families of his command. He has been removed under fire . . .
>
> "The Defense Department has made it increasingly clear during recent weeks that the pro-fascist groups are not to the liking of the Kennedy Administration, and their association with the military was a source of increasing embarrassment."

Kushner then rehashed Thomas Ross's story on the suppression of anti-Communist activities at Glenview and at Great Lakes, but without naming Ross as the reporter. He dealt at length with the anti-Communist activities of Lt. Commander C. E. Bigler, who is assigned to Glenview Air Base, and asked this question:

"Will Lt. Commander Bigler walk the plank as General Walker did? The evidence against Bigler is much more substantial."

Another story in the same issue of *The Worker,* with a Chicago dateline was headed "Midwest Writers Confirm Military-Right-Wing Ties," and is worth quoting:

"During the past several years, *The Worker* has regularly spot-lighted the insidious alliance between military leaders — active and retired — and right-wing groups in the United States . . .

. . . *The Worker* . . . was the only national publication to expose the Glenview Naval Air Base 'anti-Communist seminar' last September.

The article then cited Thomas B. Ross's July 13 story in the *Chicago Sun-Times.*

The Reporter magazine, a publication for which John Dornberg of the *Overseas Weekly* has written, featured two articles in its July 20 issue: "A New Army for the New Germany," which paralleled Dornberg's line in his book, *Schizophrenic Germany,* and "Revivalism on the Far Right." The latter article attacked the Military Crusaders at length, named *Rear Admiral Louis J. Kern,* Chief of Naval Air Advanced Training at Corpus Christi, Texas; *Rear Admiral W. G. Schindler,* Commandant of the Eighth Naval District headquartered in New Orleans; his successor, *Rear Admiral F. B. Warders; Major General William C. Bullock,* head of the XIX Army Reserve Corps Area (covering Oklahoma, Arkansas, and Louisiana); *Lt. General Ridgely Gaither,* Commanding General, XXI U.S. Army Corps; *Captain I. M. Hampton,* Commanding Officer of the Glenview Naval Air

Station; *Captain Kenneth J. Sanger*, Commanding Officer of the Sand Point Naval Air Station; *Vice Admiral Robert Goldthwaite*, Chief of Naval Air Training at Pensacola, Florida.

The article cited McNamara's statement during a press conference he had held on May 26, at which time he said,

"In public discussions all officials of the Department should confine themselves to defense matters."

As a result of the Glenview anti-Communist seminar, the American Civil Liberties Union had drawn up a bill of particulars on the matter and sent it along with a letter of protest to the then Secretary of the Navy, W. B. Franke, who retorted, in part,

"I am sure that you do not consider that information regarding the dangers of the international Communist conspiracy is 'political propaganda' which should not be given to the American people."

Thus, the General Walker case became the pivot on which major political issues of this decade began to turn.

Continuing development of this issue revealed not only the reasons for the "purge" of General Walker, but also the motives and objectives of the Fabian-Socialists. We now know that it is their intent that all pro-American and anti-Communist programs shall be erased from army troop information programs and that all pro-Constitution personnel in the armed forces of the United States shall be eliminated to make way for the Fabian-Socialist "take-over" — aided and abetted by international Communism, its agents, and its sympathizers.

"In you," I wrote General Walker on August 5th, 1961, "the opinion-molders in our Congress have an instrument through which they can dramatize the counter-attack against Fabian-Socialists, particularly that element which would ban all pro-American indoctrination programs in the United States military establishment."

On July 26, Senator Strom Thurmond made the first of several addresses on the Senate floor attacking the *Fulbright Memorandum* and the "muzzling" of military officers who attempted to implement the National Security Council Directive on "Cold War" education.[2] "The Friends of General Walker" campaign thus gained its immediate and central objective; action leading to a Congressional investigation of "military muzzling."

"Another important fighter who has joined our effort," I reported to General Walker, "is Mr. Fulton Lewis Jr., who began what he called a 'crusade' last week which he stated will reveal the 'dastardly' attempt by the 'New Frontier' to crush anti-Communism seminars and anti-Communist officers in the armed forces.

"There are many grass roots workers now pushing the General Walker case with us and who are part of our national team of determined and dedicated fighters," I said. "These, with an increasing number of high-talent commentators, writers, and publishers in mass media;

[2] "The Role of Military Officers in Public Forums," *Congressional Record*, August 10, 1961; "The Nature of Communism," *Congressional Record*, August 11, 1961; "The Anti-Anti-Communist Campaign Directed at Military Personnel," *Congressional Record*, August 15, 1961.

e.g.:

George Sokolsky (columnist)

Paul Harvey (radio news commentator)

William Buckley (*National Review*)

Holmes Alexander (newspaper columnist)

Richard Berlin (*Hearst* Newspapers)

James Copley (*Copley* Newspapers)

Dan Smoot (Dan Smoot Report)

Walter Trohan (*Chicago Tribune*)

Irene Kuhn (newspaper columnist)

Edith Kermit Roosevelt (newspaper columnist)

Willard Edwards (*Chicago Tribune*)

. . . have joined with veterans' organizations, patriotic societies, women's organizations, and plain citizens to expose and explain the problem of alien subversion within the American armed services."

Through a "direct mail" technique, "The Friends of General Walker" brought home to the American people the facts and concealed issues involved in the Walker Case. This operation successfully circumvented the captive wire and press services which attempted to impose a code of silence on the Walker Case and on the explosive Washington developments attending the struggle to lift the curtain on "military muzzling."

As our Capitol mentors stressed in their counsels, by arousing and informing Americans to the implications inherent in the Walker Case and by suggesting courses of action which would support a Congressional investigation, we assured a continuation of the strategy battles then in progress at the National Legislative level.

On September 6, 1961, four and one-half months after

our launching of the "Friends of General Walker" campaign, the Committee on Armed Services, United States Senate called Secretary of Defense Robert S. McNamara to testify pursuant to Senate Resolution 191, "To Authorize a Study of the Use of Military Personnel and Facilities to Arouse the Public to the Menace of the Cold War," which had been introduced by the Honorable J. Strom Thurmond, a member of the Committee.[3]

And, on September 10, I received notice terminating a ten-year career assignment in the army information field. Within a month I was transferred from the New York office, OCINFO, to the Second Logistical Command, Fort Lee, Virginia. I was no longer "suitable for continued duty in the army information field." [4]

This sacrifice proved to be a bitter exercise in frustration.

The administration succeeded in delaying the report on the Pentagon's cold war policies until the height of the Cuban crisis.

"Thus ended, in relative obscurity, an inquiry into the entire range of American foreign policy and strategy," said Willard Edwards, *Chicago Tribune,* on December 2, 1962.[5]

"Senator J. W. Fulbright, (Dem., Arkansas), Chairman

[3] "A Resolution to Authorize the Committee on Armed Services to Study the use of Military Personnel and Facilities to Arouse the Public to the Menace of the Cold War," Senate Resolution 191, 87th Congress, First Session.

[4] "Probe Shift of Walker Aide, Legion Asks," *Chicago Tribune,* October 2, 1961.

[5] "Muzzling Probe Report Hustled out to Obscurity in Fog of Crisis," Willard Edwards, *Chicago Tribune* Press Service, December 2, 1962.

of the Senate foreign relations committee, was presumably gratified," Mr. Edwards stated. "Little or no publicity was given to a stinging repudiation of the views he had advanced in a celebrated memorandum on the dangers of a military clique in the United States."

A press release in October, 1962 made by Senator J. Strom Thurmond immediately following publication of the Senate Report, "Military Cold War Education and Speech Review Policies," was similarly muted.[6]

". . . censorship and other official action reflected the application of a 'no-win' foreign policy which has had a 'paralytic effect' on cold war alertness and awareness," said Senator Thurmond in his October statement.

His statement contained a detailed analysis of each phase of the investigation . . . censorship of speeches, troop education programs, and cold war seminars . . . and also a section on civil-military relations. In introducing his summary, the Senator discussed at length Communist success in employing what he termed "revolutionary antimilitarism." He said this is a fundamental tenet of Soviet strategy" designed to "undermine, disintegrate, or neutralize the military establishment of the non-Communist nation through all available means including subversion, infiltration, propaganda, and psychopolitical operations."

To our dismay, the Senate "military muzzling" hearings failed to arouse the American people. Our sights were set too low. In retrospect, it is apparent that instead of accepting "Communism" as the conventional "enemy" we

[6] News Release, U.S. Senator J. Strom Thurmond, October 25, 1962.

should have pursued our line of investigation to the Department of State, the United Nations organization, and to those concealed planners who manipulate Communists and Communism to achieve a one-world, totalitarian empire.

The penalty for failing clearly to identify the assassins of liberty is cogently revealed in a study of the techniques of betrayal prepared by Prince Michel Sturdza, former Rumanian Foreign Minister. The Prince Sturdza work will be reproduced in a succeeding chapter titled, "Voice from an Iron Curtain Country."

Before citing this case history of international subversion, I should like to illustrate by personal example the propaganda climate which precedes revolution.

The forces now at work undermining U.S. Army principles of "Honor, Duty, Country" have been identified and the indictment supported by considerable documentation. This study reveals that the role and mission of America's fighting forces is being remolded to conform to international, rather than national, objectives, and that United States soldiers are being trained to serve under the United Nations banner.

The obvious corollary to military infiltration is the elimination of resistance forces within the military.

The Sam Yorty case, therefore, is a significant example of the use of power politics to "muzzle" and eliminate from active service army personnel who do not conform to the new military morality. Officers and enlisted men who militantly resist actions which place U.S. Armed Forces in the untenable position of aiding and abetting international communism are now "undesirable." Those who question directives which violate provisions of the United States Constitution are the targets of the Pentagon drive against anti-Communists.

I am the proof that such a Pentagon anti-anti-Communist policy exists — as we shall prove in the chapter titled, "Is Sam Yorty a Communist?"

CHAPTER XI

IS SAM YORTY A COMMUNIST?

"But you insist again, how do we spot a Communist? Well, first, every concealed Communist denies he is a Communist, indignantly and with a show of outraged innocence. Second, Communists say and advocate the same things that the Communist press and Communist text books say and advocate. This is important, for actual party membership is of little consequence if the individual is a propagandist for the party program. He may be even more dangerous outside the party and able to deny membership under oath. In fact, we think that some of the most effective agents of the Kremlin are deliberately put outside the party to continue subversion without the hazard of identification and exposure."
— *A Freedom Manifesto,* by Senator Nelson S. Dilworth, California Legislature, April 16, 1955.

The "Yorty Case" began with my speech before the Seventy-First Congress, National Society, Daughters of the American Revolution, April 19, 1962 in Washington, D.C. and resulted in my separation from active duty on May 7 by order of the Army Secretary.[1]

[1] "Soldiers, Politics and Civilian Control," Arch E. Roberts, Major, USAR., Proceedings of the 71st Continental Congress, National Society, Daughters of the American Revolution, April 16-20, 1962, pages 382-391.

During the course of the DAR talk, I made three specific charges:

(a) One channel of civilian control over the army terminates in the office of a Soviet Communist.

(b) *Overseas Weekly* staff, policy, and character is pro-Communist.

(c) Sam Yorty, Mayor of Los Angeles, has a Communist background.

The documented argument presented in preceding chapters, specifically and in detail, confirm indictments (a) and (b). We have, therefore, established the techniques of subversion directed at the United States military establishment.

Now a word about the pattern of infiltration of U.S. armed services by Communist agents.

"In this respect," said Dr. Beerstecher during the "military muzzling" hearings, "going back to the outbreak of World War II, within a matter of months after the 7th of December of 1941, more than fifteen thousand members of the Communist Party and Young Communist League, both men and women, went into the Armed Forces of the United States according to one prominent Communist, although another set figures at something less. They went in under directives of the party." [2]

"It follows that the job of Communist agents is not necessarily to foment 'revolutionary action' as that is popularly conceived — and as it was understood by Lenin — but to use their positions in order to serve the

[2] "Military Cold War and Speech Review Policies," Committee on Armed Service, USS, Report, page 221.

immediate interests of the party and the USSR. For example, the main work of American Communist soldiers during World War II was not to foment discontent but to gain positions useful to the international movement." [3]

During World War II, Communist propaganda and agitation against the U.S. Armed Forces virtually ceased since the Communist Party line dictated support of the common war effort against Nazi Germany. In 1945, the Committee on Military Affairs of the House of Representatives made a study of "Communist Activities Directed Against the U.S. Armed Forces." The study was prompted by the fact that on February 22, 1945 the War Department made public the information that it had inaugurated a new policy by removing the ban on Communists. [4]

The committee noted in its report that although "army men in high authority denied that any Communists held commissions in the army," the *Chicago Tribune* "gave the names of ten army officers about whose Communist connections there can be little doubt in the light of official records." [5]

One example is that of Major William L. Ullman, United States Air Force, who in 1945 acted as go-between for Soviet spy, Nathan G. Silvermaster and who, as was noted in chapter two, passed the D-Day date to the Soviets. Ullman was tried and convicted in 1956.

[3] "The Organizational Weapon," U.S. Air Force Rand Project, 1952, page 112.
[4] "Investigation of the National War Effort," H. Rept. 839, 79th Congress, First Session, June 29, 1945, page 1.
[5] ibid, page 2.

Another example is that of Brigadier General Evans F. Carlson, of "Carlson's Raiders" fame. Distinguished and decorated in combat, this general, upon release from service in 1946, became the publicly vocal co-chairman, with Paul Robeson, of the "National Committee to Win Peace." The headquarters of this organization was at 23 West 26th Street, New York City (the address of the Communist Party, USA.) Prior to World War II, Carlson had accompanied, for an extended period, the Communist Eighth Route Army in North China, where, according to an article in the June 9, 1947 issue of the *Nation* magazine, "Carlson got the ideas about democratic indoctrination and training that he put to such effective use in his Marine Raider Battalion."

An even more recent example is that of Brigadier General Hugh B. Hester, USA (retired), whose extensive record of pro-Communist activities is documented in the hearings (H-2701-2713.) Hester's activities include writing and lecturing about his visit in Cuba, from which he returned in May, 1962. About the Cuban situation, Hester stated,

> "Castro is still unquestionably the boss, the most popular leader in the entire Western Hemisphere, with seventy-five percent of his people solidly behind him. It is simply not true that Cuba is now a Communist satellite." [6]

Of the Cubans who were taken prisoner by the Castro government in the ill-fated Bay-of-Pigs invasion in April, 1961, Hester states,

[6] *Orlando Sentinel*, Orlando, Florida, May 4, 1962, page 13-A.

"These prisoners were found guilty and are guilty of treason."

It must be perfectly obvious that this pro-communist policy interlock in the Pentagon, State Department, and United Nations can exist only under the protective power of highly placed international planners, and that these planners manipulate communists and communism to further a larger objective. That objective is a one-world totalitarian supra-government controlled through the United Nations apparatus.

No other interpretation can explain the deliberate elevation of the Alger Hisses and the vicious destruction of the General MacArthurs in the course of contemporary history.

A salient factor of the interlock is the political and propaganda team-play used to frustrate and defeat action by military commanders which threaten the concealed design of the Planners. A typical example of the propaganda power play was the use made of congressmen and national newspapers to reverse the military ban on *Overseas Weekly*.

During our investigation of *Overseas Weekly*, we learned that Congressman Samuel W. Yorty of California helped Marion von Rospach get *Overseas Weekly* reinstated on *Stars and Stripes* newsstands after this "repulsive" publication was removed in 1953. A combination of congressional pressure and "press freedom" articles in U.S. newspapers did the trick.

It was felt, therefore, that Congressman Yorty, now Mayor of Los Angeles, California, merited attention. The results of the Yorty investigation were published in our series "Inside *Overseas Weekly*." A part of this information was subsequently revealed in the course of my talk before the Daughters of the American Revolution.

Sam Yorty, it should be noted, was a commissioned officer assigned to intelligence duties during World War II.

In the April 19 address, I stated,

"I can assure you that it is the responsibility of all Americans, in and out of uniform, when the mayor of a great city in the United States has a Communist background." [7]

In support of this serious charge I presented two pages of documentation extracted from public records which I introduced with the following remarks:

"Sam Yorty has a very interesting background. On November 4, 1938 one Arthur James Kent, a member of the Communist Party in San Francisco in 1936 and 1937, had entered into the record of the hearings, Special Committee on Un-American Activities, Investigation of Un-American Propaganda Activities in the United States, Volume 3, a sworn affidavit in which he stated:

'For almost a year hereto, a Strategy Committee of the Communist Party would meet with members of the California Legislature, particularly John G. Clark, Ellis Patterson, Ben Rosenthal, Jack Tenney, and Sam Yorty, all members of the Communist Party, and sometimes also with other sympathetic persons not actually members of the Party.'" [8]

Within four hours after I had revealed the Communist background of Mayor Samuel Yorty the army suspended

[7] Proceedings NS, DAR, 4th Day, page 384.
[8] Affidavit of Arthur James Kent, House Un-American Propaganda Activities, Volume 3, page 2083, November 2, 1938.

me from duty and confined me to the limits of the post at Fort Lee, Virginia.

On the following day newspapers across the nation carried the indignant and outraged denials of Mr. Samuel Yorty and quoted him as saying he, ". . . regarded it as proper for the army to take such steps against 'irresponsible statements'." [9]

In explanation of the "Communist background" charge, Mr. Yorty offered the statement that, "this allegation is a complete fabrication originated by a convicted burglar and placed into the . . . record by an irresponsible congressman."

The "irresponsible congressman" was the Honorable Martin Dies.

Support for Yorty's pose of outraged innocence appeared in an Associated Press story of the same date alleging that Chairman Francis E. Walter (now deceased), Committee on Un-American Activities, had told a reporter that Committee records, ". . . disclose that Mayor Sam Yorty of Los Angeles not only does not have a Communist background but has been one of the most effective fighters against internal Communism in this country."

During the days immediately following my suspension, anti-anti-Communist elements of the national press launched a vicious and slyly deluding attack which deliberately ignored and concealed the documentation which I had presented outlining the Communist background of Yorty. This campaign of vilification achieved

[9] "Army Suspends Major on Yorty Red Charge," *Los Angeles Herald Examiner*, April 20, 1962.

the desired effect of discrediting me and materially contributed to the hardening of the public mind against a
fair and impartial investigation into these salient charges
and facts in the case. The anti-anti-Communists had
successfully created a propaganda climate which would
deprive me of the provisions of due process of law.

Typical of the slander and misrepresentation foisted
upon the American public by these professional character assassins was a column by Inez Robb titled, "You
Can't Turn Back and Defy Authority." [10]

"Just as Walker has done," said Robb, "Roberts on
the DAR rostrum accused his victims of being Communists, Communist sympathizers, or 'far leftists'
without offering one shred of proof or one iota of
evidence."

This lie was followed by the further libel:

"The 20th Century is a difficult and perilous one,"
observed the mother superior of the *Hearst* newspapers. "But no group in the United States — be
it military, so-called patriotic or simply crackpot
Fascist — can turn back the clock by calumny and
self-seeking defiance of authority."

Al Capp, in his column "Who Would They Shoot,"
with willful malice stated,

"A guy from Cheboygan, Michigan, named Arch
Roberts, who could never quite make it in an as-
sortment of jobs in civilian life but who made it up
to Major in the army, certainly earned his pay last

---

[10] "You Can't Turn Back and Defy Authority," Inez Robb, *Detroit
News*, April 29, 1962.

week. He," said Capp with accustomed elegance,
"alerted us to the possibility that the army may
have others like him in its Information Service who
accept and spread as 'information' the equivalent
of obscenities scrawled on a washroom wall." [11]

Even some who wear the label of "conservative"
joined the pack and retched on cue. One of these was
George Todt who, writing in the *Los Angeles Herald-
Examiner*, said with more heat than illumination,

"Anybody who has ever been an officer in the armed
services ought to know that you cannot go flagrantly
against expressed military orders by those in higher
authority — as Roberts did when he insisted on
making a highly controversial speech which officially
had been turned down — unless we are asking for
trouble."

"I have long felt very strongly," said professional
conservative Todt, "that untactful, uncouth and un-
thinking loudmouths do more to hurt than to help
our conservative movement." [12]

Defeat of the Inez Robbs, the Al Capps and the
George Todts was to involve me in three years of litiga-
tion and a cost of over twenty thousand dollars in legal
fees.

Vindication came on June 18, 1964 when the United
States Court of Appeals, District of Columbia Circuit
in Washington found that the Secretary of the Army had
violated public law and army regulations in separating

---

[11] "Who Would They Shoot," Al Capp, *New York News*, April 26,
1962.
[12] "Arch Should Read Manual," George Todt, *Denver Post*, May
23, 1962.

me from active duty status because of my speech before the Daughters of the American Revolution on April 19, 1962.

A year later, on August 5, 1965 the Department of the army returned me to active duty status with, ". . . all the rights, privileges and emoluments;" including three years back-pay and allowances. However on April 27, 1962, influenced by writers who had elected to offer themselves to the American public as judge, jury and reviewing authority in a newspaper trial of the Roberts case, the Secretary of the Army relieved me of active duty and — in an unprecedented violation of Public Law and Constitutional principle — returned me to civil life after eighteen years and nine months of military service.

Denied a military hearing, I subsequently brought suit against the Secretary of the Army and other officials in the Pentagon in a complaint which stated:

> "The present action involves the failure on the part of the predecessor of Defendant 1 and Defendant 2 and 3 lawfully and properly to act pursuant to the provisions of applicable law . . . This action by defendants was without any notice or statement of charges or opportunity to appear before a Court Martial or Board of Officers and to present his defense; it thus deprived him of valuable property rights, without due process of law, as will hereinafter appear."

The incomprehensible withholding of justice by the military, the studied aloofness of the national legislature which ignored a resolution by the Daughters of the American Revolution requesting Congress, ". . . to investigate this arbitrary exercise of power" and the continued hostility of the anti-anti-Communist press to legal rights, all demand that the facts pertaining to the Communist background of Mr. Samuel Yorty now be presented for public examination.

The first fact is the affidavit by Arthur James Kent identifying Yorty, with several others as members of the Communist Party. This statement appears in the Dies Committee Hearings, Volume 3, 1938, which is of course, an official record of the House Committee on Un-American Activities.

Kent's information, never in dispute before my DAR speech, was corroborated by many other witnesses who appeared before the Dies Committee.

George Bertholon, an ex-Communist Party member, in testimony in the Executive Hearings, July 19, 1940, explained how Labor's Non-Partisan League was organized around a hard-core Communist Party membership. Admitting that, in order to get positions in the various counties and municipalities, it was necessary to ". . . go to Labor's Non-Partisan League for endorsement," Bertholon agreed that the League, ". . . followed the Communist Party Line."

Extracts of this testimony reveal that the Non-Partisan League supported Samuel Yorty in his 1938 campaign.[13]

Mr. Stedman

"But in order to get positions in the various counties and municipalities do you go to Labor's Non-Partisan League for endorsement, is that correct?"

[13] Bertholon Testimony, Cong. Dies Sp. Comm., Executive Hearings, July 19, 1940, page 1156.

Mr. Bertholon

"I would say correct."

Mr. Stedman

"Do you know from your own experience whether or not Labor's Non-Partisan League followed the Communist Party Line?"

Mr. Bertholon

"I did."

Mr. Stedman

"Can you cite any instance of this?"

Mr. Bertholon

"In choosing candidates it selected only those who were completely in accord with the party line or that the party felt they could control."

Mr. Stedman

"Mr. Bertholon, what other prominent candidates did Labor's Non-Partisan League support in the 1938 campaign?"

Mr. Bertholon

"Culbert Olson for Governor; Ellis E. Patterson for Lieutenant-Governor, Robert Kenney for State Senator; and Samuel Yorty, Augustus Hawkins, and Paul Ritchie for the assembly, besides many others. Those are the ones I happened to know."

It should be recalled that Samuel Yorty addressed the convention of Labor's Non-Partisan League of California in San Francisco on December 11, 1937.

Further Dies Committee Testimony reveals many Communist affiliations of Mr. Yorty.

One of these, an affidavit by W.B. Holther, entered in the record on July 25, 1939 lists the prominent California Communists who brought into existence the Committee For Political Unity, which was organized by the Communist Party for the purpose of influencing the political structure of Southern California by inserting into public office those candidates who were sympathetic to the Communist Party.[14]

Holther's testimony concerning the Committee For Political Unity has critical significance when examined in conjunction with an article which appeared in the *Western Worker* of October 21, 1937. This Communist paper announced that Assemblyman Samuel Yorty was on the Executive Committee of the California Committee of 100 for Political Unity.[15]

Holther identified a number of California political figures who were chosen by the Committee for Political Unity who were to receive Communist Party support to assure their election to positions of public trust. Among these was Assemblyman Samuel Yorty, selected for the Fourteenth District.

In the same testimony, Holther described the manner in which the California Federation for Political Unity drafted Samuel Yorty, ". . . a prominent liberal," and the techniques subsequently employed by the California Communist Party to secure the election of their candidates.

Additional statements by Rena Vale regarding the Communist Party support for Sam Yorty and an affidavit

---

[14] Holther testimony, Cong. Dies Sp. Comm., Executive Hearings, July 25, 1939, page 1178.
[15] "Progressive Political Unity Charted at Fresno Meeting," *Western Worker*, October 21, 1937.

by Marguerite Miller concerning "Yorty's speech for the sympathizers of Loyalist Spain," appear in the same hearings.

In light of comments attributed to Yorty that Kent's testimony had been "repudiated" and the witness "discredited," it is interesting to read the testimony of Captain John Keegan, Chief of Detectives, Portland Police Bureau. On December 7, 1938 Captain Keegan, then on the force for twenty-seven years, presented the following testimony (which was entered in volume 4 of the Dies Committee Hearings) in support of Kent's veracity:[16]

"I have every reason in the world to believe this man. Through him we did an enormous amount of work. He has never lied to any of my men once. Everything he told us we have proved before submitting it to the immigration authorities."

Pertinent also is the expert testimony of Mr. Harper L. Knowles, then Chairman, Radical Research committee, California American Legion; now head of the Western Research Foundation, 660 Market Street, San Francisco. Mr. Knowles quoted directly from an affidavit by Arthur Kent regarding Kent's relationship with various California Communists and identified Kent (known in the Party as Arthur Scott) as a high-ranking member of the Communist Party.

"During this period," said Knowles, "Kent was married to Norma Perrie, the secretary of Harry Bridges."

Observing that Norma Perrie was also a high-ranking member of the Communist Party, Knowles then stated

---

[16] Captain Keegan testimony, Cong. Dies Sp. Comm., December 7, 1938.

that the apartment of Arthur Kent and Norma Perrie became the strike headquarters for the Communist Party during the San Francisco maritime strikes in 1934.

Confirmation of Kent's reliability as a government witness is noted in "The Maritime Brief," of which Kent's affidavit is a part. This is the most important evidence ever produced before the Committee on Un-American Activities regarding Harry Bridges's Communist background and was never questioned.

Furthermore in the House Committee Report on the CIO Political Action Committee, dated March 29, 1944 which was published six years after Knowles's testimony, Kent's affidavit of December 22, 1937 was again entered in the record as proof of Harry Bridges's affiliation with the Communist Party in the United States.

In a letter to me dated May 9, 1962 former Senator Jack B. Tenney, who headed the California Legislative Committee on Un-American Activities in the 1940's (now an attorney, 176 North San Gorgonia Avenue, Banning, California), noted that, "The entire Yorty story is told in *The Tenney Committee: The American Record.*"

On pages twenty and twenty-one of his book Senator Tenney, writing in the third person, says,

> "Assemblyman Samuel W. Yorty, near the end of the 1939 Session of the Legislature, asked Tenney to meet with two men at Yorty's apartment in Sacramento. 'These fellows can help you with your problems in the union,' Yorty explained carelessly. 'Anyway, you've got nothing to lose by talking to them.' The 'two men' turned out to be William Schneiderman and Paul Cline, who frankly announced their official position with the Communist Party of California."

Mr. Tenney, in the *Tenney Committee* book, had this to say about the Arthur Kent affidavit and about his (Tenney's) alleged membership in the Communist Party of California,

> "With the exception of the various allegations made by Kent as to Tenney's membership in the Communist Party, many of the events referred to in the affidavit appear accurate enough. The Democratic members of the Assembly were continuously being called into meetings with so-called 'progressive leaders' . . . Tenney, in company with other members of the Legislature, attended several such meetings and was induced to either introduce or co-author legislation proposed by such meetings." [17]

Significantly the California Legislative Committee on Un-American Activities was generally referred to as the *Tenney Committee*.

Now Sam Yorty has publicly stated, "I took my public stand against Communism many years ago and it has never changed."

Yet on pages ninety-one and ninety-two of his book, Senator Tenney describes how — after returning to the California Assembly in 1949 — Yorty destroyed the entire California anti-Communist program.

The bills which were blocked by Yorty in this action (which Yorty proudly called his "Two Uncle Sams") included:

— Senate Bill 132, requiring candidates for public office to subscribe to a non-Communist oath;

— Senate Bill 280, requiring a loyalty oath for public employees;

[17] *The Tenney Committee . . . The American Record*, by Senator Jack B. Tenney, page 23.

— Senate Bill 515, permitting employers with defense contracts to discharge and to refuse to hire Communists;

— Senate Constitutional Amendment 14, requiring a loyalty oath for all public officials.

Mr. Tenney observes that Assemblyman Stanley Tomlinson, Willard Huyck, and Harold K. Levering placed a statement in the *Assembly Journal* in which they expressed disapproval of Yorty's motion and said:

"We are satisfied the motion was designed to cut off debate on these bills and cause them to die in committee. We believe these bills are of such importance to the people of this state that we should have a recorded roll call after a full and complete debate thereon."

On June 25, 1949, Mr. Chester Hanson, writing in the *Los Angeles Times*, explained in detail how Yorty had ". . . pulled a parliamentary knife from his legislative toga and sank it deep in Tenney's back with a swift stroke."

On April 12, 1962, ex-Congressman Thomas H. Werdel, an attorney at 458 Haberfelde Building, Bakersfield, California, wrote to me concerning the DAR talk. In this letter Mr. Werdel said,

"I was a member of Congress from Kern, Kings, and Tulare Counties, California (then the 19th District) in the 81st and 82nd Congresses, and on May 7, 1951 (during the first session of the 81st Congress) I found it necessary to defend myself against privileged attacks by Mr. Yorty in his first session of Congress."

In his candid talk on the floor of the House, Mr. Werdel described the Communist Party support extended to Congressman Samuel Yorty, he identified the Communist Press which had promoted Congressman Yorty, and he listed the Communist associations and affiliations of Congressman Yorty.[18]

In his speech, which occupies over four pages of the *Congressional Record,* Congressman Werdel observed,

> "The gentleman from California (Sam Yorty). . .by his voting record is a good Communist in the opinion of the *Daily People's World* (Communist newspaper). . .
>
> "Perhaps the same should be said in connection with the report in the Communist *Western Worker* in an issue for July 26, 1937. At that time they announced that the gentleman from California (Mr. Yorty) was the speaker for Worker's Alliance, a Communist-dominated group of agitators."

Despite loud protestations by the friends of Samuel W. Yorty that he is not a Communist and the indignant claim to outraged innocence voiced by Sam Yorty, the record proves that Yorty's occasional support of anti-Communist causes is a mask employed to conceal his real identity.

In fact, it is prudent at this point to question the political acuity and professional responsibility of spokesmen, both public and private, who have conspired to ignore or conceal the Communist background of an

[18] "Congressman Werdel Reveals Communist Background of Congressman Samuel W. Yorty," U.S. Congressman Thomas H. Werdel, *Congressional Record,* May 7, 1951, pages 5008-5012.

elected government official, *Mr. Samuel W. Yorty, Mayor of Los Angeles, California.*

The Communist background of Sam Yorty also explains the affinity existing between the Mayor of Los Angeles and Marion von Rospach, and why Congressman Yorty rushed to the aid of *Overseas Weekly* in 1953.

CHAPTER XII

VOICE FROM AN IRON CURTAIN COUNTRY

"Freedom of speech doesn't mean that you have a right to speak up in agreement with popular view. Even in the most backward and regimented countries the sorriest slave can do that. Freedom of speech means your right to speak up against established opinion; to challenge that which has been long accepted; to defy even the authoritarian position with logic, reason, and persuasion."
—*Gazette Telegraph*, October 21, 1963, Colorado Springs, Colorado.

On Bill of Rights Day, December 16, 1963, I submitted to the Honorable John A. Love, Governor of Colorado, and to members of the Colorado State Legislature a charge and complaint indicting the United Nations as a subversive organization.

Noting that the United States Senate continues to delegate power and authority over the American military establishment and over American citizens in the State of Colorado to the Communist-dominated United Nations Organization, I requested that the State of Colorado reveal to the citizens of Colorado the concealed objectives of the U.N.

"An informed citizenry," I said, "may then direct the

promulgation of state laws in consonance with the provisions of the U.S. Constitution, rejecting the U.N. Charter and outlawing United Nations agencies in the state."

Attached to my petition were some twenty-four position papers prepared by business, professional, and military leaders, as well as statements by publishers, heads of veterans organizations, and political authorities.

One of the statesmen who responded to my appeal for assistance in presenting United Nations facts to our Colorado legislators was Prince Michel Sturdza, former Rumanian Foreign Minister. Prince Sturdza's study, arising from his personal experience suffered under the international convulsion which destroyed his country, is of such penetration that a portion of it demands inclusion in this work.

"It seems presumptuous for a foreigner to submit to an American Legislature an uncalled for and critical statement about United States policy towards the United Nations Organization," Prince Sturdza began. "The writer, however, respectfully asks the Colorado Legislature to bear in mind:

"That this statement represents the opinions, the hopes and the fears of one hundred twenty million Europeans sold in slavery in Teheran, Yalta, and Potsdam; that the United States was chiefly responsible for the Teheran, Yalta and Potsdam agreements.

"That it is, nevertheless, upon the United States' independence of action and eventually upon United States power that the enslaved European millions, despite so many bitter disappointments, are still founding their hopes of resuscitating their national life, of shaking finally the yoke of their oppressor.

"That those millions are convinced that this independence of action is about to be lost and this power about to be transferred to an organization already controlled — and soon totally dominated — by Soviet Russia and the communist world, because of the constantly increasing number of Communists and so-called Neutralists in the Assembly, because of the unavoidable pro-Communist submissiveness of the General Secretaries, always chosen by Moscow, and of a great majority of its permanent personnel; and last but not least, thanks to the in-built snares and traps in a Charter which, after all, was the exclusive product of the collaboration between a Soviet spy on the side of the United States, and Soviet conspirators.

"Indeed, the representatives of the Free World were blind enough in San Francisco to accept a text which, concerning the price at which world peace could be preserved, was putting it entirely at the mercy of the greatest and most artful of aggressors, and which fulfilled, by what it included and what it did not include, all the conditions essential to the pursuit of the policy and of the objectives prescribed by Lenin twenty-eight years before the Communist adventure."

Pointing out the incongruity of Russia, violator of all pacts of non-aggression it has signed, being a charter member of a world "Peace and Security" Organization, Prince Sturdza then stated,

"After San Francisco no member of the Organization

of the United Nations that had, without protest, accepted Soviet Russia and its stooges Yugoslavia and Poland among the co-founder countries, could have logically, legally, and morally pretended that these three Communist governments . . . (fulfilled) all the conditions prescribed by Articles 2 and 4. That is, as long as such a member had not broken with the counterfeit organization. It is for the same logical, legal, and moral reasons that Soviet Russia and the Communist puppet governments — permanent violators of the most fundamental human rights — cannot be indicted by other members of the Human Rights Commission so expertly presided over by the late Mrs. (Franklin D.) Roosevelt, and cannot be declared unable to emit an impartial verdict in an international issue by any country which has recognized the authority of the International High Court — another United Nations dependency.

"The bill of permanent immunity and impunity thus conferred in San Francisco to Soviet Russia and to Yugoslavia and Poland — and later extended to all the puppet governments — was singularly reinforced by the facts that to Russia alone, among the nations of the world, three seats and three votes were allowed in the Assembly and that it was upon a Polish and Yugoslavian suggestion that Spain was banned from the Organization . . . as a menace to peace.

"Concerning any future offense, the immunity of the criminals was guaranteed by the lack of any explusion procedure, a condition expressly required by Stalin who, as the Yalta documents inform us, asked to be insured against a repetition of what happened in Geneva on the first of January, 1940 when Russia was condemned for its aggression against Finland and expelled from the League of Nations."

Explaining how the U.N. veto power protects Soviets against similar "inconveniences" the writer then said,

"It is such casuistry that made it possible for the government of Messrs. Benes and Masaryk and that of Mr. Nagy to be replaced by those of their assassins and forced the Free World to accept the package formula of compensatory admissions which has already completely transformed the nature of the Assembly and will, by the admission of Red China, completely transform that of the Council.

"Besides the written Law established in San Francisco, there was, we later learned, an unwritten one of which we will perhaps never know the whole content, that probably explains the crushing percentage of Communists, pro-Communists, fellow-travellers, one-worlders, security cases, and down-right spies in the United Nations administrative staff. But at least one of the stipulations of what has been called 'a gentleman's agreement' has finally come to light. Only a Russian may hold the United Nations Under-Secretariat for special political, military and security affairs: And only a Russian has held it since its establishment in 1947. It was, by the way, General A. Ph. Vasiliev who, in April 1947 drew up the first plan for the organization of an armed United Nations — soon to become an armed World Government, we fear. It is not irrelevant to the subject matter to remind the reader that this same General Vasiliev, on leave of absence as Chairman of the Military

Staff Committee of the United Nations Organization, acted as adviser to Chinese and North Korean troops, fighting what was purported to be a United Nations Armed Force."

Following a lengthy presentation of historical fact including references from Mr. Trygve Lie's book, *In the Cause of Peace*, which reveal that the Communists desired United States involvement in the Korean War, Prince Sturdza observed,

"The most salient trait, however, of the part played by the United Nations in the Korean Affair, was that the real culprit was never indicted nor punished, but on the contrary invited in person or in the person of his stooges (as he would later be invited in the Indo-China, the Korean, and the Laos Affairs) to serve as arbiter and judge for the victims of his outrages.

"Nothing could better epitomize the fact that the Kremlin has found in the United Nations Organization — its own and Alger Hiss's creature — the best protection and safeguard for its illicit activities, not only in Korea, but, as has so often been proved afterwards, in every continent and country and, it seems, for all time to come.

"The frustrating end to the Korean War, imposed by the United Nations Organization and accepted by the American Command, was, on the other hand, the first tangible sign of the always increasing conformity of American foreign policy with the directives of the United Nations Secretariat, a conformity which seems to increase with the communist world in the organization and today threatens to extend itself to the most important and critical domestic problems of the United States.

"The present negotiations concerning a general disarmament are the result of a Soviet gambit in 1955 on the chessboard of the United Nations. The Western Powers have let themselves get so deeply involved in them that they could not pull out even if they wanted to without giving the Soviets a wonderful opportunity for accusing them of bellicism or even, if it should suit then at the moment, of a precise or immediate aggressive intention.

"The only Western delegation to the U.N. which seemed to wake up to the pitfalls and dangers of the Soviet initiative, was the Australian one, which insisted that a specially appointed body of experts proceed, before the beginning of any disarmament negotiation, to a careful on-the-spot inventory of the armaments and forces of all the countries concerned and to an investigation of every circumstance bearing on the comparative military capacities of the two parties involved. The Western powers joined the Soviets in opposing the Australian proposition.

"If such an investigation were to be carried out today, not by gutless diplomats or handpicked experts, but by uninfluenceable military and intelligence personnel, it would not fail to show:

1. "That facing the one hundred and seventy-five Soviet divisions destined to the European Front, and in front of what has justly been called 'the deadliest international menace in recorded history,' the NATO troops with nineteen to twenty-

one divisions are a little more than one-third of what they were initially intended to be. That with thirty-eight divisions instead of one hundred and twenty, the entire peace establishment of the NATO Powers is about one-fourth what it was in 1948. That of all the non-Communist European Powers, only Spain with eleven divisions and Switzerland with the equivalent of nine, have kept a constant and adequate peacetime defense effort.

2. "The fact that two oceans and about five hundred Soviet submarines, an indefinite number of them armed with atomic artillery and all of them probably provided with the Snorkel dispositif, stand between the United States Army and its Allies in Europe and Asia.

3. "The fact that on both continents the Communist troops have the important advantage of the inner lines of communication, constantly perfected by the Soviet Command. It is with Soviet engineers and Soviet capital, for instance, that new strategic railway lines were built in 1957 and 1958 between Red China and the Viet-Minh, towards Laos, Cambodia, the Viet-Nam, Thailand, and Birmania in view of a premeditated violation of both the Indo-China and the Laos Geneva Agreements. In 1959, with the same financial and technical support, similar constructions were taking place on the India-Tibet border, once more giving the lie to the 'War-Between-Two-Giants' hoax cherished by our co-existence advocates.

4. "That the high mobility of modern armies in general and of the Russian Army in particular (in 1954 the Red Army already had eighteen airborne divisions against two of the U.S. Army — of which eight were of parachutists) and the hazards of surprise plus probably tactical atomic warfare, makes the mobilization of reserves a very problematical proposition for the NATO Command.

5. "The fact that the political pro-Communist landslide in Italy and the profound demoralization and turmoil, provoked among the French military forces by General de Gaulle's policy of abandonment, highly diminishes the estimate of what one has a right to expect the two countries to contribute to Europe's defense.

6. "That almost all of Asia is under Communist, pro-Communist, or Neutralist rule. That thanks to the joint efforts of the U.N., the USSR, and the U.S.A. under the pretext of their so-called 'anti-colonialist', policy and the stampede of Europeans provoked thereby, the same can be said of the African Continent. And that consequently the United States and the European Powers have been forced to abandon in Asia, in the Mediterranean, and in Morocco all their Air Force and Navy bases, built at the price of two billion dollars, conservatively estimated.

7. "The fact that Soviet Russia and Red China have an unmatched record of broken pledges, treaty violations, aggressions, subversion, and terror which, reasonably estimated and in association with Western apathy, confers them in advance the

appreciable advantage of the initiative in any kind of armed encounter.

8. "The fact that in every country the Communist powers are entertaining, under the guise of Communist parties and other more concealed organizations, unsurpassed intelligence services and regular fifth columns — the disarmament of which has never been considered — and the importance of which increases at the square power in proportion to the arithmetical diminution of the officially armed troops.

9. "That only political nitwits could believe that Yugoslavia's army, carefully armed and partly trained by the United States, would side with the West, or that Red China would bite a chunk out of Soviets' tail — as Lord Home so nicely put it — in case of an armed conflict between the Free and the Communist worlds.

10. "That it was only after a first violation of a Test Ban Agreement and after having secured the superiority in research and results won by about seventy extra nuclear explosions that Soviet Russia has consented to sign the Moscow Test Ban Pact to which the Coexistence Conspiracy (helped by the kept Press and News Agencies) has given such a ridiculous and misleading importance.

11. "That despite the shameless brainwashing and bamboozling of public opinion, the signing of this Pact by Soviet Russia is no sign at all of a change in the direction and the objectives of its policy. That Soviet Russia and Red China have

never been engaged in a more extended and more insolent aggressive and conspirative activity — as proved in Laos and Viet Nam, at the Himalayan border, in Yemen, and in Saudi Arabia, where such activities were backed by the United Nations. Also in Africa, where with the same amazing support they are behind any subversion, any infiltration, and every massacre; in the Caribbean, where Mr. Khrushchev has, calmly and unmolested, built a formidable Communist stronghold — a thing which even Stalin would not have dared to attempt — from where his agents, his rabble rousers, his murderers have already infested all the Latin American countries.

12. "That by the continuous occupation of the territories it controls in Eastern and Central Europe and its strategical positions in the Baltic, Warsaw, Berlin, Prague, Budapest, Bucharest, Sofia, and — we insist — Belgrade and Tyranna, the Red Army has already won as many victories and captured as many potential allies of the NATO even before the first shot of a Third World War.

"It is obvious, therefore, that from a statistical and positional military point of view, disarming the Free World, beginning at the present level of armament and troops and the present lines of demarcation, would be disarming an already disarmed and defeated world. And it is also obvious that it would be folly for the Western Powers to renounce one battalion or one bomb before a proportional reduction of the Soviet Forces to the level the European countries have condemned themselves to in London and later, and before the total evacuation, political and military, of the irruption zones the Soviets already control in European territory.

"The still living peril of a general insurrection among the captive nations represents for the Soviets a much greater menace than their atomic armament represents for the Western Powers. It is those nations, indeed, and only they, which can wring out of the Soviet's hands the initiative that has been granted them by the continuously retreating Western policy, and leave the Western Powers as arbiter in a fight in which they have otherwise already been virtually defeated.

"It is this undisputable truth that General Eisenhower had in mind when declaring over Radio Europe, in the understatement of the year 1957,

> 'While we maintain our vigilance at home and abroad we must help intensify the will for freedom behind the Iron Curtain. Those countries are in the Soviet back yard and only as long as their people are reminded that the outside world has not forgotten them—only that long do they remain as a potential deterrent to Soviet aggressiveness.'

"On October 24, 1956 the Hungarian patriots were controlling the situation in Budapest and in the greatest part of Hungary. On November 2, President Eisenhower asked Tito to communicate to his Kremlin friends that . . . 'the government of the United States will not grant any support to any government unfriendly to the Soviet Union on the borders of the Soviet Union.' On November 4, after having received this assurance, Moscow unlashed friend Zhukov's armies and threw them against the Hungarian People."

The writer then denounced the disarmament convention as formalizing and recognizing the boundaries between the free world and the enslaved world.

"If the West is too cautious to take towards the atrocious situation created at Yalta in Eastern and Central Europe the intelligent, ethical, and categorical position adopted by Generalissimo Franco or even to consider the possibility of giving the enslaved nations whatever positive help it can, it could at least avoid giving their tyrants an advance guarantee of impunity, no matter what new atrocities they may commit under the protection of a new agreement and of newly and permanently recognized boundaries. This is, however, exactly what was done recently in Warsaw when the United States Government formally promised the Peiping Government that Chiang Kai-shek would never be allowed to try to land on the Continent and liberate his people. One can easily guess what effect such a strange step has had on the resisting and fighting elements in enslaved China. It might very well have saved the Peiping Government from the dangerous consequences of a growing popular unrest which otherwise could have brought about its doom. Is that what the Washington Government wanted to do?

"It is not the eighteen or twenty-one divisions of the NATO nor the thirty-eight divisions which represent the total military establishment of the NATO Powers that can stop the one hundred and seventy-five divisions grouped in depth on the other side of the frontier of doom, nor is it the fear of atomic disasters, the menaces of which cancel each other reciprocally by their very horror and enormity, even more than those of the gasses and germs during the last wars. What stops the Soviets, and can stop them only as long as it exists, is the menace of a simultaneous and unanimous upheaval behind the battle lines in the event of a new armed conflict.

"Those forces of resistance and revolt that represent the greatest vulnerability of the Communist Empire and the only certain military superiority of the West, have so far resisted the repeated blows, the bitter disappointments inflicted on them by the Western attitude of oblivion and contempt, characterized more than anything else by the tolerance of the United Nations Organization, the stronghold of their tyrants in its present fraudulent structure and activities, on free world territory.

"We must look for the weak place in Communism, its Achilles heel, its neuralgic spot. We must start from the fact that the hate against the invaders grows everyday in the occupied countries. They are masters only of the ground upon which they materially stand. The homes, the country live their own life, accumulating their rancours and imperviousness to Communist action . . . Here is the potential weapon that the West possesses. But in order to have it, one must stay faithful to Western ideals. We must not abandon the people behind the Iron Curtain; we must not betray them by shameful concessions to the aggressor . . . Victory must be deserved." (Generalissimo Francisco Franco's speech on the XXV Anniversary of the only decisive military defeat inflicted on Communism, October 3, 1962.)

Expressing pained amazement at the active or passive

participation of Western members of the United Nations in the geographical, political, and prestige expansion of the Communist Empire, and the betrayal into Communist hands of eleven countries and one hundred-thirty million Christians, Ambassador Sturdza declared,

"In Vienna in 1955 the Western Powers did not exercise the rights which were conferred to them by Treaties, signed by Soviet Russia also, which compelled the Soviets to evacuate Rumania and Hungary together with Austria; and that they instead accepted without protest the stratagem of the Warsaw Treaty. It was not only for Rumania and Hungary but for all the countries treacherously represented in Warsaw that Vienna was a tacit confirmation by the Western Powers of what had been resolved in Yalta against their national existence. It is an explicit confirmation which will be granted by a disarmament and non-aggression agreement with the so-called governments of Warsovia (Warsaw Pact Nations), whose representatives are nothing other than groups of scoundrels in Moscow's service.

"It is in the United Nations Organization that resides the constitutional lie, the Master Imposture by which the Western Civilization is imperceptibly dying: That Soviet Russia, its methods and its designs are not what they are. Indeed, how could Soviet Russia be a member of an organization purported to be the champion of liberty, justice, and human rights and to promote good-will among nations, if it were the bloodiest and most inhuman of tyrannies, if its methods were those preached by Lenin, and if its constant purpose were the ruin of the nations' community?

"It is this imposture which has permitted the growing and today the almost total oblivion, by the Western Powers, of the nations they have sold in slavery as a price for a precarious and mendacious peace. It must be considered as a miracle that those nations have not yet lost their faith in a belated revival of courage and reason among the World of the Free. But human endurance has its limits. The eight hundred million captives between the Iron and the Bamboo Curtains still form a compact mass of unique explosive power, provided they are helped at least in the measure the U.N. Secretariat and the State Department are helping, politically and indirectly materially, rabbles organized in Egypt, Algeria, and Tunisia to spread destruction and terror in quiet, orderly, and peaceful Portuguese Africa.

"This tremendous asset will not maintain itself permanently at the disposal of the Western Commands. Subjected to a technique of moral and physical disintegration unknown until now in human history, profoundly discouraged by the disinterest of the West, the organized elements of resistance will gradually disappear. The leaderless masses will submit to attrition and terror or, maddened by them, will rebel without direction or organization in uncoordinated efforts condemned in advance, as in Hungary, East Germany, Poland, and Rumania, to an inevitable defeat. The mere fact that the West has consented to negotiate a Disarmament and Non-Aggression Agreement with their tyrants — without stipulating a previous evacuation of all the territories presently illegally occupied or controlled by the Soviet armies, will suffice to convince the enslaved nations that they have been completely forgotten by those who nevertheless bear the entire responsibility for their martyrdom.

"It would be tragic if the best weapon of the Western Powers — the only one in any case that they, alone, possess — were to fail them in the moment of the greatest need."

The Administration's strange policy of accommodation with International Communism and its determined efforts to dismantle the American Consitution — enunciated by the late President Kennedy in his "Declaration of Interdependence" on July 4, 1962 — elicited the following comment by Prince Sturdza:

"Mr. Walter Whitman Rostow from the White House staff, who was sent on November, 1960 to Moscow in order to discuss American-Soviet relations and disarmament, proclaims in his book, *The U.S. In the World Arena,* that, 'It is in the American interest to put an end to nationhood.' It is reported that as a result of his conversations with Mr. Kutnetzof, he recommended that the manufacture of the BS-70 superbomber be stopped as being considered a provocative weapon by the Soviet Command . . . and very likely too national by Mr. Rostow himself.

"Mr. Paul H. Nitze, in a paper published in 1960, asked for a unilateral U.S. disarmament designed, 'to produce a reciprocal action on the part of our Allies and also on the part of our enemies.' He recommended the scrapping of American missile and atom bases and placing American Strategic Air Command first under NATO control, then under the control of the United Nations

Assembly. It was after the publication of this paper that President Kennedy appointed Mr. Nitze Under-Secretary of Defense.

"It is, however, in the Proposal for a General Disarmament made by the United States in April, 1962 at Geneva, and more specially and tragically in the Plan for American Disarmament presented to the General Assembly of the United Nations, that we find the full meaning of Mr. Kennedy's 'interdependence.' This Plan provides:

1. that the United States will retain only enough military strength to maintain order within its own borders, and

2. that the remaining U.S. military establishment will be turned over to the United Nations Organization as a police force to insure world peace.

"We, from the forgotten millions, we beg to ask, 'What Peace?' What could be the peace defended by the Police Force of an organization of which two years ago already General Charles de Gaulle has said that, 'Given the way in which the United Nations Organization is now composed, given the frenetical and chimerical currents which convulse it and the state of permanent violation of its own Charter in which it maintains itself, we will not recognize in it any right of jurisdiction or of arbitration.' What peace but that of Teheran, Yalta, and Potsdam can be expected from an organization where Russia chooses the Secretary General, where it has three seats instead of one in the Assembly, where the enslaved countries are represented by crooks and murderers chosen also by their tyrants?

"It is inconceivable for any responsible government to accept the idea of sharing leadership of a United Nations transformed into a World Government with a partner who has sworn to 'bury you.'

"That is, however, what occurs today for anyone who has eyes to see and ears to hear," says Sturdza.

"There is something more amazing than the cynical frankness of the World Government conspiracy, a frankness which shows how confident they are of victory; it is the apathy with which public opinion has accepted its purposeful and far-reaching machinations. Not that the alarm has not been sounded in the really free press, or by legislators like Taft, McCarran, Knowland, McCarthy, Bricker, Connally, and by those who so far-sightedly passed Public Law Number 85474, which forbids the use of public funds for the purpose of advancing the cause of a world government.

"In an editorial dated June, 1961 of *The New Age,* the official organ of North American Free-masonry, Mr. N.S. Meese complains that despite Public Law Number 85474 the State Department has obtained an annual credit of $400,000 and is asking for another of $600,000 to subsidize an agency which, under the direction of Mr. E.A. Gullion, works, 'for the purpose of expediting the substitution of our present constitutional government for a World Government that could succeed only in shackling us to a totalitarian tyranny.' And further on: 'It should be remembered that the State Department officials are known to favor the abandonment of the Connally Reservation, a step that would place the nation in the power of Communism by the way of the International Court, an arm of the United Nations . . . Those who have regard for their own freedom and the maintenance unimpaired of our national sovereignty should ask their elected representatives in Congress what they can and shall do about this new threat to our liberty.'

"No sentiment of revolt was arisen by that and other flagrant violations of a Public Law which, if correctly applied, should have been sufficient to defend the United States and all those countries which count on them to protect the liberty they still keep or to reconquer that which they have lost. It is with public funds that Mr. E.A. Gullion, the apostle of World Government in the State Department operates. It is also with the tax-exempted public funds of the Ford Foundation that Mr. Charles S. Rhyne, Mr. Saul Mendelovitz, Harry B. Holmes, etc., travel around the world selling the same kind of goods. It is also with U.S. public funds, those of the U.S. massive contribution to United Nations expenditures, that Mr. Moses Moscovitz and the swarm of the U.N. international agitators do exactly the same thing. It is with public funds also, those of the State and Defense Departments, that the instrument has been prepared by which the United States renounces on behalf of the United Nations Organization its right to have an independent national army; therefore, the right to its independence.

"This apathy, this false feeling of security is created chiefly by the counterfeit image of the U.N. conjured by the formidable force of persuasion of the proselytizing, brain-washing, and suborning agencies. Besides the countless 'affiliated' newspapers and magazines, the radio, television, the movies, almost every university, every high school, every church, every tax-exempted Foundation (Carnegie, Ford, Rockefeller, etc.), many important industrial companies (United States Rubber, Union Carbide, Texaco, Coca-Cola, etc.), every Administrative Department, concur in some way or other in this deceitful and nefarious opinion-creating and educational program; in presenting the United Nations Organization as a guarantee of peace, justice, and security.

"The real secret weapon of the Communist Empire," concludes Prince Sturdza in this powerful, erudite examination of internationalism, "is the United Nations."

"A prompt reaction is necessary. The Big Imposter has to be dissipated and truth be allowed to prevail again, if Western Civilization is to be saved before the consummation of the invisible surrender."

CHAPTER XIII

TO SUPPORT
AND DEFEND
THIS CONSTITUTION

"This led me to think that the nations of Christendom would perhaps eventually undergo some oppression like that which hung over several of the nations of the ancient world."

—*"De la Democratic en Amerique"*, Alexis Henri Charles Maurice Clerel, Comte de Tocqueville, 1840

Our examination of interlocking subversion in governmental departments and the malignant power block comprising internationalists and their agents, now forces upon us the hard necessity of a realistic reassessment of the United Nations and its Charter.

A paramount issue revealed in this study is the ugly fact that concealed international planners manipulate the highest echelons of our government. They organize world-wide political apparatuses and they generate long-range revolutionary movements so as to infiltrate and destroy existing American social, economic, and religious disciplines with the objective of erecting upon the ruins a one-world collectivist state.

It is now conclusively revealed that the United Nations is a prime agency for the accomplishment of these subversive objectives.

It is revealed that Planners are working to have the Charter of the United Nations supersede the United States Constitution as the "Law of the Land."

It is revealed that the United Nations Security Council, not the Congress of the United States, now directs the deployment of American armed forces throughout the world.

It is revealed that American military forces have been surreptitiously transferred to a United Nations army.

It is revealed that the Commander-in-Chief of the United Nations army is, and always will be, a Soviet Communist.

It is revealed that the prime justification for the existence of the United Nations Organization is found in the Security Council, the war-waging arm of the U.N., and that this whole set-up has nothing to do with "peace."

It is revealed that the first objective of the United Nations is to get control of enough military power — U.S. military power — to force all of the nations of the world into line and to deliver them up to a one-world government.

And it is revealed that the U.S. Department of State and other governmental agencies are actively engaged in promoting these felonious objectives.

The United Nations is, in fact, a revolutionary apparatus designed for global conquest. It is obvious that continuing U.S. membership in the United Nations constitutes a real and present danger to the sovereignty, to the freedom, to the proper interest, and to the security of the United States and to its people.

Frequent requests and demands have been made upon the Senate of the United States to review the Charter of the United Nations and to what may be necessary to protect the interests of the United States and the people. The Senate has not only failed to comply with these demands, but has delegated more power over our people and over our military establishment to the subversive United Nations.

Therefore, in the light of these failures and because events in Washington disclose that Americans have lost control of the Federal Government, I propose that, ". . . We, the People" act to force our State Governments to do what may be necessary to ". . . Support and Defend the Constitution of the United States," and to protect the interests of the people.

I suggest that you and I, being the last reserves in the struggle against United Nations tyranny, generate appropriate state legislative action so that we may ". . . maintain our Freedom on this Continent."

It must be stressed that citizen action through the respective state legislatures is the last practicable means (excepting revolution) remaining to the people for the correction of Constitutional abuse.

"Executive failure to conform to the Constitution, principally through abuse of the treaty power," states Warren Jefferson Davis, Constitutional lawyer in his book, *Law of the Land*, "is the most dangerous form which subversion within the governmental structure has taken. This has been recognized by the American Bar Association, which, because of its composition of leading lawyers throughout the country, has since 1949 constituted the first line of defense against attempts which have successively been made to subvert the Constitution of the United States." [1]

Needless to say, the American Bar Association has failed to deter the tide of internationalism and subversion.

"The thoroughly corrupt plan to subvert the Constitution from within," Mr. Davis then noted, "has been exposed, but it remains for the people to take back the republic from the alien hands and ideologies into which it has fallen and reconstruct it and confine it within the limits of the Constitution." [2]

Mr. T. David Horton, nationally recognized authority on Constitutional law, [3] explicitly defined the character of the attack upon the Constitution in correspondence to me date April, 1964.

"Federal Agencies created by the Constitutional Compact are attempting to change and destroy that Constitution by exercising powers that were not delegated to them and which they do not have."

[1] *"Law of the Land,"* by Warren Jefferson Davis, page 61.
[2] ibid, page 63.
[3] T. DAVID HORTON, Atty, Pioche, Nevada, member District of Columbia, Virginia, and Nevada Bar; member United States 9th Circuit Court of Appeals, California; member United States Circuit Court of Appeals for the District of Columbia; Chairman Executive Council, Defenders of the American Revolution, Inc.; Publisher, Square Dollar Series; Professional witness before numerous Congressional Committees in matters pertaining to Constitutional inquiries; Graduate Ohio State University, American University, Washington, D.C., Catholic University, Washington, D.C. and Hamilton College, Clinton, New York.

Only the states which won their independence as sovereign nations as a result of the Treaty of Peace that closed the Revolutionary War can be the source of power in the federal agencies which they later created by Constitutional compact.

Mr. Horton then pointed out the action required to correct the usurpation of governmental power and the responsibility of the State Legislatures in defending the Constitutional Compact.

"State Legislators," he said, "are aiding and abetting this subversion of the Constitution by failing to clarify the law and enforce the provisions of the Constitution within their respective states.

"The failure of the state to act," Mr. Horton continued, "creates a presumption which law enforcement officers cannot overturn. This presumption is that the inaction of the states is tacit approval of the unauthorized attempt by the agent to exercise power beyond the authority granted.

"The ordinary citizen also lacks the capacity to overturn the presumption. Failure of the state to clarify the law by statute allows the limits of authority placed upon the federal agencies by the Constitution to become dimmed and in this confusion, usurpation flourishes."

This counsel was subsequently formalized and incorporated in our campaign to arouse meaningful Constitutional action in the respective sovereign State Legislatures; the objective of this effort being to generate legislative investigations of the United Nations Treaty agreement and enactment of statutes which will enforce the limits of the U.S. Constitution.

The proposal for State Legislation to enforce the Constitution and to prevent the U.N. Charter from gaining "law effect" by default will be discussed in this chapter.

This State Legislation is more than political theory. It is the lawful means for thwarting traitors and Communist dupes.

Grass roots, citizen-generated, Constitutional programs are currently being implemented in a number of States of this Republic. Among those states in which a public demand for investigation of the U.N. Charter has reached important proportions is the State of Alabama.

On March 31, 1965 I addressed a joint session of the Alabama Legislature and presented, "A Proposal to Insure that the Limits of the U.S. Constitution are Respected within the Borders of the State of Alabama."[4]

At the conclusion of my speech the Alabama Legislature adopted a resolution, "To Investigate the Legality of the Action of Federal Agents with Regard to the United Nations and to Provide Means for the Enforcement of the Constitution of the United States in Relation Thereto." Succeeding legislative investigations by the Alabama Commission to Preserve the Peace have produced an exhaustive study of the problem of attempts to illegally transfer governmental powers to foreign governments by treaty.

The Alabama Legislature is now prepared to call wit-

---

[4] "A Proposal to Insure that the Limits of the U.S. Constitution are Respected within the Borders of the State of Alabama," Arch E. Roberts, Major, USAR, *Congressional Record*, April 13, 1965.

nesses in a public hearing concerning United Nations Treaty agreements to determine whether the U.N. Charter relates to the relinquishment of any rights affecting the State of Alabama or its people, or would involve any attempt to change any of the law of Alabama or any of the provisions of the Constitution of the United States without the consent of the government of the people of the State of Alabama.

The Alabama campaign, therefore, offers a convenient example of the procedures and techniques by which Americans can re-establish the United States Constitution as the "Supreme Law of the Land." My address before the Alabama Legislature presents this detail in succinct form and, for that reason, will be quoted at some length.

"I believe that the Alabama syndrome reveals our sister states in the South comprise the target area for a centrally directed revolution which is intended to eventually engulf the entire United States," I said in the Montgomery speech.

"I believe that we must determine the causes for this revolution.

"And, I believe that 'we, the people,' must do whatever is necessary to '. . . insure domestic tranquillity.'

"It is no accident that Montgomery, Alabama — former capitol for the Confederacy — is the focal point for today's anarchist. In fact, Dr. John A. Morsell, Assistant Executive Director, National Association for the Advancement of Colored People, declared in Denver on

March 20 that 1965 has the 'potential of a real revolution.' [5]

"Under the guise of a crusade for minority rights, Dr. Martin Luther King and other trained revolutionaries are engaged in a plan to inflame Americans to a point where our citizens defy legally constituted authority, flout private property rights and finally, generate violence, bloodshed, and murder.

"These are techniques of subversion familiar to everyone who has studied the Spanish Revolution and other examples of Communist control of populations by mass terror. [6]

"It is now apparent that certain agents provocateur, acting in consonance with a master plan, are attempting to create an atmosphere of crisis in the South which will favor the declaration of a state of national emergency."

"It can be predicted that a state of national emergency will lead to the implementation of a series of Executive Orders now held in readiness to place control of all phases of our society in the hands of a few 'elite directors' in the Federal Government. [7]

"We begin to see the emerging outline of a Soviet America.

"I hope," I said, "to place in your hands a weapon with which to defend the sovereign State of Alabama, a procedure for arresting this incipient revolution and the

[5] "NAACP Official Hails 1965 as Banner Year," *Rocky Mountain News,* March 21, 1965.

[6] "Text of Instructions for the Red Militia," *Echo de Paris,* April, 1936.

[7] Title 3, Code on Federal Regulations, Federal Register Publications, Archives of Records, U.S.

legislative act needed to insure that the limits of the U.S. Constitution are respected within the borders of the State of Alabama.

"Our examination of the rise and progress of revolution in Alabama, however, must be prefaced by a word on a contributing factor to this terror," I stated in the Alabama Senate.

I then noted that this peril may be attributed in part to a false economy in the affairs of our state governments.

Americans have long failed to recognize the responsibilities to preserve Constitutional liberties which were placed in the hands of our State Legislators by Constitutional Compact. We have, in fact, condoned a system which denies just compensation for public service and which places a "part-time" sentry on the ramparts of freedom.

"The preservation of our Constitutional republic now — as never before — urgently demands the attention of full-time legislators," I suggested.

Many State Legislatures are limited by their State Constitutions to sessions lasting a couple of months. For ordinary domestic legislation this is generally enough. But in time of Constitutional crisis, the limitation on the length of legislative sessions ties the hands of the state at a time when the state's powers are needed full-time to arrest the full-time subversion by concealed manipulators.

One of the first moves that the state should take in arresting the overthrow of the Constitutional Compact is to free its own hands. No military leader would fight a battle on a "Sunday only" basis.

A State Legislature that is out of session deprives that state of its power to speak "in its Highest Sovereign capacity," as it must speak when arresting the excesses of one of the agents created by the state in Constitutional Compact.

The state should enable its legislature to meet continuously, if necessary, to put down usurpation. In this way the state can discharge its responsibility and state office-holders can hold to their oath of office "to support this Constitution."

"The State Legislature," I told the Alabama Legislature, "being the reservoir of all true political power (as the states are the reservoir of all true national wealth) may thus defend the Constitution and protect the freedoms guaranteed to the people by this Constitution."

I then explained the significance of the policy talk by Secretary of State, John Foster Dulles before the American Bar Association at Louisville, Kentucky on April 12, 1952.

"Treaties," Mr. Dulles said, "can take powers away from the Congress and give them to the President, they can take powers from the state and give them to the Federal Government or to some international body, and they can cut across the rights given the people by the Constitutional Bill of Rights."

This monstrous impertinence is, of course, utterly false, as voiced by the Honorable Henry St. George Tucker, former President, American Bar Association,

"The treaty power can never make Constitutional that which without its sanction is unconstitutional," said Attorney Tucker.

The record of usurped governmental power which Mr. Dulles presumed to sanction is dramatically demonstrated in the record of hundreds of U.N.-enforcing "treaties" which were surreptitiously "ratified" by as few as two or three U.S. Senators convening in secret during the months immediately following passage of the United Nations treaty agreement.

This astonishing information was initially reported by the *Chicago Tribune* on December 8, 1952.[8]

"In at least one instance," said the *Tribune*, "one Senator convened himself at 6:30 p.m. on the empty floor of the Senate; ratified a 'treaty' binding upon every citizen in the United States and then adjourned himself at 6:31 p.m."

"That man was Senator John P. Sparkman, of Alabama," I told Alabama legislators.

This abuse of privileges prompted Senator Bricker and fifty-three other alarmed Senators to propose Senate Joint Resolution 1 (the Bricker Resolution, June 15, 1953) in an attempt to contain by Constitutional amendment the treaty-making powers of the Senate.

These men saw the need to prevent attempts to abuse the treaty-making powers of the Senate. This abuse was represented by numerous efforts to use these powers in areas where there was no authority for such claimed power.

[8] "Vote by Single Senator Makes Treaties Legal," *Chicago Tribune*, December 8, 1952, page 13.

Assurance by the President that such questionable action would be terminated, led to the defeat of the Bricker Amendment by one vote.

A recently conducted search for these secret "treaties," however, has revealed that the total now stands at three thousand U.N.-implementing treaties.[9]

The claim of authority to agree to these secret "treaties" has never been challenged by a single State Legislature.

These interrelated events confirm a chilling fact: The United Nations Charter is the master plan for a Communist-style revolution in America.

It is clear that the so-called United Nations Treaty agreement, if valid, would surrender to foreign governments rights and liberties retained by the people, under the Constitution.

The President and Senate have purported to agree to this treaty, but they lack the power to do so.

These federal agents have no authority to exceed the limited and enumerated powers delegated by the states in the Constitution of the United States.

No federal agent has the power or authority to modify or change the Constitutional Compact.

The so-called United Nations Treaty, of course, is no treaty within the meaning of that word. The U.N. Charter is a constitution for one-world government and its aim is to abrogate the U.S. Constitution and to erect in its place the United Nations Charter as the "Supreme Law of the Land."

[9] "Treaties in Force," U.S. *Department of State Publication*, January, 1964.

"The United Nations now overtly and arrogantly proclaims its preeminence in the affairs of our state governments. Dr. Ralph J. Bunche, U.N. Undersecretary, marches in the vanguard of defiant mobs who assault your state capitol," I said in the Alabama talk.

Of course, the pro-Communist leanings of Mr. Bunche are well advertised. In fact, on August 9, 1948 after Alger Hiss had been exposed as a Communist agent, Bunche assured Hiss by letter that, "I want you to know that I am in your corner." [10]

It is now clear that Federal agents, acting under what they assert to be a legal use of the limited powers enumerated in the Constitution, have negotiated with foreign governments in an attempt to coerce these United States into a United Nations Treaty agreement. This U.N. Treaty, if valid, would surrender to these foreign governments the powers of government and affect a surrender of the rights and liberties assured to the people under the U.S. Constitution.

"The extent of this duplicity can now be directly assessed by example," continued the Montgomery speech.

"We have witnessed attempts by members of the Supreme Court to overturn the sovereignty of state governments: Example — the reapportionment innovation.

"We have been burdened with attempts at Congressional Legislation which directly attacks the Constitutional premise of private property rights: Example — the so-called 'Civil Rights Act.'

"And now we are confronted by the arbitrary use of

[10] "The Fearful Master" by G. Edward Griffin, page 103.

claimed Presidential power to override the Constitutional guarantees of universal suffrage: Example — the 'voting rights law'."

These attempted acts by judicial, legislative, and executive agents violate specific articles in the U.S. Constitution and in the constitutions of the several states and they are in contradiction to the intent of these constitutions. They are bold lawlessness.

These acts are not, however, in contradiction to the United Nations Treaty agreement. They are, in fact, demanded by the articles of the United Nations Charter.

"The General Assembly," states Article 13 of the Charter, "shall initiate studies and make recommendations for the purpose of promoting international cooperation in the political field and encouraging the progressive development of international law and its codification; promoting international cooperation in the economic, social, cultural, educational, and health fields, and assisting in the realization of human rights and fundamental freedom for all without distinction as to race, sex, language, or religion." [11]

The conclusion is inescapable.

Since its ratification by the U.S. Senate on July 28, 1945, the United Nations Charter has been alleged to be the "Supreme Law of the Land," and our elected and appointed agents in judicial, legislative, and executive office have conducted our affairs in consonance with the provisions of the U.N. Charter.

[11] "Charter of the United Nations," Chapter IV, Article 13, The General Assembly.

Furthermore, the agony in Alabama promises that the technique of "silent revolution" to change our government from one of limited and delegated powers to a centralized, totalitarian regime, is to be reinforced by planned violence which will expedite the change-over.

Americans, of course, have been assured that the Constitutional legality of the United Nations Treaty agreement is found in Article VI of our Constitution, Secretary of State Dulles, remember, stated that "Treaty law can override the Constitution."

A treaty, however, cannot authorize what the Constitution forbids.

No federal agent has the power or the authority to modify or to dissolve the Constitutional Compact.

In Reid vs. Covert, 1957, the United States Supreme Court observed,

> "It would be manifestly contrary to the objectives of those who created the Constitution as well as those who were responsible for the Bill of Rights—let alone alien to our entire Constitutional history and tradition—to construe article VI as permitting the United States to exercise power under an international agreement without observing constitutional prohibitions. In effect, such contruction would permit amendment of that document in a manner not sanctioned by article V. The prohibitions of the Constitution were designed to apply to all branches of the national government and they cannot be nullified by the Executive or by the Executive and Senate combined."

Well-concealed Planners in our federal government, however, have clearly demonstrated that they would amend the Constitution "in a manner not sanctioned by Article V."

It must be said, too, that the Supreme Court cannot declare a statute of Congress "Unconstitutional." The court can exercise only the judicial power conferred upon it by the Constitution. It can no more "unmake" a legislative act than it can make one.

To strike down a legislative act requires legislative power. No court has such power.

The ordinary citizen also lacks the power to overturn breaches of the Constitution.

Only a state acting in its highest sovereign capacity can repudiate unauthorized acts of its agents.

"Therefore, the proper party to now challenge the validity of the United Nations Treaty agreement is a party to the Constitutional Compact, a sovereign state — the State of Alabama," I stated in the Alabama capitol.

The sovereign power of the state, through its legislative apparatus can legally clarify this question of attempted usurpation of governmental power.

The sovereignty of the thirteen nations that later entered into the Constitutional Compact was established by the Treaty of Peace at the end of the Revolutionary War. Years passed before these sovereignties contracted with one another in the Agreement known as the Constitution of the United States.

"It is by so understanding the subject," wrote Martin Van Buren, eighth President of the United States, "that the Preamble (to the Constitution) is reconciled with facts and that it is a Constitution established by 'the people of the United States,' not as one consolidated body but as members of separate and independent communities each acting for itself. It was in this form," he said, "that the Constitution of the United States was established by the people of the different states . . ."

In so doing, the people of the different states acted in "their highest sovereign capacity." "It is in this capacity," said Van Buren, "that each state is a party to the Constitutional Compact."

"It is well established," he observed, "that, in that sense, the Constitution was submitted to the states; that, in the term 'states' that they form the constituency from which the Federal Constitution emanated and it is by the states, acting either by their Legislatures or in Convention, that any valid alterations of the instrument can alone be made."

Under this Constitution so established by "The People of the United States" (i.e., the governments of the several states,) are fixed three separate and distinct agencies of government, each with clearly defined and strictly limited powers.

The action which is proposed for each State Legislature is to clarify the confusion that arises from the attempt by the agencies created by the agreement between the states to exercise a power which was not delegated and which, therefore, these agents do not have.

The Constitution was binding on the thirteen original states when approved and ratified by the people of those states, and the states that have since joined in the contract share in its privileges and obligations.

Each has the same obligation to the others to insure that the provisions of the Contract are enforced within its borders. All state officeholders are sworn to achieve this result.

Attempts by federal agents to exceed the limited powers of the Constitution are void and, in law, are no acts at all.

However, when the state fails to repudiate the un-authorized act of its agents, a presumption arises that the state has approved. The vitality that is thus given to the purported act of the agent arises from the power of the state in question. The power does not come from the limited agents who had no power to act.

As the Constitutional authority, Mr. Horton, explained to me in his correspondence, "The farmer who sends his hired hand to market to sell part of his potato crop is in the same position when the hired hand sells the team and wagon. Other hired hands can deplore his conduct but they are powerless to correct it. Only the farmer, the principal, can correct the excess of his agent. He must do this by an affirmative act of repudiation. If he acquiesces in the unauthorized act of his agent, he will be bound by it. It is not his agent's act, but his own that makes it binding upon him. If he either does nothing or affirmatively ratifies the agent's act, then he is bound by what the agent did. Only an affirmative repudiation of the agent's act can correct the situation."

In the case of the Cherokee Tobacco (11 Wall 616 1870), Mr. Justice Swayne observed,

"It need hardly be said that a treaty cannot change

the Constitution or be held valid if it be in violation of that instrument."

"The so-called United Nations 'Charter,' and other matters arising under the purported authority of the United Nations Organization, are neither executing the laws passed by Congress, as the Chief Executive is obligated to do, nor are they judicial. They are attempts to exercise powers which can be made lawful only by the affirmative action of three-fourths of the states (i.e., by amending the Constitution.) Because these purported acts seek to have general application within the state, they are legislative in nature and require legislative power to correct," Mr. Horton observed during the formative stages of our legislative program.

"Judicial power only is accorded to Federal Courts by the terms of the Constitution. Such authority is confined to the application of the law to a particular controversy as it affects the particular parties before a court. A court is denied authority to exercise any form of legislative power. The assumption that the Supreme Court, in Marbury vs. Madison, declared a statute of Congress 'unconstitutional' is a misunderstanding," Mr. Horton told me.

"The Supreme Court has no such power. It can exercise only the judicial power conferred upon it by the Constitution. Judicial power does not include the right, or the ability, to declare an act of Congress 'unconstitutional.'

"The confused understanding of this case arises from a failure to see what the court did. The court decided that as far as concerned the case before it, there was no

Act of Congress. What was before the court was an unauthorized and *ultra vires* and therefore void act of the members of Congress.

"But, in the exercise of its judicial function, it is the right and the duty of the court to determine what is and what is not, evidence in the case that is before it. In the case of Marbury vs. Madison, the court did not declare an 'Act of Congress,' 'unconstitutional.' It exercised, in that case, judicial power, not legislative power. The court examined what was claimed to be an Act of Congress and found it to be beyond the authority granted by the Constitution, and therefore void. There was no Act of Congress. Thus in excluding, as void, the purported act of Congress as evidence in the case before it, the court exercised its judicial power, not any legislative power which it did not have.

"In exercising its judicial power," Mr. Horton counseled, "the Supreme Court could no more un-make an act of Congress than it could make one. To do so requires the exercise of legislative power and all legislative power granted by the agreement between the states is given to the Congress, not to the Supreme Court. However, since there was no legislative act of the Congress, the court proceeded without recognizing as evidence in the case before it the attempt of the Congress to exceed its powers."

How we translated these basic legal propositions into legislative action will be told in the concluding chapter of this work.

CHAPTER XIV

GRASS ROOTS LEADERSHIP

"Let us not make it a blank paper (the Constitution) by construction. I say the same as to the opinion of those who consider the grant of the treaty-making power as boundless. If it is, then we have no Constitution."
—Thomas Jefferson . . . *Law of the Land* by Warren Jefferson Davis, p. 76.

The reason that the people of each State have been burdened with the acts of federal agents in their surrender of the powers of government to the United Nations is because that State has not repudiated the attempts of its agents to act beyond their authority. These acts had the effect of "law" not by reason of any nonexistent authority of the Federal agents, but because of the authority that State gave to these acts by failing to challenge the attempts of its Federal agents to exceed their authority.

The power to correct these excesses by federal agents is found in the Constitution.

"We, the People of the United States," declares the preamble to the Constitution, "in Order to form a more perfect Union, establish Justice, insure domestic Tranquillity, provide for the common Defense, promote the general Welfare, and secure the Blessings of Liberty to ourselves and our Posterity, do ordain and establish this CONSTITUTION for the United States of America,"

The preamble thus clearly defines the sovereignty and the authority of the States as parties to the Constitutional Compact.

The United Nations Treaty agreement is not the first instance in which the sovereign States have found it necessary to reaffirm the restrictions placed upon the Federal Government by the Constitutional Compact. The oppressive Sedition Act of July 14, 1798 by which the U.S. Congress attempted to abridge freedom of the press, elicited the Kentucky Resolution of November 19, 1799, repudiating the unauthorized acts of the Congress.

"Resolved that the several States composing the United States of America," said the Kentucky Legislators, "are not united on the principles of unlimited submission to their general government; but that by Compact under the style and title of a Constitution for the United States and of amendments thereto, they constituted a general government for special purposes, delegated to that government certain definite powers, reserving each State to itself the residuary mass of right to their own self-government; and that whensoever the general government assumes undelegated powers, its acts are unauthoritative, void, and of no force; that to this Compact each State acceded as a State and is an integral party, its co-states forming as to itself the other party; that the government created by this Compact was not made the exclusive or final judge of the extent of the powers delegated to itself since that would have made its discretion, and not the Constitution, the measure of its powers; but that as in all other cases of Compact among parties having no common judge, each party has an equal right to judge for itself, as well of infractions as of the mode and measure of redress."

It is a matter of historical record that the agencies in Washington have fallen into the hands of those who would not only alter the Constitution but would completely abrogate it by means of the so-called United Nations Treaty.

This emasculation of our Constitution most certainly was not authorized by the parties to the Constitutional Compact. Lacking this authority it is against the law. Being unlawful, it must be put down.

In this respect, State officeholders have a positive duty to enforce the provisions of the Constitution. It is a continuing obligation and may not be met merely by an empty oath taken upon accepting public office.

"The language of Article VI, paragraph 3, U.S. Constitution, '. . . shall be bound by Oath or Affirmation to support this Constitution, . . .' imposes a continuing duty upon these officeholders as long as they continue in office.

"In like manner," I stated in the Alabama address, "the State at the time of its admission into the Union assumes all obligations to the people of that State and to the people of the several States which are parties to the same agreement, to insure that all provisions of the Constitution are respected and enforced within the boundaries of the State.

"Therefore, in conformity with these duties and obligations, I propose that the legislators of the State of Alabama now do what is necessary to defend the Constitution and to protect the rights of the people."

"To this end the limits of authority given by the Constitution must be enforced and violations of those limits must be punished. Events in Washington and in the States disclose a systematic attack upon the liberties and freedoms guaranteed to the people under this Constitution.

"I, therefore, suggest that the legislators of the State of Alabama appoint a special committee comprising members of the House and Senate to investigate the legality of the action of Federal agents with regard to the United Nations and to provide means for the enforcement of the Constitution of the United States in relation thereto. (f)

"I suggest that such committee be authorized and directed to investigate the question of whether the United Nations Treaty agreement, purportedly entered into by Federal agencies acting as representatives of these United States and of the State of Alabama, be within the power and authority granted to said agents under the Constitution of the United States.

"I suggest that this committee be further authorized and directed to investigate the question of whether this purported U.N. Treaty agreement affects the State of Alabama or relates to the relinquishment of any of the laws or rights affecting the State of Alabama or its people.

F Exhibit—"A Bill to Investigate the Legality of the Action of Federal Agents with Regard to the United Nations and to Provide Means for the Enforcement of the Constitution of the United States in Relation Thereto."

"This committee must determine whether there is any change proposed to be made under this United Nations Treaty agreement which would deprive the State of Alabama or its people of rights and privileges, or would involve any change in any of the provisions of the Constitution of the United States without the consent of the State of Alabama or of the several States.

"And I suggest that this committee inquire into what measures may be taken by the State of Alabama to enforce the Constitution of the United States and to punish any infraction thereof that may appear to be indorsed by any unlawful attempt to use authority by any agency not sanctioned by the Constitution of the United States.

"Upon determining that the United Nations Treaty agreement is beyond the authority granted to Federal agents by Constitutional Compact, I propose that the legislators of the State of Alabama introduce 'a bill to provide for the enforcement of the Constitution of the United States with regard to the so-called United Nations Organization.' (g)

"I suggest that this statute declare that the agreements relating to the United Nations Organization are beyond the authority granted to agencies purporting to make these treaties and agreements — and are, therefore, null, void, and of no effect within the jurisdiction of the State

---

G Exhibit—"A Bill to Provide for the Enforcement of the Constitution of the United States with Regard to the so-called United Nations Organization."

of Alabama and that any attempt to enforce the provisions of any said treaties or agreements within the State of Alabama is unlawful.

"And lastly, I suggest that any person who shall commit an act in violation of the provisions of this statute shall be guilty of a felony and upon conviction thereof shall be fined not more than $100,000, or be confined in the State penitentiary not more than twenty years, or both."

In providing criminal penalties for attempts to enforce acts that have no authority under the U.S. Constitution, the State Legislature is not asked to declare "unconstitutional" a treaty that is made with regard to the United Nations. The State Legislature is requested to first inquire into the question of whether there was authority to enter into such a treaty. Upon finding that there was not, the State Legislature is asked to provide criminal sanctions for attempts to effectuate in the State that which was never in legal existence.

The Legislature of the State, by adopting this proposed statute, will clarify and make definite the law in the state and will discharge the state's obligation to insure that the limits of the U.S. Constitution are respected within its borders.

"At such time as the Alabama Legislature commissions a committee to investigate the United Nations Treaty," I promised the Southern Solons, "I will be pleased to suggest qualified witnesses to offer testimony regarding the usurpation of governmental powers and the attempt to surrender our liberties to the United Nations Organization without the consent of the people of the State of

Alabama or of the several States comprising the Union.

"These witnesses will include Constitutional attorneys, general officers of the U.S. military establishment, civilian experts on the subject of U.N. subversion, and U.S. Senators.

If we are to preserve individual liberty as defined by our Constitution and not the constitutions of Communist Nations, "We must destroy the United Nations banner," I said in concluding my address before the Alabama Legislature.[1]

The legislative response to this talk has been recorded in chapter thirteen. The manner in which the Alabama action was initiated and the technique now being employed by conscientious citizens in many other States of the Union, north, south, east, and west, may provide a guide to conservative action by other concerned Americans.

The following actions have been found to be effective and successful tactics for resisting United Nations tyranny:

1. Establish legislative liaison committees. Make personal contact with State senators and representatives within each State political subdivision. Press for official action on the petition for a public hearing on the legality of the action of federal agents concerning the United Nations Treaty agreement and for passage of a State Statute providing for the enforcement of the Constitution

---

[1] "Solons asked to check U.N. Programs," Mobile, Alabama *Register*, April 1, 1965.

of the United States with regard to the so-called United Nations Organization.

2. Institute reciprocal working relations with, and promote the active support of religious, fraternal, civic, patriotic, veteran, youth, and women's organizations. Motivate aid in publicizing conservative American intelligence so as to counter alien United Nations propaganda. Generate vocal "Grass Roots" resistance programs and seek organizational participation in the promotion of state legislative action on the U.N. treaty issue.

3. Organize letter-writing groups for the production of continuous letters and petitions to state executive and legislative officeholders demanding adherence to their oaths of office, to ". . . support this Constitution." Generate a series of letters-to-the-editor to all state-located newspapers and publications bringing attention to "Grass Roots" repudiation of the United Nations Treaty.

4. Disseminate constitutional opinions and reviews on the U.N. to members of your State legislature, to State opinion leaders and to your friends.

5. Arrange patriotic rallies and public speaking engagements for the presentation of factual information regarding U.N. control over our military establishment. Arouse citizen-support for a State campaign seeking rejection of the U.N. Treaty.

The United Nations stands indicted as a subversive organization. The cabalistic planners who manipulate the U.N. have been shown to be dedicated to the overthrow of the United States of America.

Those who occupy executive, legislative, and judicial offices at the federal level of government have demonstrated that they are unwilling or unable to defend the freedom, the proper interest, and the security of the people of the United States.

Effective resistance to United Nations tyranny, therefore, now devolves to the absolute source of all governmental power; the American citizen acting through his State legislature.

"We hold from God the gift which includes all others," said the French economist Frederic Bastiat in *The Law.*[2]

This nineteenth century writer then stated:

"Life, faculties, production — in other words, individuality, liberty, property — this is man. And in spite of the cunning of artful political leaders, these three gifts from God precede all human legislation, and are superior to it.

"Life, liberty, and property do not exist because men have made laws. On the contrary," said Bastiat, "it was the fact that life, liberty, and property existed beforehand that causes men to make laws in the first place.

"What, then, is the law? It is the collective organization of the individual right to lawful defense.

"Each of us," the writer said, "has a natural right — from God — to defend his person, his liberty, and his property. These are the three basic requirements of life,

---

[2] *The Law,* by Frederic Bastiat, June, 1850. Translated from the French by Dean Russell, The Foundation for Economic Education, Inc., 1961.

the preservation of any one of them is completely dependent upon the preservation of the other two. For what are our faculties but the extension of our individuality? And what is property but an extension of our faculties?"

Mr. Bastiat, a Deputy in the Legislative Assembly, then proclaimed in words which ring with particular urgency today:

"If every person has the right to defend — even by force — his person, his liberty, and his property, then it follows that a group of men have the right to organize and support a common force to protect these rights constantly. Thus the principle of collective right — its reason for existing, its lawfulness — is based on individual right."

"Individual right" so eloquently defended by Frederic Bastiat over one hundred years ago is embodied in the provisions of the United States Constitution.

The United States Constitution created a new and unique political power in the world: *The sovereign individual.* To "support and defend the Constitution of the United States," and to preserve those rights of person, liberty, and property which are the foundation of the Constitution, all that is necessary is that Americans assert the authority of their citizenship.

Let each American, individually and in concord, assert that authority.

EXHIBITS
&
INDEX

Exhibit A

NORTH ATLANTIC TREATY

Washington D.C., 4 April, 1949*

The Parties to this Treaty reaffirm their faith in the purposes and principles of the Charter of the United Nations and their desire to live in peace with all peoples and all Governments.

They are determined to safeguard the freedom, common heritage and civilization of their peoples, founded on the principles of democracy, individual liberty and the rule of law.

They seek to promote stability and well-being in the North Atlantic area.

They are resolved to unite their efforts for collective defence and for the preservation of peace and security.

They therefore agree to this North Atlantic Treaty:

---

* The Treaty came into force on 24 August, 1949, after the deposition of the ratifications of all signatory states.

ARTICLE 1

The Parties undertake, as set forth in the Charter of the United Nations, to settle any international dispute in which they may be involved by peaceful means in such a manner that international peace and security and justice are not endangered, and to refrain in their international relations from the threat or use of force in any manner inconsistent with the purposes of the United Nations.

ARTICLE 2

The Parties will contribute toward the further development of peaceful and friendly international relations by strengthening their free institutions, by bringing about a better understanding of the principles upon which these institutions are founded, and by promoting conditions of stability and well-being. They will seek to eliminate conflict in their international economic policies and will encourage economic collaboration between any or all of them.

ARTICLE 3

In order more effectively to achieve the objectives of this Treaty, the Parties, separately and jointly, by means of continuous and effective self-help and mutual aid, will maintain and develop their individual and collective capacity to resist armed attack.

ARTICLE 4

The Parties will consult together whenever, in the opinion of any of them, the territorial integrity, political independence or security of any of the Parties is threatened.

ARTICLE 5

The Parties agree that an armed attack against one or more of them in Europe or North America shall be considered an attack against them all, and consequently they agree that, if such an armed attack occurs, each of them, in exercise of the right of individual or collective self-defence recognized by Article 51 of the Charter of the United Nations, will assist the Party or Parties so attacked by taking forthwith, individually and in concert with the other Parties, such action as it deems necessary, including the use of armed force, to restore and maintain the security of the North Atlantic area.

Any such armed attack and all measures taken as a result thereof shall immediately be reported to the Security Council. Such measures shall be terminated when the Security Council has taken the measures necessary to restore and maintain international peace and security.

ARTICLE 6*

For the purpose of Article 5 an armed attack on one or more of the Parties is deemed to include an armed attack on the territory of any of the Parties in Europe or North America, on the Algerian Departments of France, on the occupation forces of any Party in Europe, on the islands under the jurisdiction of any Party in the North Atlantic area north of the Tropic of Cancer or on the vessels or aircraft in this area of any of the Parties.

ARTICLE 7

This Treaty does not affect, and shall not be interpreted as affecting, in any way the rights and obligations under the Charter of the Parties which are members of the

---

* The definition of the territories to which Article 5 applies was revised by Article 11 of the Protocol to the North Atlantic Treaty on the accession of Greece and Turkey.

United Nations, or the primary responsibility of the Security Council for the maintenance of international peace and security.

ARTICLE 8

Each Party declares that none of the international engagements now in force between it and any other of the Parties or any third State is in conflict with the provisions of this Treaty, and undertakes not to enter into any international engagement in conflict with this Treaty.

ARTICLE 9

The Parties hereby establish a council, on which each of them shall be represented to consider matters concerning the implementation of this Treaty. The Council shall be so organized as to be able to meet promptly at any time. The Council shall set up such subsidiary bodies as may be necessary; in particular it shall establish immediately a defence committee which shall recommend measures for the implementation of Articles 3 and 5.

ARTICLE 10

The Parties may, by unanimous agreement, invite any other European State in a position to further the principles of this Treaty and to contribute to the security of the North Atlantic area to accede to this Treaty. Any State so invited may become a party to the Treaty by depositing its instrument of accession with the Government of the United States of America. The Government of the United States of America will inform each of the Parties of the deposit of each such instrument of accession.

ARTICLE 11

This Treaty shall be ratified and its provisions carried out by the Parties in accordance with their respective constitutional processes. The instruments of ratification shall be deposited as soon as possible with the Government of the United States of America, which will notify all the other signatories of each deposit. The Treaty shall enter into force between the States which have ratified it as soon as the ratifications of the majority of the signatories, including the ratifications of Belgium, Canada, France, Luxembourg, the Netherlands, the United Kingdom and the United States, have been deposited and shall come into effect with respect to other States on the date of the deposit of their ratifications.

ARTICLE 12

After the Treaty has been in force for ten years, or at any time thereafter, the Parties shall, if any of them so requests, consult together for the purpose of reviewing the Treaty, having regard for the factors then affecting peace and security in the North Atlantic area, including the development of universal as well as regional arrangements under the Charter of the United Nations for the maintenance of international peace and security.

ARTICLE 13

After the Treaty has been in force for twenty years, any Party may cease to be a party one year after its notice of denunciation has been given to the Government of the United States of America, which will inform the Governments of the other Parties of the deposit of each notice of denunciation.

ARTICLE 14

This Treaty, of which the English and French text are equally authentic, shall be deposited in the archives of the Government of the United States of America. Duly certified copies will be transmitted by that Government to the Governments of the other signatories.

Exhibit B

UNITED NATIONS FORCES MILITARY GOVERNMENT OF AGRESSI

PROCLAMATION NUMBER I

TO THE PEOPLE OF AGRESSI:

WHEREAS, in prosecuting the war against AGRESSI, it has become necessary for the armed forces of the UNITED NATIONS under my command, to occupy this town, adjacent areas and OTHER PORTIONS OF AGRESSI, and

WHEREAS, it is the policy of the armed forces of the UNITED NATIONS not to make war upon the civilian inhabitants of the occupied territory but to protect them in the peaceful exercise of their legitimate pursuits, insofar as the exigencies of war and their own behaviour will permit, and

WHEREAS, in order to preserve law and order and to provide for the safety and welfare both of the forces under my command and of yourselves, it is necessary to establish MILITARY GOVERNMENT in the occupied territory.

NOW, THEREFORE, I, JONES SMITHMAN, General, United States Army Commanding United States Forces Oceania, and Military Governor of Agressi, by virtue of the authority vested in me by the United Nations Security Council, do hereby proclaim as follows:

I

All powers of government and jurisdiction in the occupied territory and over the inhabitants thereof, and final administrative responsibility are vested in me as Commanding General of the Forces of Occupation and as Military Governor of UNITED NATIONS FORCES MILITARY GOVERNMENT OF AGRESSI is hereby established to exercise these powers under my direction.

II

All persons in the occupied territory will obey promptly all orders given by me or under my authority and must not commit any act hostile to the forces under my command or helpful to the

Agressi forces; must not commit acts of violence or acts which may disturb public order in any way.

III

Your existing customs, religious beliefs and property rights will be fully respected and your existing laws will remain in force and effect except insofar as it may be necessary for me in the exercise of my powers and duties to change them by proclamation or order issued by me or under my direction.

IV

All Agressi civil and criminal courts and all universities, schools and educational establishments will be closed until further order of United Nations Forces Military Governor of Agressi.

V

All administrative and police officials of towns, cities, counties and states and all other government and municipal functionaries and employees, and all officers and employees of state, municipal or other public services, except such officials and political leaders as are removed by, or under my direction, are required to continue in the performance of their duties subject to my direction or the direction of such of the officers of the armed forces of the United Nations as may be deputed for the purpose.

VI

So long as you remain peaceable and comply with the orders of the forces of occupation, you will be subject to no greater interference than is made necessary by war conditions, and may go about your normal vocations without fear.

VII

Further proclamation, orders and regulations will be issued by me or under my authority from time to time. They will state what is further required of you, and what you are forbidden to do, and will be displayed in court houses, city halls, or other public places.

VIII

In case of conflict or ambiguity between the English text of this proclamation or any other proclamation, order, or regulation issued under my authority, and any translations thereof, the English text is to prevail.

> JONES SMITHMAN
> Commanding United Nations Forces Oceania
> General, United States Army
> MILITARY GOVERNOR OF AGRESSI

Exhibit C

FACTORS OPERATIVE IN A POST - ARMS CONTROL SITUATION

CONTRACT NO. AF 49(638)-1411

NORTH AMERICAN AVIATION, INC.

SPACE AND INFORMATION SYSTEMS DIVISION

AEROSPACE SCIENCES DIVISION

OPERATIONS ANALYSIS DEPARTMENT

APRIL 1965

Exhibit C-1

NUCLEAR FREE ZONE CHRONOLOGY

EVENTS	TIME			
	1964	1965	1966	1967
POLITICAL AND ARMS CONTROL DEVELOPMENTS	▲ MORE LIBERAL ECONOMIC POLICIES BETWEEN EAST AND WEST BECOME EFFECTIVE ▲ U.S. AND U.S.S.R. CURTAIL FISSIONABLE MATERIALS	▲ INCREASED COOPERATION AT GENEVA CONFERENCE ▲ COMMUNIST CHINESE GOVERNMENT LEADERS COMMIT SUICIDE ▲ BILATERAL U.S.-U.S.S.R AGREEMENT FOR DESTRUCTION OF OBSOLETE BOMBER AIRCRAFT ▲ FRENCH POLICIES REORIENTED TOWARD U.S., U.K., AND NATO ▲ COMMUNIST CHINA ADMITTED TO U.N.	▲ DEVELOPMENT OF NONPROLIFERATION TREATY ▲ DESTRUCTION OF BOMBERS COMPLETED ▲ EXECUTION OF MULTINATION NONPROLIFERATION TREATY ▲ U.S.S.R. PROPOSES NUCLEAR-FREE ZONE IN CENTRAL EUROPE ▲ SPAIN AGREES TO ADDITIONAL U.S. BASE PRIVILEGES IN SPANISH TERRITORY ▲ NUCLEAR-FREE ZONE TREATY SIGNED	▲ U.S. GOVERNMENT RATIFIES CENTRAL EUROPEAN NUCLEAR-FREE ZONE TREATY ▲ EFFECTIVE DATE FOR NUCLEAR-FREE ZONE TREATY
MILITARY DEVELOPMENTS		▨ AGGRESSIVE ACTS BY COMMUNIST CHINA AND NORTH VIETNAM AGAINST U.S. AND SEATO ▲ U.S.S.R.R ABROGATES U.S.S.R.-CHINA MUTUAL DEFENSE TREATY ▨ U.S. PUNITIVE WAR VS COMMUNIST CHINA AND NORTH VIETNAM		▲ U.S. JCS ORDER IMPLEMENTING ACTION CONFORMING TO CENTRAL EUROPEAN NUCLEAR-FREE ZONE TREATY ▲ U.S. JCS APPROVE REDEPLOYMENT PLAN WITH NATO CONCURRENCE ▲ U.S. HAS 41 FRAG (SSBN) IN COMMISSION ▲ 6 SHIPS OF NAVAL MLF IN OPERATION ▲ ACTION COMPLETED TO DENUCLEARIZE TREATY ZONE ▲ ESSENTIAL ELEMENTS OF U.S. & NATO REDEPLOYMENT PLAN EXECUTED 30 SEPT

LEGEND: ▲ = ACTION OCCURING AT SPECIFIC TIME   ▨ = ACTION OR ACTIONS OCCURING OVER A PERIOD OF TIME

45 PS 82206

Exhibit C-2

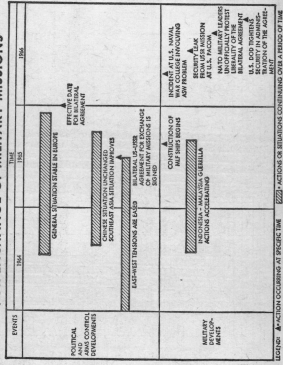

CHRONOLOGY OF SCENARIO FOR
BILATERAL U.S.-USSR AGREEMENT
FOR EXCHANGE OF MILITARY MISSIONS

EVENTS	TIME		
	1964	1965	1966
POLITICAL AND ARMS CONTROL DEVELOPMENTS	GENERAL SITUATION STABLE IN EUROPE		
		CHINESE SITUATION UNCHANGED SOUTHEAST ASIA SITUATION IMPROVES	
	EAST-WEST TENSIONS ARE EASED	BILATERAL US-USSR AGREEMENT FOR EXCHANGE OF MILITARY MISSIONS IS SIGNED	EFFECTIVE DATE FOR BILATERAL AGREEMENT
MILITARY DEVELOPMENTS		CONSTRUCTION OF MLF SHIPS BEGINS	INCIDENT AT U.S. NAVAL WAR COLLEGE INVOLVING ASW PROBLEM
	INDONESIA - MALAYSIA GUERRILLA ACTIONS ACCELERATING		SECURITY LEAK FROM USSR MISSION AT U.S. PACOM
			NATO MILITARY LEADERS UNOFFICIALLY PROTEST LIBERALITY OF THE BILATERAL AGREEMENT
			U.S. DOD TIGHTENS SECURITY IN ADMINISTRATION OF THE AGREEMENT

LEGEND: ▲ = ACTION OCCURRING AT SPECIFIC TIME   ▨ = ACTIONS OR SITUATIONS CONTINUING OVER A PERIOD OF TIME

45PS82212

Exhibit C-3 CHRONOLOGY FOR PARTIAL DISARMAMENT & FINAL GENERAL DISARMAMENT TREATIES

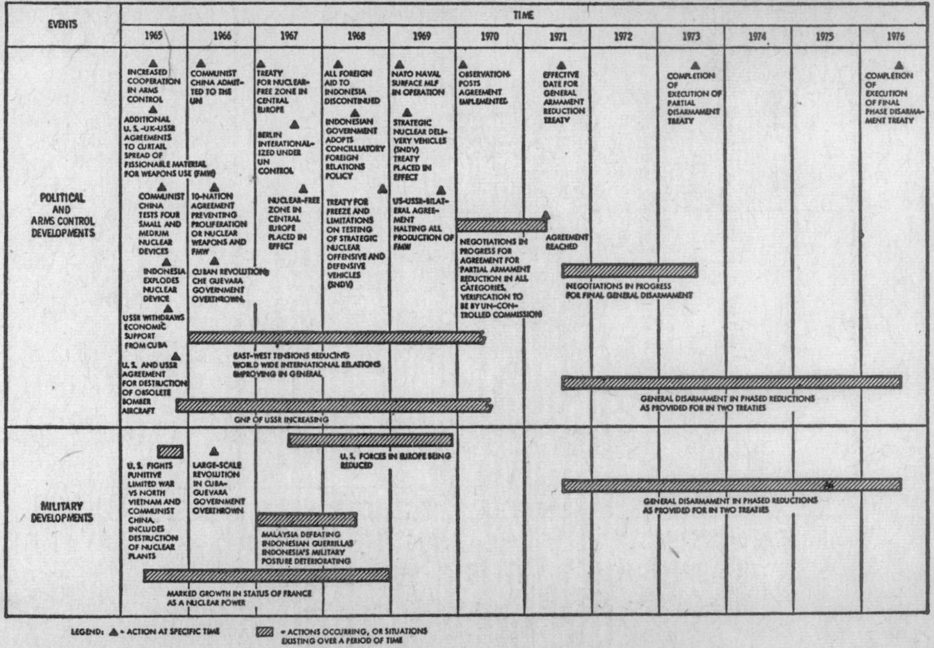

457582225

Exhibit D

DEPARTMENT OF STATE
PUBLICATION 7277
Disarmament Series 5
Released September 1961
Office of Public Services
BUREAU OF PUBLIC AFFAIRS
For sale by the Superintendent of Documents,
U.S. Government Printing Office
Washington 25, D.C.   Price 15 cents

INTRODUCTION

The revolutionary development of modern weapons within a world divided by serious ideological differences has produced a crisis in human history. In order to overcome the danger of nuclear war now confronting mankind, the United States has introduced at the Sixteenth General Assembly of the United Nations a program for *General and Complete Disarmament in a Peaceful World.*

This new program provides for the progressive reduction of the war-making capabilities of nations and the simultaneous strengthening of international institutions to settle disputes and maintain the peace. It sets forth a series of comprehensive measures which can and should be taken in order to bring about a world in which there will be freedom from war and security for all states. It is based on three principles deemed essential to the achievement of practical progress in the disarmament field:

First, there must be immediate disarmament action:
A strenuous and uninterrupted effort must be made toward the goal of general and complete disarmament at the same time, it is important that specific measures be put into effect as soon as possible.

Second, all disarmament obligations must be subject to effective international controls:
The control organization must have the manpower, facilities, and effectiveness to assure that limitations or reductions take place as agreed. It must also be able to certify to all states that retained forces and armaments do not exceed those permitted at any stage of the disarmament process.

Third, adequate peace-keeping machinery must be established:
There is an inseparable relationship between the scaling down of national armaments on the one hand and the building up of international peace-keeping machinery and institutions on the other. Nations are unlikely to shed their means of self-protection in the absence of alternative ways to safeguard their legitimate interests. This can only be achieved through the progressive strengthening of international institutions under the United Nations and by creating a United Nations Peace Force to enforce the peace as the disarmament process proceeds.

There follows a summary of the principal provisions of the United States Program for General and Complete Disarmament in a Peaceful World. The full text of the program is contained in an appendix to this pamphlet.

FREEDOM FROM WAR
THE UNITED STATES PROGRAM FOR
GENERAL AND COMPLETE DISARMAMENT
IN A PEACEFUL WORLD

SUMMARY

DISARMAMENT GOAL AND OBJECTIVES

The over-all goal of the United States is a free, secure, and peaceful world of independent states adhering to common standards of justice and international conduct and subjecting the use of force to the rule of law; a world which has achieved general and complete disarmament under effective international control; and a world in which adjustment to change takes place in accordance with the principles of the United Nations.

In order to make possible the achievement of that goal, the program sets forth the following specific objectives toward which nations should direct their efforts:

•The disbanding of all national armed forces and the prohibition of their reestablishment in any form whatsoever other than those required to preserve internal order and for contributions to a United Nations Peace Force;

•The elimination from national arsenals of all armaments, including all weapons of mass destruction and the means for their delivery, other than those required for a United Nations Peace Force and for maintaining internal order;

•The institution of effective means for the enforcement of international agreements, for the settlement of disputes, and for the maintenance of peace in accordance with the principles of the United Nations;

•The establishment and effective operation of an International Disarmament Organization within the framework of the United Nations to insure compliance at all times with all disarmament obligations.

TASK OF NEGOTIATING STATES

The negotiating states are called upon to develop the program into a detailed plan for general and complete disarmament and to continue their efforts without interruption until the whole program has been achieved. To this end, they are to seek the widest possible area of agreement at the earliest possible date. At the same time, and without prejudice to progress on the disarmament program, they are to seek agreement on those immediate measures that would contribute to the common security of nations and that could facilitate and form part of the total program.

GOVERNING PRINCIPLES

The program sets forth a series of general principles to guide the negotiating states in their work. These make clear that:

•As states relinquish their arms, the United Nations must be progressively strengthened in order to improve its capacity to assure international security and the peaceful settlement of disputes:

•Disarmament must proceed as rapidly as possible, until it is

completed, in stages containing balanced, phased, and safe-guarded measures;
•Each measure and stage should be carried out in an agreed period of time, with transition from one stage to the next to take place as soon as all measures in the preceding stage have been carried out and verified and as soon as necessary arrangements for verification of the next stage have been made;
•Inspection and verification must establish both that nations carry out scheduled limitations or reductions and that they do not retain armed forces and armaments in excess of those permitted at any stage of the disarmament process; and
•Disarmament must take place in a manner that will not affect adversely the security of any state.

DISARMAMENT STAGES

The program provides for progressive disarmament steps to take place in three stages and for the simultaneous strengthening of international institutions.

FIRST STAGE

The first stage contains measures which would significantly reduce the capabilities of nations to wage aggressive war. Implementation of this stage would mean that:
•The nuclear threat would be reduced:
All states would have adhered to a treaty effectively prohibiting the testing of nuclear weapons.
The production of fissionable materials for use in weapons would be stopped and quantities of such materials from past production would be converted to non-weapons uses.
States owning nuclear weapons would not relinquish control of such weapons to any nation not owning them and would not transmit to any such nation information or material necessary for their manufacture.
States not owning nuclear weapons would not manufacture them or attempt to obtain control of such weapons belonging to other states.
A Commission of Experts would be established to report on the feasibility and means for the verified reduction and eventual elimination of nuclear weapons stockpiles.
•Strategic delivery vehicles would be reduced:
Strategic nuclear weapons delivery vehicles of specified categories and weapons designed to counter such vehicles would be reduced to agreed levels by equitable and balanced steps; their production would be discontinued or limited; their testing would be limited or halted.
•Arms and armed forces would be reduced:
The armed forces of the United States and the Soviet Union would be limited to 2.1 million men each (with appropriate levels not exceeding that amount for other military significant states); levels of armaments would be correspondingly reduced and their production would be limited.
An Experts Commission would be established to examine and report on the feasibility and means of accomplishing verifiable reduction and eventual elimination of all chemical, biological and radiological weapons.

•Peaceful use of outer space would be promoted:

The placing in orbit or stationing in outer space of weapons capable of producing mass destruction would be prohibited.

States would give advance notification of space vehicle and missile launchings.

•U.N. peace-keeping powers would be strengthened:

Measures would be taken to develop and strengthen United Nations arrangements for arbitration, for the development of international law, and for the establishment in Stage II of a permanent U.N. Peace Force.

•An International Disarmament Organization would be established for effective verification of the disarmament program:

Its functions would be expanded progressively as disarmament proceeds.

It would certify to all states that agreed reductions have taken place and that retained forces and armaments do not exceed permitted levels.

It would determine the transition from one stage to the next.

•States would be committed to other measures to reduce international tension and to protect against the chance of war by accident, miscalculations, or surprise attack:

States would be committed to refrain from the threat or use of any type of armed force contrary to the principles of the U.N. Charter and to refrain from indirect aggression and subversion against any country.

A U.N. peace observation group would be available to investigate any situation which might constitute a threat to or breach of the peace.

States would be committed to give advance notice of major military movements which might cause alarm; observation posts would be established to report on concentrations and movements of military forces.

SECOND STAGE

The second stage contains a series of measures which would bring within sight a world in which there would be freedom from war. Implementation of all measures in the second stage would mean:

•Further substantial reductions in the armed forces, armaments, and military establishments of states, including strategic nuclear weapons delivery vehicles and countering weapons;

•Further development of methods for the peaceful settlement of disputes under the United Nations;

•Establishment of a permanent international peace force within the United Nations;

•Depending on the findings of an Experts Commission, a halt in the production of chemical, bacteriological, and radiological weapons and a reduction of existing stocks or their conversion to peaceful uses;

•On the basis of the findings of an Experts Commission, a reduction of stocks of nuclear weapons;

•The dismantling or the conversion to peaceful uses of certain military bases and facilities wherever located; and

•The strengthening and enlargement of the International Disarmament Organization to enable it to verify the steps taken in Stage II and to determine the transition to Stage III.

THIRD STAGE

During the third stage of the program, the states of the world building on the experience and confidence gained in successfully implementing the measures of the first two stages, would take final steps toward the goal of a world in which:

•States would retain only those forces, non-nuclear armaments, and establishments required for the purpose of maintaining internal order; they would also support and provide agreed manpower for a U.N. Peace Force.

•The U.N. Peace Force, equipped with agreed types and quantities of armaments, would be fully functioning.

•The manufacture of armaments would be prohibited except for those of agreed types and quantities to be used by the U.N. Peace Force and those required to maintain internal order. All other armaments would be destroyed or converted to peaceful purposes.

•The peace-keeping capabilities of the United Nations would be sufficiently strong and the obligations of all states under such arrangements sufficiently far-reaching as to assure peace and the just settlement of differences in a disarmed world.

APPENDIX

DECLARATION ON DISARMAMENT

THE UNITED STATES PROGRAM FOR GENERAL AND COMPLETE DISARMAMENT IN A PEACEFUL WORLD

The Nations of the world,

Conscious of the crisis in human history produced by the revolutionary development of modern weapons within a world divided by serious ideological differences;

Determined to save present and succeeding generations from the scourge of war and the dangers and burdens of the arms race and to create conditions in which all people can strive freely and peacefully to fulfill their basic aspirations;

Declare their goal to be: A free, secure, and peaceful world of independent states adhering to common standards of justice and international conduct and subjecting the use of force to the rule of law; a world where adjustment to change takes place in accordance with the principles of the United Nations; a world where there shall be a permanent state of general and complete disarmament under effective international control and where the resources of nations shall be devoted to man's material, cultural, and spiritual advance;

Set forth as the objectives of a program of general and complete disarmament in a peaceful world:

(a) The disbanding of all national armed forces and the prohibition of their reestablishment in any form whatsoever other than those required to preserve internal order and for contributions to a United Nations Peace Force;

(b) The elimination from national arsenals of all armaments, including all weapons of mass destruction and the means for their delivery, other than those required for a United Nations Peace Force and for maintaining internal order;

(c) The establishment and effective operation of an International Disarmament Organization within the framework of the United Nations to ensure compliance at all times with all disarmament obligations;

(d) The institution of effective means for the enforcement of international agreements, for the settlement of disputes, and for the maintenance of peace in accordance with the principles of the United Nations.

Call on the negotiating states:

(a) To develop the outline program set forth below into an agreed plan for general and complete disarmament and to continue their efforts without interruption until the whole program has been achieved;

(b) To this end to seek to attain the widest possible area of agreement at the earliest possible date;

(c) Also to seek — without prejudice to progress on the disarmament program — agreement on those immediate measures that would contribute to the common security of nations and that could facilitate and form a part of that program.

Affirm that disarmament negotiations should be guided by the following principles:

(a) Disarmament shall take place as rapidly as possible until it is completed in stages containing balanced, phased and safeguarded measures, with each measure and stage to be carried out in an agreed period of time.

(b) Compliance with all disarmament obligations shall be effectively verified from their entry into force. Verification arrangements shall be instituted progressively and in such a manner as to verify not only that agreed limitations or reductions take place but also that retained armed forces and armaments do not exceed agreed levels at any stage.

(c) Disarmament shall take place in a manner that will not affect adversely the security of any state, whether or not a party to any international agreement or treaty.

(d) As states relinquish their arms, the United Nations shall be progressively strengthened in order to improve its capacity to assure international security and the peaceful settlement of differences as well as to facilitate the development of international cooperation in common tasks for the benefit of mankind.

(e) Transition from one stage of disarmament to the next shall take place as soon as all the measures in the preceding stage have been carried out and effective verification is continuing and as soon as the arrangements that have been agreed to be necessary for the next stage have been instituted.

Agree upon the following outline program for achieving general and complete disarmament:

STAGE I

A. *To Establish an International Disarmament Organization:*

(a) An International Disarmament Organization (IDO) shall

be established within the framework of the United Nations upon entry into force of the agreement. Its function shall be expanded progressively as required for the effective verification of the disarmament program.

(b) The IDO shall have: (1) a General Conference of all the parties; (2) a Commission consisting of representatives of all the major powers as permanent members and certain other states on a rotating basis; and (3) An Administrator who will administer the Organization subject to the direction of the Commission and who will have the authority, staff, and finances adequate to assure effective impartial implementation of the functions of the Organization.

(c) The IDO shall: (1) ensure compliance with the obligations undertaken by verifying the execution of measures agreed upon; (2) assist the states in developing the details of agreed further verification and disarmament measures; (3) provide for the establishment of such bodies as may be necessary for working out the details of further measures provided for in the program and for such other expert study groups as may be required to give continuous study to the problems of disarmament; (4) receive reports on the progress of disarmament and verification agreements and determine the transition from one stage to the next.

B. To Reduce Armed Forces and Armaments:

(a) Force levels shall be limited to 2.1 million each for the U.S. and U.S.S.R. and to appropriate levels not exceeding 2.1 million each for all other militarily significant states. Reductions to the agreed levels will proceed by equitable, proportionate, and verified steps.

(b) Levels of armaments of prescribed types shall be reduced by equitable and balanced steps. The reductions shall be accomplished by transfers of armaments to depots supervised by the IDO. When, at specified periods during the Stage I reduction process, the states party to the agreement have agreed that the armaments and armed forces are at prescribed levels, the armaments in depots shall be destroyed or converted to peaceful uses.

(c) The production of agreed types of armaments shall be limited.

(d) A Chemical, Biological, Radiological (CBR) Experts Commission shall be established within the IDO for the purpose of examining and reporting on the feasibility and means for accomplishing the verifiable reduction and eventual elimination of CBR weapons stockpiles and the halting of their production.

C. To Contain and Reduce the Nuclear Threat:

(a) States that have not acceded to a treaty effectively prohibiting the testing of nuclear weapons shall do so.

(b) The production of fissionable materials for use in weapons shall be stopped.

(c) Upon the cessation of production of fissionable materials for use in weapons, agreed initial quantities of fissionable materials from past production shall be transferred to non-weapons purposes.

(d) Any fissionable materials transferred between countries for peaceful uses of nuclear energy shall be subject to appropriate safeguards to be developed in agreement with the IAEA.

(e) States owning nuclear weapons shall not relinquish control of such weapons to any nation not owning them and shall not transmit to any such nation information or material necessary for their manufacture. States now owning nuclear weapons shall not manufacture such weapons, attempt to obtain control of such weapons belonging to other states, or seek or receive information or materials necessary for their manufacture.

(f) A Nuclear Experts Commission consisting of representatives of the nuclear states shall be established within the IDO for the purpose of examining and reporting on the feasibility and means for accomplishing the verified reduction and eventual elimination of nuclear weapons stockpiles.

D. To Reduce Strategic Nuclear Weapons Delivery Vehicles:

(a) Strategic nuclear weapons delivery vehicles in specified categories and agreed types of weapons designed to counter such vehicles shall be reduced to agreed levels by equitable and balanced steps. The reduction shall be accomplished in each step by transfers to depots supervised by the IDO of vehicles that are in excess of levels agreed upon for each step. At specified periods during the Stage I reduction process, the vehicles that have been placed under supervision of the IDO shall be destroyed or converted to peaceful uses.

(b) Production of agreed categories of strategic nuclear weapons delivery vehicles and agreed types of weapons designed to counter such vehicles shall be discontinued or limited.

(c) Testing of agreed categories of strategic nuclear weapons delivery vehicles and agreed types of weapons designed to counter such vehicles shall be limited or halted.

E. To Promote the Peaceful Use of Outer Space:

(a) The placing into orbit or stationing in outer space of weapons capable of producing mass destruction shall be prohibited.

(b) States shall give advance notification to participating states and to the IDO of launchings of space vehicles and missiles, together with the track of the vehicle.

F. To Reduce the Risk of War by Accident, Miscalculation, and Surprise Attack:

(a) States shall give advance notification to the participating states and to the IDO of major military movements and maneuvers, on a scale as may be agreed, which might give rise to misinterpretation or cause alarm and induce countermeasures. The notification shall include the geographic areas to be used and the nature, scale and time span of the event.

(b) There shall be established observation posts at such locations as major ports, railway centers, motor highways, and air bases to report on concentrations and movements of military forces.

(c) There shall also be established such additional inspection arrangements to reduce the danger of surprise attack as may be agreed.

(d) An international commission shall be established immediately within the IDO to examine and make recommendations on the possibility of further measures to reduce the risks of nuclear war by accident, miscalculation, or failure of communication.

G. To Keep the Peace:

(a) States shall reaffirm their obligations under the U.N. Charter to refrain from the threat or use of any type of armed force — including nuclear, conventional, or CBR — contrary to the principles of the U.N. Charter.

(b) States shall agree to refrain from indirect aggression and subversion against any country.

(c) States shall use all appropriate processes for the peaceful settlement of disputes and shall seek within the United Nations further arrangements for the peaceful settlement of international disputes and for the codification and progressive development of international law.

(d) States shall develop arrangements in Stage I for the establishment in Stage II of a U.N. Peace Force.

(e) A U.N. peace observation group shall be staffed with a standing cadre of observers who could be dispatched to investigate any situation which might constitute a threat to or breach of the peace.

STAGE II

A. International Disarmament Organization:

The powers and responsibilities of the IDO shall be progressively enlarged in order to give it the capabilities to verify the measures undertaken in Stage II.

B. To Further Reduce Armed Forces and Armaments:

(a) Levels of forces for the U.S., U.S.S.R., and other militarily significant states shall be further reduced by substantial amounts to agreed levels in equitable and balanced steps.

(b) Levels of armaments of prescribed types shall be further reduced by equitable and balanced steps. The reduction shall be accomplished by transfers of armaments to depots supervised by the IDO. When, at specified periods during the Stage II reduction process, the parties have agreed that the armaments and armed forces are at prescribed levels, the armaments in depots shall be destroyed or converted to peaceful uses.

(c) There shall be further agreed restrictions on the production of armaments.

(d) Agreed military bases and facilities wherever they are located shall be dismantled or converted to peaceful uses.

(e) Depending upon the findings of the Experts Commission on CBR weapons, the production of CBR weapons shall be halted, existing stocks progressively reduced, and the resulting excess quantities destroyed or converted to peaceful uses.

C. To Further Reduce the Nuclear Threat:

Stocks of nuclear weapons shall be progressively reduced to the minimum levels which can be agreed upon as a result of the findings of the Nuclear Experts Commission; the resulting excess of fissionable material shall be transferred to peaceful purposes.

D. *To Further Reduce Strategic Nuclear Weapons Delivery Vehicles:*

Further reductions in the stocks of strategic nuclear weapons delivery vehicles and agreed types of weapons designed to counter such vehicles shall be carried out in accordance with the procedure outlined in Stage I.

E. *To Keep the Peace:*

During Stage II, states shall develop further the peace-keeping processes of the United Nations, to the end that the United Nations can effectively in Stage III deter or suppress any threat or use of force in violation of the purposes and principles of the United Nations:

(a) States shall agree upon strengthening the structure, authority, and operation of the United Nations so as to assure that the United Nations will be able effectively to protect states against threat to or breaches of the peace.

(b) The U.N. Peace Force shall be established and progressively strengthened.

(c) States shall also agree upon further improvements and developments in rules of international conduct and in processes for peaceful settlements of disputes and differences.

STAGE III

By the time Stage II has been completed, the confidence produced through a verified disarmament program, the acceptance of rules of peaceful international behavior, and the development of strengthened international peace-keeping processes within the framework of the U.N. shall have reached a point where the states of the world can move forward to Stage III. In Stage III progressive controlled disarmament and continuously developing principles and procedures of international law would proceed to a point where no state would have the military power to challenge the progressively strengthened U.N. Peace Force and all international disputes would be settled according to the agreed principles of international conduct.

The progressive steps to be taken during the final phase of the disarmament program would be directed toward the attainment of a world in which:

(a) States would retain only those forces, non-nuclear armaments, and establishments required for the purpose of maintaining internal order; they would also support and provide agreed manpower for a U.N. Peace Force.

(b) The U.N. Peace Force, equipped with agreed types and quantities of armaments, would be fully functioning.

(c) The manufacture of armaments would be prohibited except for those of agreed types and quantities to be used by the U.N. Peace Force and those required to maintain internal order. All other armaments would be destroyed or converted to peaceful purposes.

(d) The peace-keeping capabilities of the United Nations would be sufficiently strong and the obligations of all states under such arrangements sufficiently far-reaching as to assure peace and the just settlement of differences in a disarmed world.

Exhibit E

Public Law 87-297
87th Congress, H. R. 9118
September 26, 1961

An Act

75 STAT. 631.

To establish a United States Arms Control and Disarmament Agency.

*Be it enacted by the Senate and House of Representatives of
United States of America in Congress assembled,*

SHORT TITLE

Section 1. This Act may be cited as the "Arms Control and
Disarmament Act."

PURPOSE:

Sec. 2. An ultimate goal of the United States is a world which
is free from the scourge of war and the dangers and burdens of
armaments; in which the use of force has been subordinated to
the rule of law; and in which international adjustments to a changing world are achieved peacefully. It is the purpose of this Act to
provide impetus toward this goal by creating a new agency of
peace to deal with the problem of reduction and control of armaments looking toward ultimate world disarmament.

Arms control and disarmament policy, being an important aspect of foreign policy, must be consistent with national security
policy as a whole. The formulation and implementation of United
States arms control and disarmament policy in a manner which
will promote the national security can best be insured by a central organization charged by statute with primary responsibility
for this field. This organization must have such a position within
the Government that it can provide the President, the Secretary
of State, other officials of the executive branch, and the Congress
with recommendations concerning United States arms control and
disarmament policy, and can assess the effect of these recommendations upon our foreign policies, our national security policies, and our economy.

This organization must have the capacity to provide the essential scientific, economic, political, military, psychological, and
technological information upon which realistic arms control and
disarmament policy must be based. It must be able to carry out
the following primary functions:

(a) The conduct, support and coordinations of research for
arms control and disarmament policy formulation;

(b) The preparation for and management of United States
participation in international negotiations in the arms control and
disarmament field;

(c) The dissemination and coordination of public information
concerning arms control and disarmament; and

(d) The preparation for, operation of, or as appropriate, direction of United States participation in such control systems as may

become part of United States arms control and disarmament
activities.

DEFINITIONS

Sec. 3. As used in this Act —

(a) The terms "arms control" and "disarmament" mean the
identification, verification, inspection, limitation, control, reduction, or elimination, of armed forces and armaments of all kinds
under international agreement including the necessary steps taken
under such an agreement to establish an effective system of international control, or to create and strengthen international organizations for the maintenance of peace.

(b) The term "Government agency" means any executive department, commission, agency, independent establishment, corporation wholly or partly owned by the United States which is an
instrumentality of the United States, or any board, bureau, division, service, office, officer, authority, administration, or other establishment in the executive branch of Government.

(c) The term "Agency" means the United States Arms Control and Disarmament Agency.

TITLE II — ORGANIZATION

UNITED STATES ARMS CONTROL AND DISARMAMENT AGENCY

Sec. 21. There is hereby established an agency to be known as
the "United States Arms Control and Disarmament Agency."

DIRECTOR

Sec 22. The Agency shall be headed by a Director, who shall
serve as the principal adviser to the Secretary of State and the
President on arms control and disarmament matters. In carrying
out his duties under this Act the Director shall, under the direction of the Secretary of State, have primary responsibility within
the Government for arms control and disarmament matters, as
defined in this Act. He shall be appointed by the President, by
and with the advice and consent of the Senate. He shall receive
compensation at the rate of $22,500 per annum.

DEPUTY DIRECTOR

Sec. 23. A Deputy Director of the Agency shall be appointed by
the President, by and with the advice and consent of the Senate.
He shall receive compensation at the rate of $21,100 per annum.
The Deputy Director shall perform such duties and exercise such
powers as the Director may prescribe. He shall act for, and exercise the powers of, the Director during his absence or disability or
during a vacancy in said office.

ASSISTANT DIRECTORS

Section 24. Not to exceed four Assistant Directors may be appointed by the President, by and with the advice and consent of
the Senate. They shall receive compensation at the rate of $20,-
000 per annum. They shall perform such duties and exercise such
powers as the Director may prescribe.

BUREAUS, OFFICES, AND DIVISIONS

Sec. 25. The Director, under the direction of the Secretary of State, may establish within the Agency such bureaus, officers, and divisions as he may determine to be necessary to discharge his responsibilities under this Act, including, but not limited to, an Office of the General Counsel.

GENERAL ADVISORY COMMITTEE

Sec. 26. The President, by and with the advice and consent of the Senate, may appoint a General Advisory Committee of not to exceed fifteen members to advise the Director on arms control and disarmament policy and activities. The President shall designate one of the members as Chairman. The members of the committee may receive the compensation and reimbursement for expenses specified for consultants by section 41(d) of this Act. The Committee shall meet at least twice each year. It shall from time to time advise the President, the Secretary of State, and the Disarmament Director respecting matters affecting arms control, disarmament, and world peace.

TITLE III — FUNCTIONS

RESEARCH

Sec 21. The Director is authorized and directed to exercise his powers in such manner as to insure the acquisition of a fund of theoretical and practical knowledge concerning disarmament. To this end, the Director is authorized and directed, under the direction of the President, (1) to insure the conduct of research, development, and other studies in the field of arms control and disarmament; (2) to make arrangements (including contracts, agreements, and grants) for the conduct of research, development, and other studies in the field or arms control and disarmament by private or public institutions or persons; and (3) to coordinate the research, development, and other studies conducted in the field of arms control and disarmament by or for other Government agencies in accordance with procedures established under section 35 of this Act. In carrying out his responsibilities under this Act, the Director shall, to the maximum extent feasible, make full use of available facilities, Government and private. The authority of the Director with respect to research, development, and other studies shall be limited to participation in the following insofar as they relate to arms control and disarmament:

(a) the detection, identification, inspection, monitoring, limitation, reduction, control, and elimination of armed forces and armaments, including thermonuclear, nuclear, missile, conventional, bacteriological, chemical, and radiological weapons;

(b) the techniques and systems of detecting, identifying, inspecting, and monitoring of tests of nuclear, thermonuclear, and other weapons;

(c) the analysis of national budgets, levels of industrial

production, and economic indicators to determine the amounts spent by various countries for armaments;

(d) the control, reduction, and elimination of armed forces and armaments in space, in areas on and beneath the earth's surface, and in underwater regions;

(e) the structure and operation of international control and other organizations useful for arms control and disarmament;

(f) the training of scientists, technicians, and other personnel for manning the control systems which may be created by international arms control and disarmament agreements;

(g) the reduction and elimination of the danger of war resulting from accident, miscalculation, or possible surprise attack, including (but not limited to) improvements in the methods of communications between nations;

(h) the economic and political consequences of arms control and disarmament, including the problems of readjustment arising in industry and the reallocation of national resources;

(i) the arms control and disarmament implications of foreign and national security policies of the United States with a view to a better understanding of the significance of such policies for the achievement of arms control and disarmament;

(j) the national security and foreign policy implications of arms control and disarmament proposals with a view to a better understanding of the effect of such proposals upon national security and foreign policy;

(k) methods for the maintenance of peace and security during different stages of arms control and disarmament;

(l) the scientific, economic, political, legal, social, psychological, military, and technological factors related to the prevention of war with a view to a better understanding of how the basic structure of a lasting peace may be established;

(m) such related problem as the Director may determine to be in need of research, development, or study in order to carry out the provisions of the Act.

PATENTS

Sec. 32. All research within the United States contracted for, sponsored, cosponsored, or authorized under authority of this Act, shall be provided for in such manner that all information as to uses, products, processes, patents, and other developments resulting from such research developed by Government expenditure will (with such exceptions and limitations, if any, as the Director may find to be necessary in the public interest) be available to the general public. This subsection shall not be so construed as to deprive the owner of any background patent relating thereto of such rights as he may have thereunder.

POLICY FORMULATION

Sec. 33. The Director is authorized and directed to prepare for the President, the Secretary of State, and the heads of such other

Government agencies, as the President may determine, recommendations concerning United States arms control and disarmament policy: Provided, however. That no action shall be taken under this or any other law that will obligate the United States to disarm or to reduce or to limit the Armed Forces or armaments of the United States, except pursuant to the treaty making power of the President under the Constitution or unless authorized by further affirmative legislation by the Congress of the United States.

NEGOTIATIONS AND RELATED FUNCTIONS

Sec. 34. Under the direction of the Secretary of State—

(a) the Director, for the purpose of conducting negotiations concerning arms control and disarmament or for the purpose of exercising any other authority given him by this Act, may (1) consult and communicate with or direct the consultation and communication with representatives of other nations or of international organizations and (2) communicate in the name of the Secretary with diplomatic representatives of the United States in this country and abroad.

(b) the Director shall perform functions pursuant to section 2 (c) of Reorganization Plan 8 of 1953 with respect to providing to the United States Information Agency official United States positions and policy on arms control and disarmament matters for dissemination abroad.

(c) the Director is authorized (1) to formulate plans and make preparations for the establishment, operation, and funding of inspection and control systems which may become part of the United States arms control and disarmament activities, and (2) as authorized by law, to put into effect, direct, or otherwise assume United States responsibility for such systems.

COORDINATION

Sec. 35. The President is authorized to establish procedures to (1) assure cooperation, consultation, and a continuing exchange of information between the Agency and the Department of Defense, the Atomic Energy Commission, the National Aeronautics and Space Administration and other affected Government agencies, in all significant aspects of United States arms control and disarmament policy and related matters including current and prospective policies, plans, and programs, (2) resolve differences of opinion between the Director and such other agencies which cannot be resolved through consultation, and (3) provide for presentation to the President of recommendations of the Director with respect to such differences, when such differences involve major matters of policy and cannot be resolved through consultation.

TITLE IV — GENERAL PROVISIONS

GENERAL AUTHORITY

Sec. 41. In the performance of his functions, the Director is authorized to —

(a) utilize or employ the services, personnel, equipment, or facilities of any other Government agency, with the consent of the agency concerned, to perform such functions on behalf of the Agency as may appear desirable. It is the intent of this section that the Director rely upon the Department of State for general administrative services in the United States and abroad to the extent agreed upon between the Secretary of State and the Director. Any Government agency is authorized, notwithstanding any other provision of law, to transfer to or to receive from the Director, without reimbursement, supplies and equipment other than administrative supplies or equipment. Transfer or receipt of excess property shall be in accordance with the provisions of the Federal Property and Administrative Services Act of 1949, as amended;

(b) appoint officers and employees, including attorneys, for the Agency in accordance with the civil service laws and fix their compensation in accordance with the Classification Act of 1949, as amended;

(c) enter into agreements with other Government agencies, including the military departments through the Secretary of Defense, under which officers or employees of such agencies may be detailed to the Agency for the performance of service pursuant to this Act without prejudice to the status or advancement of such officers or employees within their own agencies;

(d) procure services of experts and consultants or organizations thereof, including stenographic reporting services, as authorized by section 15 of the Act of August 2, 1946 (5 U.S.C. 55a), at rates not to exceed $100 per diem for individuals, including transportation and per diem in lieu of subsistence while away from their homes or regular places of business, as authorized by section 5 of said Act, as amended (5 U.S.C. 73b-2) Provided. That no such individual shall be employed for more than one hundred days in any fiscal year unless the President certifies that employment of such individual in excess of such number of days is necessary in the national interest: And provided further, That such contracts may be renewed annually;

(e) employ individuals of outstanding ability without compensation in accordance with the provisions of section 710 (b) of the Defense Production Act of 1950, as amended (50 U.S.C. App. 2160), and regulations issued thereunder;

(f) establish advisory boards to advise with and make recommendations to the Director on United States arms control and disarmament policy and activities. The members of such boards may receive the compensation and reimbursement for expenses specified for consultants by section 41 (d) of this Act;

(g) delegate, as appropriate, to the Deputy Director or other officers of the Agency, any authority conferred upon the Director by the provisions of this Act; and

(h) make, promulgate, issue, rescind, and amend such rules and regulations as may be necessary or desirable to the exercise of any authority conferred upon the Director by the provisions of this Act.

FOREIGN SERVICE RESERVE AND STAFF OFFICERS

Sec. 42. The Secretary of State may authorize the Director to exercise, with respect to Foreign Service Reserve officers and Foreign Service Staff officers and employees appointed or employed for the Agency, the following authority: (1) The authority available to the Secretary of State under the Foreign Service Act of 1946, as amended, (2) the authority available to the Secretary under any other provision of law pertaining specifically, or generally applicable, to such officers or employees, and (3) the authority of the Board of Foreign Service pursuant to the Foreign Service Act of 1946, as amended.

CONTRACTS OR EXPENDITURES

Sec. 43. The President may, in advance, exempt actions of the Director from the provisions of law relating to contracts or expenditures of Government funds whenever he determines that such action is essential in the interest of United States arms control and disarmament and security policy.

CONFLICT OF INTEREST AND DUAL COMPENSATION LAW

Sec. 44. The members of the General Advisory Committee created by section 26 of this Act, and the members of the advisory boards, the consultants, and the individuals of outstanding ability employed without compensation, all of which are provided in section 41 of this Act, may serve as such without regard to the provisions of section 281, 283, 284, or 1914 of title 18 of the United States Code, or of section 190 of the Revised Statutes (5 U.S.C. 99), or of any other Federal law imposing restrictions, requirements, or penalties in relation to the employment of individuals, the performance of services, or the payment or receipt of compensation in connection with any claim, proceeding, or matter involving the United States Government, except insofar as such provisions of law may prohibit any such individual from receiving compensation from a source other than a nonprofit educational institution in respect of any particular matter in which the Agency is directly interested. Nor shall such service be considered as employment of holding of office or position bringing such individual within the provisions of section 13 of the Civil Service Retirement Act (5 U.S.C. 2263), section 212 of the Act of June 30, 1932, as amended (5 U.S.C. 59a), or any other Federal law limiting the reemployment of retired officers or employees or govern-

ing the simultaneous receipt of compensation and retired pay or
annuities.

SECURITY REQUIREMENTS

Sec. 45. (a) The Director shall establish such security and loyalty requirements, restrictions, and safeguards as he deems
necessary in the interest of the national security and to carry out
the provisions of this Act. The Director shall arrange with the
Civil Service Commission for the conduct of full-field background
security and loyalty investigations of all the Agency's officers,
employees, consultants, persons detailed from other Government
agencies, members of its General Advisory Committee, advisory
boards, contractors and subcontractors, and their officers and
employees, actual or prospective. In the event the investigation
may be or may become a security risk, or may be of doubtful
loyalty, the report of the investigation shall be turned over to the
Federal Bureau of Investigation for a full-field investigation. The
final results of all such investigations shall be turned over to the
Director for final determination. No person shall be permitted to
enter on duty as such an officer, employee, consultant, or member
of advisory committee or board, or pursuant to any such detail,
and no contractor or subcontractor, or officer or employee thereof
shall be permitted to have access to any classified information,
until he shall have been investigated in accordance with this subsection and the report of such investigations made to the Director, and the Director shall have determined that such person is
not a security risk or of doubtful loyalty. Standards applicable
with respect to the security clearance of persons within any category referred to in this subsection shall not be less stringent, and
the investigation of such persons for such purposes shall not be
less intensive or complete, than in the case of such clearance of
persons in a corresponding category under the security procedures
of the Government agency or agencies having the highest security
restrictions with respect to persons in such category.

(b) The Atomic Energy Commission may authorize any of its
employees, or employees of any contractor, prospective contractor, licensee, or prospective licensee of the Atomic Energy Commission or any other person authorized to have access to
Restricted Data by the Atomic Energy Commission under section
2165 of title 42, to permit the Director or any officer, employee,
consultant, person detailed from other Government agencies,
member of the General Advisory Committee or of any advisory
board established pursuant to section 41 (f), contractor, subcontractor, prospective contractor, or prospective subcontractor, or
officer or employee of such contractor, subcontractor, prospective
contractor, or prospective subcontractor, to have access to Restricted Data which is required in the performance of his duties
and so certified by the Director, but only if (1) the Atomic Energy
Commission has determined, in accordance with the established
personnel security procedures and standards of the Commission,
that permitting such individual to have access to such Restricted

Data will not endanger the common defense and security, and (2) the Atomic Energy Commission finds that the established personnel and other security procedures and standards of the Agency are adequate and in reasonable conformity to the standards established by the Atomic Energy Commission under section 2165 of title 42, including those for interim clearance in subsection (b) thereof. Any individual granted access to Restricted Data pursuant to this subsection may exchange such date with any individual who (A) is an officer or employee of the Department of Defense, or any department or agency thereof, or a member of the Armed Forces, or an officer or employee of the National Aeronautics and Space Administration, or a contractor or subcontractor of any such department, agency, or armed force, or an officer or employee of any such contractor or subcontractor, and (B) has been authorized to have access to Restricted Data under the provisions of sections 2163 or 2455 of title 42.

COMPTROLLER GENERAL AUDIT

Sec. 46. No moneys appropriated for the purpose of this Act shall be available for payment under any contract with the Director, negotiated without advertising, except contracts with any foreign government, international organization or any agency thereof, unless such contract includes a clause to the effect that the Comptroller General of the United States or any of his duly authorized representatives shall, until the expiration of three years after final payment, have access to and the right to examine any directly pertinent books, documents, papers, and records of the contractor or any of his subcontractors engaged in the performance of, and involving transactions related to such contracts or subcontracts: Provided, however, That no money so appropriated shall be available for payment under such contract which includes any provisions precluding an audit by the General Accounting Office of any transaction under such contract: And provided further, That nothing in this section shall preclude the earlier disposal of contractor and subcontractor records in accordance with records disposal schedules agreed upon between the Director and the General Accounting Office.

TRANSFER OF ACTIVITIES AND FACILITIES TO AGENCY

Sec. 47. (a) The United States Disarmament Administration, together with its records, property, personnel, and funds, is hereby transferred to the Agency. The appropriations and unexpended balances of appropriations transferred pursuant to this subsection shall be available for expenditure for any and all objects of expenditure authorized by this Act, without regard to the requirements of apportionment under section 665 of title 31.

(b) The President, by Executive order, may transfer to the Director any activities or facilities of any Government agency which relate primarily to arms control and disarmament. In connection with any such transfer, the President may under this section or other applicable authority, provide for appropriate transfers of records, property, civilian personnel, and funds. No transfer shall be made under this subsection until (1) a full and complete report concerning the nature and effect of such proposed transfer has been transmitted by the President to the Congress, and (2) the first period of sixty calendar days of regular session of the Congress following the date of receipt of such report by the Congress has expired without adoption by either House of the Congress of a resolution stating that such House does not favor such transfer. The procedures prescribed in title II of the Reorganization Act of 1949 shall apply to any such resolution.

USE OF FUNDS

Sec. 48. Appropriations made to the Director for the purposes of this Act, and transfers of funds to him by other Government agencies for such purposes, shall be available to him to exercise any authority granted him by this Act, including, without limitation, expenses of printing and binding without regard to the provisions of section 11 of the Act of March 1, 1919 (44 U.S.C. 111); purchase or hire of one passenger motor vehicle for the official use of the Director without regard to the limitations contained in section 78 (c) of title 5 of the United States Code; entertainment and official courtesies to the extent authorized by appropriation; expenditures for training and study; expenditures in connection with participation in international conferences for the purposes of this Act; and expenses in connection with travel of personnel outside the United States, including transportation expenses of dependents, household goods, and personal effects, and expenses authorized by the Foreign Service Act of 1946, as amended, not otherwise provided for.

APPROPRIATION

Sec. 49 (a) There are hereby authorized to be appropriated not to exceed $10,000,000 to remain available until expended, to carry out the purposes of this Act.

(b) Funds appropriated pursuant to this section may be allocated or transferred to any agency for carrying out the purpose of this Act. Such funds shall be available for obligation and expenditure in accordance with authority granted in this Act, or under authority governing the activities of the agencies to which such funds are allocated or transferred.

REPORT TO CONGRESS

Sec. 50. The Director shall submit to the President, for transmittal to the Congress, not later than January 31 of each year, a report concerning activities of the Agency.

Approved September 26, 1961, 12:45 p.m.

Exhibit F

A BILL TO INVESTIGATE THE LEGALITY OF THE ACTION OF FEDERAL AGENTS WITH REGARD TO THE UNITED NATIONS AND TO PROVIDE MEANS FOR THE ENFORCEMENT OF THE CONSTITU TION OF THE UNITED STATES IN RELATION THERETO:

WHEREAS, the State of____at the time of its admission into the union of states as attested by its ratification of the agreement known as the Constitution of the United States, assumed all obligations to the People of____and to the People of the several States that were parties to the same agreement, to insure that all provisions of the Constitution of the United States shall be respected and enforced within the boundaries and under the jurisdiction of the State of____and:

WHEREAS, three Federal Agencies of Government were created by Article I, Article II, and Article III of that compact; and:

WHEREAS, it appears, under what has been asserted to be a legal use of these limited and enumerated delegated powers, that certain of these Federal Agencies have purported to negotiate with foreign Governments and to coerce these States as so united into an agreement which would constitute a surrender to foreign Governments of the rights and liberties assured to the people under the Constitution of the United States, and to surrender the powers of government this Constitution guarantees to preserve to our People.

BE IT ENACTED BY THE GENERAL ASSEMBLY OF THE STATE OF____that:

1. A Special Joint Committee of the Legislature of this State, comprised of four members elected by and from the House of Representatives and four members from the Senate be chosen and elected by the members thereof in session,

2. Such Committee shall be authorized and directed to investi-

gate the question of whether the agreement which is represented to be entered into by Federal Agencies acting as representatives of these United States with regard to the so-called United Nations Organization be within the power and authority granted to said Agencies under the Constitution of the United States; and

3. The Committee shall be further authorized and directed to investigate the question of whether this purported agreement affects the State of___, or relates to the relinquishment of any of the laws or rights affecting the State of___or its People, and whether there is any change proposed to be made which would deprive the State of___or its People of rights and privileges, or would involve any change in any of the provisions of the agreement known as the Constitution of the United States without the consent of the Government of the People of this State or of the several States.

4. The Committee inquire into what measures may be taken by this State to enforce the Constitution of the United States and to punish any infractions thereof that may appear to be sanctioned by any unlawful use of purported authority by an Agency not sanctioned by the Constitution of the United States,

5. Said Committee shall report their findings to each House of the State Legislature of___not later than two months following the passage of this act, and

6. The sum of $100,000,000 be appropriated for the uses and purposes of said Committee.

Exhibit G

A BILL TO PROVIDE FOR THE ENFORCEMENT OF THE CONSTITUTION OF THE UNITED STATES WITH REGARD TO THE SO-CALLED UNITED NATIONS ORGANIZATION:

WHEREAS, by agreement with her Sister States, the State of _____is duty-bound to enforce the Constitution of the United States within its borders; and

WHEREAS, as the Legislature of this State has inquired into the question of whether certain purported agreements made by certain Federal Agencies created by the Constitution of the United States were within the authority granted by the Constitution of the United States; and

WHEREAS, authority for said purported acts was not granted under the terms of the Constitution of the United States; and

WHEREAS, said agreements purport to abridge rights and liberties of this State and its People without lawful authority

BE IT ENACTED BY THE GENERAL ASSEMBLY OF THE STATE OF____in conformity with the duty of the State of____ to its People and to her Sister States, and in further conformity with the oath of office taken by the Governmental Officials thereof, that:

1. Those purported treaties and agreements relating to the United Nations Organization, now sometimes referred to as the United Nations, are beyond the authority granted to the agencies purporting to make these treaties and agreements, and are therefore, null, void and of no effect within the jurisdiction of this State, and any attempt to enforce the provisions of any of said treaties or agreements within this State is unlawful.

2. Any person who shall commit an act of violation of the provisions of this statute shall be guilty of a felony, and upon conviction thereof, shall be fined not less than $2,000 nor more than

$100,000.00, or confined in the State Penitentiary not less than 3 years nor more than 20 years, or both.

3. Any State Officeholder, or any Member of the United States Congress from the State of_____, who shall attempt to violate the provisions of this act shall, by that attempt, automatically vacate his office, and any citizen of this State may bring quo warranto proceedings in the county in which said offender last resided or was last known to be, to force the abandonment of any pretext of filling said office by the person so disqualified,

4. Any person aggrieved by a State Officeholder or by any other person acting in violation of the within statute shall retain his private action against the offender, and all of his aiders, advisors, and abettors, jointly and severally, and shall recover triple costs, besides double damages, which no jury, or Court sitting without a jury, shall assess at less than $2,500.00, and

5. Any person convicted of any criminal offense under the provisions of this statute shall be incapable of receiving pardon, and shall be incapable of receiving parole or suspension of sentence of confinement, and

6. Any person, being a defendant in a civil action brought under the provisions of this statute, who shall have had judgement rendered against him which has become final by the expiration of time for appeal or by final determination of an Appellate Court, shall be denied all exemptions from execution under said judgment, and

7. Each Representative of this State in the House of Representatives of the United States and in the Senate of the United States, before his election to office may be certified, shall be sworn, in the County of his Residence in this State, an Oath or Affirmation to be bound to support the Constitution of the United States, and for breach of this oath shall be punished as provided by any or all of the provisions of paragraphs 2 through 6 above.

Index

U. N. CHARTER ORDER FORM

Arch E. Roberts, Major, AUS, ret.
c/o Chas. Hallberg & Company Publishers
110 West Grand Avenue
Chicago, Illinois 60610

Major Roberts,

I want to participate in the investigation of the legality of federal agents with regard to the United Nations Organization.

Please mail to me one copy of:

THE CHARTER OF THE UNITED NATIONS and STATUTE OF THE INTERNATIONAL COURT OF JUSTICE, with attached chart of December, 1952, THE UNITED NATIONS SYSTEM, showing its organization structure including Commissions and Specialized Agencies.

Twenty-five cents is inclosed to cover cost and mailing.

Include with this order additional information on calling for investigation of United Nations Treaty agreements by my State Legislature.

Name   (please print)

Street

City, State & Zip code

CUT OFF HERE AND MAIL TO HALLBERG COMPANY

QUANTITY DISCOUNT
INFORMATION FORM

Chas. Hallberg & Company, Publishers
110 West Grand Avenue
Chicago, Illinois 60610

Sirs:

Please send me the address of your wholesale book dealer, nearest me, so that I may order a quantity of VICTORY DENIED for distribution.

I am interested in quantities of

_____ copies of the cloth bound library edition
and/or
_____ copies of this paperback edition.

_____
Name   (please print)

_____
Street

_____
City, State & Zip code